Religious Authority
in an Age of Doubt

RUPERT E. DAVIES

Religious Authority in an Age of Doubt

LONDON

EPWORTH PRESS

© RUPERT E. DAVIES 1968

First published in 1968
by Epworth Press
BOOK STEWARD: FRANK H. CUMBERS

SBN 7162 0047 3

Printed in Great Britain by
Latimer Trend & Co Ltd Plymouth

UXORI CARISSIMAE
OMNIUM CURARUM ET INCEPTORUM
PARTICIPI

CONTENTS

PREFACE

The problem of authority in religion has dogged me all my theological life. I tried to come to terms with it by a historical treatment in *The Problem of Authority in the Continental Reformers*, published just after the Second World War. But it has continued with me, and now the invitation to deliver the Fernley Hartley Lecture at the Methodist Conference in 1968 has given me the chance and the incentive to explore it further.

But this book is not a sequel to the earlier one. Rather it is an attempt to put the problem in the context of the critical period for Christianity in which we live, and to show that the 'shaking of the foundations' which we have experienced, so far from making the problem more difficult, in fact points towards its solution.

I am grateful to my friends with whom I have discussed the matter – many of them my colleagues in training ministers for the Methodist Church; and to my wife, for asking difficult questions and not being satisfied with unsatisfactory answers, and for making the whole enterprise possible.

I am also grateful to my colleague, John Richardson, for preparing the Index.

RUPERT E. DAVIES

Wesley College
Westbury-on-Trym
Bristol
October 1967

SELECT BIBLIOGRAPHY

K. BARTH *From Rousseau to Ritschl* Eleven chapters of *Die pro-testantische Theologie im 19 Jahrhundert,* translated by Brian Cozens: S.C.M. Press, London 1959

B. C. BUTLER *The Church and Infallibility*: Sheed & Ward, London 1954

O. CHADWICK (ed.) *The Mind of the Oxford Movement*: A. & C. Black, London 1960

O. CHADWICK *The Victorian Church* Part I: A. & C. Black, London 1966

A. O. J. COCKSHUT *Anglican Attitudes*: Collins, London 1959

J. H. COLLINS *Basis and Belief*: Epworth Press, London 1964

R. E. DAVIES *The Problem of Authority in the Continental Reformers* A Study in Luther, Zwingli, and Calvin: Epworth Press, London 1946

—— *Why I am a Protestant*: Epworth Press, London 1957

—— (with J. W. WENHAM) *Is the Bible Infallible?*: Epworth Press, London 1959

Documents of Vatican II, The, ed. Walter M. Abbott *S.J.* & Very Rev. Msgr Joseph Gallagher: Geoffrey Chapman, London/Dublin 1966

Essays and Reviews: J. W. Parker, London 1860

G. FABER *Oxford Apostles* A Character Study of the Oxford Movement: Faber, London 1933; paperback 1954

P. T. FORSYTH *The Principle of Authority in relation to Certainty, Sanctity and Society*: Hodder & Stoughton, London 1913

C GORE (ed.) *Lux Mundi* (10th edition): John Murray, London 1890

A. HANSON (ed.) *Vindications:* Essays on the historical basis of Christianity: S.C.M. Press, London 1966

R. P. C. HANSON *Origen's Doctrine of Tradition*: S.P.C.K., London 1954

—— *Tradition in the Early Church*: S.C.M. Press, London 1962

F. G. HEALEY *Religion and Reality* The Theology of John Oman: Oliver & Boyd, Edinburgh/London 1965

P. HINCHCLIFF *The One-Sided Reciprocity*: Darton, Longman and Todd, London 1966

D. E. JENKINS *Guide to the Debate about God:* Lutterworth Press, London 1966

H. KÜNG *Structures of the Church*: Burns & Oates, London 1965

J. LAWSON *The Biblical Theology of Saint Irenaeus*: Epworth Press, London 1948

J. H. NEWMAN *Apologia pro Vita sua* Fontana Books (paperback): Collins, London 1959

—— *An Essay in Aid of a Grammar of Assent*: Burns, Oates & Co., London 1870

—— *An Essay on the Development of Christian Doctrine* The New Ark Library (paperback): Sheed & Ward, London/New York 1960

J. OMAN *Vision and Authority, or The Throne of St. Peter* (2nd edition): Hodder & Stoughton, London 1928

—— *Honest Religion*: Cambridge University Press, Cambridge 1941

J. I. PACKER *Fundamentalism and the Word of God*: I.V.F., London 1958

W. PALMER *A Treatise on the Church of Christ* in Two Volumes (3rd edition): Rivington, London 1842

C. SALMON *The Infallibility of the Church* (revised edition): John Murray, London 1952

P. SCHAFF *Creeds of the Greek and Latin Churches*: London 1877

F. SCHLEIERMACHER *On Religion: Speeches to its Cultured Despisers* translated with introduction, by John Oman B.D.: London 1893; paperback New York 1958

—— *The Christian Faith* English translation of the second German edition, ed. H. R. Mackintosh & J. S. Stewart: Edinburgh 1928

O. C. THOMAS *William Temple's Philosophy of Religion*: S.P.C.K., London 1961

A. R. VIDLER *The Church in an Age of Revolution* Pelican Books: London 1961

G. D. YARNOLD *By What Authority?*: Collins, London 1964

Chapter One

THE NEW SHAPE OF AN OLD PROBLEM

Ever since men began to arrange their religious belief into a coherent scheme, or to commend them to each other in the form of persuasive propositions, there has been a problem of authority. There is a problem of authority in politics and education as well as in religion, but in religion it has a distinctive quality. In politics the problem is: What right has a government, or other duly constituted organ of administration, to enforce the carrying out of its will on those who are subject to it? What duty have the subjects to obey what is laid down for them by the government or other body? How is such a system of rights and duties set up and maintained? Or, to put the questions in more concrete forms: Has a government the right to impose income tax or has it only the *power* (embodied in the courts and the police force) to do so? and have I the duty to pay the tax, or is it just that I shall be put in prison if I do not? Or, in other words: What is the relation between duties, rights and physical force, and what is the basis of law?

In education the problem concerns itself with the teacher and the taught. Has the teacher the right, or only the power, to enforce a certain kind of conduct on the taught? Has he the right, or only the power, to inject certain ways of thinking into his pupils' minds (we are assuming that he has, in fact, the power–not all teachers have it)? So stated, the problem sounds the same as the political problem of authority. But it is not quite the same. The prime object of a government is to see that the policy which it believes (rightly or wrongly) to be for the benefit of its subjects is carried out. If

13

it has reached any degree of enlightenment, together with a desire to remain in office, it will also hope to gain the goodwill of its subjects for the policy, but this is a secondary aim. A teacher, on the other hand,–or so we may presume–makes it his main objective to persuade his pupil that the course of conduct that he enforces is the best possible one for the pupil to follow and that the ways of thinking which the school insists on are the ways of thinking that will carry him to success in life. But, although the problems of authority in politics and education are not identical, yet they are alike in this, that the exercise of physical power is part of the meaning of the word 'authority' as it is here used.

But in religion this is not so. It is, of course, true that Churches and their rulers in ancient and medieval times were not very clear about this. They seem to have thought that if people could not be persuaded to believe what was true because it seemed to them to be true, or because the Church said it was true, then the 'authority of the Church' entitled it to use coercion on them; and in order to quieten their sometimes very noisy consciences they comforted themselves with the thought that it was for the spiritual good of those so coerced, as well as of everyone else, for them to be coerced, if necessary to death. Hence the burnings of heretics and the imprisonment of schismatics, by Protestants as well as Catholics. And in our own time, though religious persecution is frowned on by all Christians, methods of psychological coercion and of indoctrination by propaganda under the guise of religious education have by no means been wholly abandoned.

Yet few would now deny that such proceedings rest on a confusion of thought no less than on a mixture of motives. For the religious man–not only for the Christian, but certainly for the Christian–the authority which he may be asked to accept has nothing to do with the enforcement of a truth or a course of action; the concepts of authority and power in this realm of thought are alien to each other, and may not be confused without danger to the integrity of religion and religious belief.

So the problem of authority in religion is a distinctive one,

perhaps a unique one. It could be stated in the terms of the
definition of 'authority' which appears in the UNESCO *Dictionary of the Social Sciences*, which runs:

> Authority denotes the mode of securing assent to a course
> of action when it is especially difficult or impossible to
> demonstrate rationally the adequacy of that course of
> action to the requirements of the situation.

We could then pose the problem thus: Does authority in the
sense defined reside in any person or persons, or any institution or writing, and, if so, how can we locate it and recognize
it? But the definition given has a faint air of disparagement,
and definitions, of all things, should be wholly neutral; nor,
surely, does authority come into play *only* when rational
demonstration is especially difficult or impossible; moreover,
the definition is limited to the mode of securing assent to a
course of action, whereas, for our purposes, it needs to be
extended to the sphere of doctrinal truths and ethical injunctions.

Let us therefore formulate the problem in another, slightly
different way: granted that many, or most, or perhaps all, of
the alleged truths of religion are not demonstrable by reason,
that is, by a logical process which all reasoning creatures
would recognize as valid, is there any person or group of
persons, any institution or document, or what-you-will, on
whose word we may legitimately accept them and legitimately expect others to do the same? It may seem rash to
assume, as this formulation does, that it is not possible for *all*
the truths of religion to be logically proved. But very few
expounders of the Christian religion—and this probably
applies to the other great religions also—have, in fact, questioned this assumption; the argument has been not about
this, but about such questions as, How many doctrinal
truths, and which of them, if any, can be demonstrated? The
assumption, then, can fairly be made; indeed, if all the truths
of the Christian faith were demonstrable by reason, there
would be no problem of authority for the Christian at all.
He would have to concern himself simply with clarifying
the concept of demonstration and reason. But we all know
that there *is* a problem of authority, and the fact that there

is shows, almost by itself, that some Christian truths at least are outside the range of demonstration.

There is, however, a logical difficulty which haunts this problem, in whatever way we formulate it. If to the question, Is there any person, or institution, etc., on whose word we may legitimately accept the alleged truths of religion?, we give an affirmative answer, and with even greater daring go on to specify the person or institution, then on what authority do we give these answers? Unless we can persuade ourselves that we are giving them on the ground of sheer reason—and this claim, as we shall soon see, has been made, implausible though it may seem—we shall find ourselves faced with the question: On what authority do we accept the person or institution on whose word, i.e., authority, we accept the truths of religion? And so on, *ad infinitum*. No resolution of this difficulty is ready to hand, but perhaps we shall see this problem in a new light before this book is finished.

Yet, in spite of the logical difficulty which attends the problem itself, and in spite of the great variety of ways in which it has been formulated, there is no doubt at all that it is a problem of great importance for all Christians and for all Churches. From time to time in these pages we shall encounter the personal perplexities of those who have sought to find the truth for themselves, and many of these perplexities will be found to centre in the problem of authority. But it is by no means purely a personal problem. It concerns the life of Christendon, and of all the communions that go to make up the Holy Catholic Church. It lies at the root of all our divisions, in the past and in the present. It severed Gnostics from Catholics in the second century; for the Gnostics based their affirmations (which we tend to call 'speculations') on a tradition which the Catholics did not recognize, and vice versa. It helped to split the Church of the West from the Church of the East at the beginning of the thirteenth century;[1] for the Easterns asserted that the Western Church had flouted the authority of the Ecumenical Councils of the Church by inserting the *filioque* clause in the Nicene Creed. More than anything else it divided Europe into contending

[1] see S. Runciman *The Eastern Schism* (London 1955), pp. 30-2

camps in the sixteenth century, for Luther and Calvin elevated the authority of the Word of God far above that of Council, Creed, Pope or Church;[1] and then it proceeded to divide still further the Churches of the Reformation. It was the main bone of contention between those who sought to reform the Church of England in the nineteenth century and reassert its title to the word 'catholic', and those who were content to rest the Church of England on the Prayer Book, the State, and sound reason. It still divides the Conservative Evangelicals in the Church of England from their fellow Anglicans. And if we now begin to think of possible reunion between Rome and the rest of Christendom the issue of authority will be the last and greatest stumbling-block in the way.

By the same token, a general agreement on the nature of religious authority could be the greatest single instrument for effecting reunion. We have already a large measure of doctrinal agreement between Churches engaged in or contemplating reunion negotiations. But this agreement is in danger while the issue of authority remains undiscussed (as in fact it does) and unresolved. All the Churches concerned agree on the central doctrine of the consubstantiality of the Son with the Father in the Holy Trinity. But some assert this doctrine because it is delivered by the sacred tradition of the Church, in the form of the Ecumenical Creeds, some because it is asserted by the New Testament, some because it is revealed to them by personal or corporate experience (of course, all communions make some reference to all these sources of authority, but in each case one of the three is basic, and the others are tested by their relation to it). Now the investigation of the meaning to be attached to the pronouncements of the Councils is still proceeding; and so still more is the investigation of the Christological statements of the New Testament; while religious experience is notoriously capable of being differently interpreted from time to time and in different contexts. If the Councils, or more probably the New Testament, or, more probably still, religious experience, were

---

[1] This was the tenor of my argument in *The Problem of Authority in the Continental Reformers* p. 11f., and I have not seen any rebuttal of it.

found to be saying something different from what they have been previously thought to say, those Churches which accept Councils, or Scripture, or experience, as their supreme authority, would have to change their Christological doctrine, and the agreement on doctrine which has been so hopefully accepted as a basis for union would immediately fall apart. But if they were to agree on the question of authority this danger would be banished, and the movement towards reunion would be immediately accelerated.[1]

To the question whether there is an authority in the sense defined above, historic Christianity has almost always given an affirmative answer. Indeed, if it were said that it has always given an affirmative answer, there is only one exception that could be adduced against the statement, and even that exception is not complete. In the Age of Reason (or, as it is more usually called on the continent of Europe, the Enlightenment) a number of Christian thinkers, many of them in highly representative positions, optimistically supposed that revelation and reason could be equated, and that it was possible to formulate a religion that was recognizable as historic Christianity without calling in the aid of anything except reason, plus a certain amount of moral feeling. It may be that Immanuel Kant's *Religion within the Bounds of Pure Reason* (1793) does not reach beyond morality into religion at all, let alone the Christian religion. But John Locke (1632–1704), who held that reason propounded a simple natural religion which was confirmed by the Bible, was widely acknowledged as an expounder and defender of the Christian faith; John Tillotson (1630–94) and Thomas Tenison (1636–1715), whose views were not very different, both became archbishops of Canterbury. But the exception which these men provide to the otherwise universal tendency of the Christian Church to believe in an authoritative revelation is only partial; for their views in this matter were never formally acknowledged as sound by their Church, which continued to

[1] These considerations seem to indicate that the problem of authority ought to find a high place on the agenda of the next round of ecumenical discussion. It is therefore pleasing to note that a study of authority was initiated by the Faith and Order Commission of the World Council of Churches, meeting in Bristol in 1967.

insist on allegiance to the Thirty-Nine Articles as a condition for ordination. Nor did their influence last long. The sunny view of human reason which their views implied collapsed from various causes. One of them was that, however much the doctrinal statements of Christianity are tailored to meet the requirements of reason, the doctrine of the Incarnation, which is not reasonable in the sense under discussion, remains; or, if it is dropped, what remains is not distinctively Christian at all. Another cause was that it turned out to be patently untrue that all reasonable men accept Christianity when it is presented in a professedly reasonable manner—and so what was for most people the whole object of the exercise was frustrated; it was concluded, very sensibly, by the Church's teachers, that if no more adherents to Christianity were gained by removing everything that might possibly offend reason, the 'unreasonable', that is, the supernatural, elements might as well be retained, since, after all, they do occupy a prominent place in the classical documents of the Faith. In any case, great numbers of the English people 'voted with their feet'; they stayed away from the parish church and attended the ministrations of the Methodist preachers, who had no hesitation in regarding Scripture as the authoritative revelation and showed no sign of burking the supernatural.

The Age of Reason apart, then, the Church in all its forms has always returned the answer Yes to the question whether there is an authority in religion. We have already hinted, in another connexion, at Scripture, tradition and experience as the main sources of authority in the judgement of the Church. And of these three, the first two have played, and still play, a much more prominent role than the third. But the Early Church was innocent of the division into three which is familiar to the modern world, and did not formulate the problem of authority in terms of any opposition between Scripture and tradition, still less between tradition or Scripture and experience. For Tertullian, for Irenaeus, for Origen, the 'rule of faith', which they persistently stressed, was identical in content with the Scripture; it did not occur to them to make any separation between them, or to think of any opposition between them, or of the subordination of one to the other (except that there are some passages in Origen in which he asks his pupils to transcend the rule of faith, though he never asks them to go beyond Scripture).[1] It is because these Fathers equated the content of Scripture and tradition that it has been possible to quote them on both sides of the modern conflict between Scripture and tradition; but such quotations always do them an injustice, for the same reason. For they did not believe that tradition could add anything to Scripture, or take anything away from it. Nor did they believe that tradition is an improvement on Scripture so far as doctrine is concerned, for the rule of faith faithfully recorded the deliverances of Scripture. If someone urged that Scripture said something that tradition rejected, e.g. in the case of the Modalists that the Son was a mode of revelation employed by the One God, and quoted 'he that hath seen me hath seen the Father', and 'I and the Father are one'; or later (in the case of the Arians) that the Son was inferior to the Father, and quoted 'my Father is greater than I', the answer to him was not that tradition overruled Scripture, but that he had misinterpreted Scripture, which was at one with tradition in affirming the true personality of the Son and his consubstantiality with the Father. In course of time, in answer to heresy and in order to instruct catechumens, the rule of faith was hardened into the Creeds of the great Councils; but these Creeds unfailingly profess to be nothing more than recitals of the central Biblical truths.

It is apparent where these writers and their contemporaries placed the source of authority. Nor is the case different with Augustine. He held, indeed, that if Scripture did not actually command the following of certain customs of great antiquity, they could be justified by being shown to belong to a 'tradition' which went back to the Apostles;[2] and here we seem to have a distinction between Scripture and tradition. But this

---

[1] see R. P. C. Hanson *Tradition in the Early Church* pp. 102–17 (cf. the same author's *Origen's Doctrine of Tradition*, pp. 105–9); J. Lawson *The Biblical Theology of Saint Irenaeus* pp. 103ff., where he rightly points out that to Irenaeus Scripture and tradition 'are manifestations of one and the same thing, the *apostolic truth* by which the Christian lives'.

[2] *de Baptismo contra Donatistas* IV, vi, 9; (Migne *P.L.* xliii, 159)

applies to customs within the life and worship of the Church, not to doctrines; and Augustine was as sure as his predecessors that Scripture and tradition were at all points harmonious so far as doctrine is concerned. There is, of course, the autobiographical sentence of Augustine which was constantly flung at the Reformers in order to confute their assertion of the prior authority of the Word: 'For my part I should not believe the Gospel except as moved by the authority of the catholic church'.[1] But this sentence will not bear the weight put upon it by the opponents of the Reformers when they claimed that it proved that Augustine placed the authority of the Church above that of Scripture. For, as Calvin says, Augustine in this passage is arguing against the Manichaeans, and asking them what they would do if they wished to persuade an unbeliever of the truth of the Gospel; he for his part, he says, when he was an unbeliever, was brought to the Gospel by the authority of the Catholic Church (which the Manichees have not got). Calvin very properly concludes that Augustine is contending that it is the *unbeliever*, not the Christian, who is convinced by the authority of the Church; and points out that elsewhere Augustine shows that he holds the faith of the *believer* to rest on the authority of Scripture.[2] It hardly needs to be added that when Augustine seeks to destroy the arguments of Manichees and others by adducing the 'consensus of the whole Church', it is very far from his mind to concede that at any point the consensus of the whole Church was in conflict with Scripture or added anything to it.[3]

For Augustine the supreme authority is the Scripture which is handed down by the Church and chimes in perfectly with the Church's tradition. But it is worth noting that it is possible to discover in Augustine the first occurrence since the New Testament of religious experience as a source of authority. Not that it appears as such explicitly. But few can doubt that Augustine's teaching on grace and predestination was derived, in whole or in part, from his experience of God

---

[1] *contra Epistolam Manichaei* I, v, 6; Migne *P.L.* xlii, 176
[2] *Institutes* I, vii, 3; cf. R. E. Davies, op. cit., p. 139
[3] cf. Calvin *Institutes* loc. cit.

as having irresistibly set the course of his life from the beginning. This experience is the main burden of the *Confessions*, and the theological positions to which he came later in his life bear very powerful testimony to the vividness and reality of the experience. But it would be wrong to suggest, even for a moment, that Augustine could ever have set experience against Scripture.

The assumption of doctrinal identity between Scripture and tradition and their joint position of supreme authority were not seriously questioned during the Middle Ages. But both were shattered by the Reformation. The reasons for the eventual break-up are highly complex; but among them must be placed the addition of various traditions to the doctrinal deposit of Scripture and early tradition. These traditions were so numerous and diverse that it became increasingly difficult to argue that they were logically developed from Scriptural truth, and it became necessary to claim that the tradition was itself a living and developing reality by which the Holy Spirit was guiding the Church into a wider and wider knowledge of the faith. It was affirmed that he was disclosing to the Church the things that the disciples 'could not bear' during the incarnate life of Jesus Christ, or, alternatively, that he was unfolding the secrets which Jesus had imparted to his disciples under the pledge of secrecy during the forty days between the Resurrection and Ascension, but was now willing to be released progressively as time went on. In either case, Scripture and tradition were beginning to live apart. Another factor in the break-up was the close assimilation of the Christian faith by the Schoolmen to the philosophy of Aristotle, justifiable, of course, in its time, but liable to be attacked very strongly when the Bible in its original languages became available to the whole learned world and was found to read so differently from scholastic treatises.

In this situation it was not difficult for the Reformers to effect a complete divorce, in their own thinking and in that of their followers, between Scripture and tradition; and by doing this they inaugurated so bitter and inconclusive a controversy that many ardent Christians cried, 'A plague on both your houses', and appealed to the Spirit and the Spirit alone–that is, to their own experience of the Spirit's working, to the inner witness which stood behind both Scripture and tradition and enabled men to find the pure Gospel without benefit of creeds or institution or written word.

Thus the Reformation achieved the tripartition of Western Christendom along the lines set by the problem as its various disputing champions saw it, and by so doing laid down the terms in which the problems of authority was to be discussed for many centuries, and still must be for many purposes.[1] 'Scripture', 'tradition', 'the testimony of the Holy Spirit', have been bandied about for so long that is is very difficult to think of them as anything but separate entities opposed to each other, or to conceive of a solution to the problem of authority except by putting one of the three in the position of primacy.

But in at least three respects the whole situation has now fundamentally changed, and the change has become apparent only in the very recent past, though its causes, as we shall see, lie much further back. First, the critical study of the Bible and of Christian history has made it impossible for any communion in Christendom, or any group of communions, to point either to Scripture or to history as validating its claims, often made in the past, to possess the authentic form of Christianity and to judge other communions by their degree of approximation to itself. When each communion pursued its Biblical and historical studies in isolation it was perfectly possible to do this, and to make out a case which was quite convincing to those who made it. It could be shown from Scripture, for instance, that a particular type of ministry was the one prescribed by the New Testament; it could then be shown from history that only certain Churches had retained this particular type of ministry. Thus, only they had preserved the apostolic faith in its purity. Each communion included itself among the preservers of the faith. This was done by Presbyterians in the Reformation

[3] For instance, the relation of Scripture and tradition was one of the subjects handed over for clarification to the Anglican–Methodist Unity Commission as an item which must be satisfactorily dealt with before the union of the two Churches can be approved.

period. It was done by Anglicans in the time of the Tractarian movement. It had been done by Rome, apparently once and for all, long before either of the other communions got to work. The fact that the conclusion of the argument was different in each case, though the premisses were allegedly the same, did not daunt men who, it must be feared, started off with the presupposition that they were right, and that all that was necessary was to prove it.

But in this century men of different denominations have begun to study the Bible and history together, and the ecumenical enterprise in this matter has now reached the point at which no reader troubles to inquire the denomination of the scholar whose work he is reading. The direct result has been that conclusions about the ministry, about the nature of the Church, and about many other doctrines of the faith, cut right across the denominations, and that differences in the doctrine of authority in particular no longer correspond in any significant way to denominational divisions. The only exception to this seems to be that it is still hard to find a Baptist scholar who believes that infant baptism was practised in New Testament times, and equally hard to find an Anglican scholar who does not. Roman Catholic and Orthodox scholars were the last to join in the co-operative activity of Biblical and historical scholarship. But Roman participation is now complete, and must surely be one of the factors which have led to the easing of Rome's attitude to other Churches and towards the Christian status of their members and ministers. It may even be not without significance in this connexion that the Second Vatican Council avoided the error of Trent which has caused so much subsequent embarrassment in the twentieth century, and omitted to pronounce its own Constitutions infallible. Nor is it likely that even so advanced a Roman theologian as Hans Küng would have opened up again the question of Papal infallibility,[1] had it not been for the fact that Roman Catholics are now as aware as Protestants of the historical difficulties of that doctrine.

Secondly, the relation between Scripture and tradition has now to be radically re-formulated. For now it is plain that

[1] in *Structures of the Church* pp. 305–36; cf. pp. 196ff. below

Scripture and tradition are fused within the pages of the New Testament itself, and that the old distinction between what the New Testament says and what tradition says does not correspond to the realities of the situation. The teaching of the New Testament Church and the way in which the New Testament Church is ordered develop considerably within the pages of the New Testament itself. The 'apostolic preaching' is one thing in Acts, another in the undisputed Pauline Epistles, yet another in the Johannine writings, yet another in the Pastoral Epistles. The question whether the various versions conflict with one another is not of primary importance; the fact of the development of one into the other, and the fact of parallel developments going on at the same time, are unmistakable. The same applies to the ordering of the Church in Acts, the Pauline Epistles and the Pastorals. In both cases a process which can only be called 'tradition' has been at work, and it is no longer reasonable to draw a sharp line of demarcation on the other side of the Pastorals, or of 2 Peter, or whichever book is taken to be the latest in the New Testament, and to say that everything on one side of the line is Scripture, and everything on the other side is tradition. Tradition is at work in the formation of Scripture, and Scripture gave the first form, or forms, to tradition.

This is now apparent in the Gospels themselves. The Form Critics some time ago established the fact that the 'forms' in which the sayings of Jesus are recorded for us–that is to say, the literary shape in which they appear and the settings in which they are found–are determined for us by the Early Church and not by historical fact; we cannot ever be sure that Jesus said what is ascribed to him at the time or in the situation which the Gospels give; nor is it at all likely that his sayings and parables were actually uttered in the chronological sequence which any of the Gospels provides. It is plain also that the Early Church *selected* the sayings and doings of Jesus which it deemed worthy of permanent record, and that it did so mainly with an eye to its own needs, and without any profound respect for the needs of later historians or the Church of the future. And now we can no longer rule out the possibility that the sayings and parables themselves have been 'doctored' (though not deliberately) to meet the current needs and answer the pressing problems of the Christian community in a difficult environment. Some scholars would go much further than this in denying historicity to the Gospel narratives,[1] but even if we go only so far as is here suggested we are compelled to the conclusion that 'tradition' has been busily at work in the formation of the Gospels as we have them, and that it is not possible any longer to say that the Gospels are pure Scripture, while every product of the Early Church outside the pages of the New Testament is pure tradition.

In fact, we have come to the point when the whole matter has to be put in a quite different way. This was taken in hand by the Theological Commission on 'Tradition and Traditions' of the Faith and Order Department of the World Council of Churches in preparation for the Fourth World Conference on Faith and Order, held in Montreal in 1963,[2] and carried further by that Conference itself.[3] On the basis of this work it is perhaps possible to re-state the position as follows:

(1) There is, first and foremost, the Apostolic Tradition. This is identical with Holy Scripture, which is Tradition *par excellence*. The Apostolic Tradition falls into three parts, according to whether the truths which it announces are (a) the central truths of the Gospel, embodied and proclaimed by Jesus himself and constituting the essence of the preaching of the Apostles, or (b) truths which are no doubt complementary to each other in the final analysis and the mind of God, but are apparently contradictory, and appear side by side, unreconciled, within the pages of Holy Scripture (e.g. the sovereign grace of God and the free will of man; justification by faith alone and the necessity of the Sacraments for salvation; the imminence of the Parousia and the

---

[1] see, for example, D. E. Nineham *The Gospel of St Mark* (Penguin Books 1963) and cf. the discussion of this by the editor in *Vindications* (ed. Anthony Hanson), pp. 74–102

[2] The Commission's Report is published in *Faith and Order Findings* Part IV, pp. 3–63.

[3] see *The Fourth World Conference on Faith and Order: The Report from Montreal 1963* pp. 50–61

growth of humanity into Christ), or (c) statements of faith made by individual authors in the New Testament, but not confirmed or denied by the New Testament as a whole (among these should perhaps be included the doctrine of the Virgin Birth, the conception of Christianity as a 'New Law', and perhaps also the doctrine of Purgatory). All these three parts are to be found within the pages of Holy Writ, and are the product of a 'traditionary process' which, so far as the record of the Christian Gospel is concerned, began with the first appearance of Jesus of Nazareth as a prophet on the arrest of John the Baptist.

Then there is (2) the Catholic tradition, based on and developed out of the Apostolic Tradition, built up, expounded and defended by the writers later recognized by the universal Church as orthodox, embodied in the liturgies of the great Churches of Christendom, in the ecumenical Creeds, and the Confessions and Articles of the great communions, and later further expounded and developed by the Schoolmen and the great Reformers. This Tradition is, of course, more fluid and less well defined and consistent than the Apostolic tradition. The division of the Church, and the differences between theologians of various schools, have sometimes caused it to be confused with other, lesser forms of tradition, and sometimes, it may be, with plain error. Yet this tradition is discernibly persistent through the vicissitudes of Church history, and certainly not confined to any one denomination.

(3) Of lesser account, but still important, are the 'traditions' developed independently, but on a world-wide scale, by the Roman, Orthodox and Protestant communions; they should perhaps be called the 'confessional traditions'. They include the doctrines of Church order and government to be found in the various Confessions, the Arminian and Calvinist approaches to the problem of election and grace, the various conceptions of sacramental grace, the differing doctrines of the Christian ministry, and so on. These traditions have been, until the present century, often engaged in a life-and-death struggle with one another. But now they have entered into the ecumenical conversation, and many of them

may emerge in due course–purified, no doubt–as integral but neglected parts of the Catholic tradition.

And finally[1] there are the denominational traditions, the peculiarities and idiosyncrasies of each denomination in belief and practice–some of them simply local or national. The words 'peculiarities' and 'idiosyncrasies' are here used in no pejorative sense; they indicate the particular possessions of groups of Christians–as it might be the Covenant Service of the Methodists, or the Confirmation Service of the Church of England (the Book of Common Prayer contains excellent examples of all the four forms of tradition which we have mentioned). These also are entering the ecumenical conversation, and some may also graduate to a higher place in the traditionary hierarchy.[1]

This analysis is certainly not final. It leaves untouched the problem of the place of the Old Testament in the Apostolic Tradition. It may still differentiate too sharply between the later New Testament and the 'sub-apostolic' writings, which resemble them so closely in spirit and content but have not received the stamp of the Church's full approval. But it indicates clearly enough that any treatment of the problem of authority which involves the disjunction, 'Scripture or tradition', does not make very good sense in the light of our present knowledge of the Bible and history.

Thirdly, the whole concept of religious authority is now under fire and in danger of being dispensed with altogether. So simple a statement as 'I believe that God is my Father on the authority of Jesus Christ', or 'on the authority of the Bible', or 'on the authority of the Church in all the ages', or 'on the authority of my personal knowledge of God', or even 'on the authority of Jesus, the Bible, the Church, *and* personal experience' is immediately under attack, inside the Church as well as outside it. Inside the Church it is now frequently said that we have no certain knowledge of what Jesus taught –but only of what the Early Church thought he taught; that the Bible is by no means uniform in its assertion of the father-

---

[1] I have developed this position rather more fully in the *London Quarterly and Holborn Review* April 1965 (pp. 133–41) under the title 'The Bible and Tradition'.

hood of God, and that we have no right to choose those passages which assert it and neglect those which do not–and that in any case the statements of the Bible spring as much from the social and economic circumstances of the writers as from any inside knowledge that they had of the ways of God; that the Church of all the ages has often denied by its practice what it has averred in its teaching about the fatherhood of God, and that there is no good reason to accept the unsupported statements which come from a historically conditioned institution; that personal experience of the fatherhood of God is easily explained away by the psychic conditions of those who have the experience, and in any case has no validity for anyone except the experiencer.

This tendency to radical scepticism is given powerful logical expression in linguistic philosophy, which has as much claim on the attention of Christians as on anyone else. The members of this school of thought often feel themselves compelled by their general philosophical position to hold that statements about God, and the unseen world in general, are either meaningless, or have meaning only within the closed world of those who believe in God and the unseen world anyway, and have no value or meaning for anyone else. In either case the notion of religious authority is stripped of its vital content, and the doctrines of the faith are reduced either to nothing at all, or to the status of a private dialect for those who wish to talk to each other about what they believe in but have no right to expect anyone else whatever to accept.

The same conclusion is often reached by another route. If it be held that Christian faith consists in total, existential self-commitment to the life and the light which are found in Jesus, and that it loses its authenticity as soon as it is translated into doctrines or any kind of propositions, or relies on historical statements (such as those commonly made about the Resurrection), or on the support of an institutional Church, the sceptical conclusion follows just as inexorably. In the first place, it is open to anyone to explain away such faith in purely psychological terms. In the second place, such faith, on the admission of those who commend it, is a purely personal affair, or at most limited to a group of people who share the same insights and experiences. And in the third place, those who have made this existential self-commitment have no common ground with those who have not or who do not think in such terms, and where there is no common ground there can be no appeal to authority. Here, as elsewhere, the concept of authority has disappeared.

Not that all Christian thinkers hold the views here described; nor do all those who hold them proceed to the sceptical conclusions which we have indicated. But the proponents of a more conservative approach now seem to find themselves perpetually on the defensive, and the argument seems often to be going against them. The advanced historical critics who refuse to proceed to radical conclusions are simply unwilling to be carried forward by the wind of their own arguments. Those who hold, for instance, that we have no reliable evidence of what Jesus said and did and of what happened to him, and in particular that we cannot say with any confidence what the Resurrection of Jesus was as an historical event, surely imply that we have no access to the historical events that formed the basis of the narrative which has come down to us, and that all we have is (a) the interpretation put upon those events by the Early Church and (b) the Early Church's account of the experience induced in the Apostles by those events, and especially by the person who is alleged by the Early Church to have been at their centre. The 'Early Church' in this connexion means, of course, not the Apostles and their contemporaries, but the community of Christians in the generation succeeding that of the Apostles.

Thus, the Christian of the second half of the twentieth century is being told that his informants about Jesus Christ are unreliable at certain key points of the narrative (such as the Resurrection) and cannot be fully trusted anywhere; and that he has to rely on the Early Church to supply him with the Christian faith. But the Early Church turns out to be identical with the informants whom he has been told not to trust on historical grounds. What kind of authority is it likely to have for him? He is at liberty with sound logic to suppose, at best, that the statements of the New Testament, lacking all authority worthy of the name, must be adjudged simply and solely on their own merits, or, at worst, that, in the absence of any solid testimony to their historicity, he is compelled in all honesty to discard them altogether. The concept of authority is once again dissolved.

The moderns who cast radical doubt on the historical reliability of the Gospels try to reinstate a doctrine of authority in one or two ways. Some of them are quite prepared to do without any historical basis, except of the barest kind ('Jesus was born, lived, had friends and enemies, and was murdered by the latter', suffices for many of them), because they believe that 'authentic Christianity' consists in the experience which Jesus and his friends had and which can be 'caught' again in every age by those who yield to the impact of Jesus upon them. Their answer to the sceptical conclusion which we have drawn from the first part of their argument is that the Early Church testifies to the same Gospel in essentials as we can believe to have been preached by Jesus and the Apostles, and to the same Gospel as they themselves hold in a de-historicized, de-mythologized form. But how do we know this? On whose word do we accept it? Only, it is to be feared, on the word of the scholars who are propounding the theory. The authority of twentieth-century scholarship takes the place of the authority of Scripture and the authority of the Church. This would be to some extent plausible if twentieth-century scholarship were unanimous or showed any sign of becoming so. But there is no sign of this. And meanwhile they are making assumptions about the expendability of historical events and the mythopoeic thought-processes of the first Christians which need a great deal of examination and discussion. The Christian faced with this version of the faith may well be excused if he detects an alarming similarity between the 'authentic Christianity' which is offered to him and the smile on the face of the Cheshire Cat after the Cat itself had disappeared.

Radicals of the other sort still adhere to the necessity of a historical basis for Christianity while claiming that the Gospels do not provide, in themselves, a reliable one. They argue that the Catholic Church has set its seal on the New Testament narrative as substantially true, and that we can therefore believe the narrative on the authority of the Church even though the narrative's own credentials are scientifically precarious. Thus they seem to have reinstated a doctrine of authority. But will it stand up to a moment's examination today? Is it at all likely that modern Christians will accept on the authority of the Church what they know on other grounds to be very probably untrue? One of the things that the Reformation did for Europe was to remove the obligation on Christians to do what is here asked of them, and there is no going back on the Reformation, at least in this respect.

If fundamental doubt of this kind about the nature and legitimacy of authority is present and growing within the Church, we cannot be surprised to discover that outside the Church the process of the disintegration of authority has gone much further. While the Church still spoke with certainty and confidence, many people outside the Church showed a surprising readiness to accept the statements on religious and ethical matters made by the Church which they had no intention of re-joining. The authority of the Church– or the Pope, or the Bible–was not, of course, regularly obeyed; in fact, it was much more often disobeyed, and there was always a great deal of grumbling at the fact that such an authority existed, and made claims, mostly of a prohibitive nature, on ordinary people. But there was always an element of bravado in the disobedience. And in the ordinary affairs and problems of life, if you could quote the Bible, or the Pope, or a bishop, to support your views, it was generally agreed that you had scored a point. This meant that in the work of evangelism or religious education the preacher or teacher had something to which he could appeal in the minds of his hearers. If he could put up a fairly good case for the Gospel, there was always the built-in authority of the Church or the Bible which might, and often did, tip the scale in favour of faith, especially in the case of the young at school or university.

But this is rapidly ceasing to be true. On the more sophisticated level the linguistic philosophers have accustomed us to refusing to consider whether a statement is true, and to confining ourselves to asking what the statement means, what 'job' it does—what 'cash-value' it has—and if the answer cannot be given in terms which make it verifiable by scientific means, to troubling no more about it. And the same philosophers have given great currency to the view that ethical consequences cannot be drawn from statements about the universe, and that therefore ethics cannot be based on theology. So the statements of Christians about God or ethics fall on equally deaf ears. And this repudiation of ecclesiastical authority has rapidly seeped through to the less sophisticated members of the population. Children in school over wide areas, as well as their immediate seniors—often to the painful surprise of their more conventional parents—simply shrug their shoulders when they are told what the Bible says or the Church teaches, and can see no reason at all why they should conform their ideas or their conduct to the prescriptions which reach them from these sources. This fact, indeed, constitutes one of the new and intractable problems of religious education today.

The age in which we live is likely to go down to history as the age which finally cast off all religious authority. It is with the fundamental changes in the mental attitude of our time, and especially with the decline of religious authority, that this book is mainly concerned. We shall endeavour to discover the stages by which the present situation came about; and at the end of the book we shall try to make some suggestions as to what should be done about it.

Chapter Two

THE LEGACY OF SCHLEIERMACHER

It is always dangerous to trace the development of an idea, or system of ideas, from one thinker to another. The connexion of thought may be very apparent to the historian of ideas, and it may be very obvious to him how one thing must have led to another by an inevitable logical process, as one thinker read and pondered the thoughts of his predecessors, and saw how to avoid their mistakes and draw the right consequences from their true insights. But the beautiful pattern which is thus created may exist solely in the mind of the historian. Each thinker may have in fact gone through the whole process for himself, without any benefit from his predecessors; or he may have derived his basic ideas from some quite other sources than the one which the historian has ascribed to them. Perhaps this is why various works with titles such as 'History of European Thought' or 'Development of Christian Doctrine' differ from each other so widely–so widely sometimes that the unfortunate student is in doubt whether a thinker with the same name is really the same thinker as the one he read about in another history of ideas. It is undoubted that historians of ideas, like other historians, may be so captivated by a connexion of thought which they have themselves observed that they impose the pattern which it seems to suggest on a series of thinkers who are not in a position to protest.

The danger is lessened in those comparatively rare cases when one thinker directly ascribes the idea which he is about to develop–or, more often, contradict–to a particular thinker whom he names and quotes. We need not doubt, for instance, the accuracy of St Thomas Aquinas when he freely ascribes

34

to Aristotle idea after idea which he discusses, and to Plato almost as many; nor is it in question that Immanuel Kant was provoked to a great deal of his more profound thinking by 'the celebrated David Hume', who 'was one of those geographers of human reason who have imagined that they have sufficiently disposed of all such [metaphysical] questions by setting them outside the horizon of human reason'.[1] But even in cases like these we cannot take the truth of such humble or sardonic acknowledgements for granted. All thinkers are influenced far more than they can ever know by ideas which have come to them from anonymous or forgotten sources, and no one can write an accurate and comprehensive history of the development of his own ideas. How much less is it possible for anyone to write an accurate and comprehensive history of the ideas of a whole civilization or a whole religion!

The danger reaches its peak if the historian traces the development of a theory or a concept from one thinker to another when there is no good evidence that the second thinker had ever read or heard about his alleged predecessor's ideas. In fact, such an enterprise is, on the face of it, entirely preposterous. It is often taken in hand, however, and the excuse for it is that ideas do not, so far as we know, take their origin from spontaneous generation in the brain of an individual, but from the effect on that brain of lectures, periodicals, newspapers, books and discussion. A man 'picks up out of the air' the ideas which are flying around in the intellectual atmosphere of his age and circle, and broods on them to good or bad effect; and we may suppose that a man whose ideas are worthy of a place in the history of thought is likely to be more sensitive than others to the thought of those who are engaged on the same problems as he is. So one idea does lead to another, if only in a roundabout way, and it is theoretically possible to write the history of thought on a particular subject. The hazard lies in attempting to select some and reject others of the influences which may have helped to mould a man's thought, especially when he gives no clue to the process himself.

[1] *Immanuel Kant's Critique of Pure Reason* tr. N. Kemp Smith (Macmillan, London 1933), p. 606

Anyone who reads this book is now invited to take the very risk which we have just described, and to take it, at least for a number of pages, in its most acute form. The attempt is about to be made to trace the decline in the doctrine of authority, which has now reached the point described in Chapter 1, from Friedrich Schleiermacher through the Oxford Movement, the publication of *Essays and Reviews*, the publication of *Lux Mundi*, the teaching of John Oman and P. T. Forsyth, and the decisions of the Second Vatican Council, down to the present day—and only then to venture any suggestions as to what the next step in the process ought to be. But there is no good reason for thinking that the Fathers of the Oxford Movement had any knowledge or fear of Schleiermacher; they shared the isolation, almost universal in the nineteenth century, of English theology from the breezes of thought blowing strongly in Germany; and it was not until the radical views of David Friedrich Strauss about the historicity of the Gospels were introduced into England that the men of the Movement took cognizance of contemporary German theology.[1] *Essays and Reviews* seems to have been produced without any awareness of Schleiermacher's influence, and the same applies to *Lux Mundi* many years later. With Oman and Forsyth we enter into a theological atmosphere that is much less parochial, and also much less patristic, than nineteenth-century Anglicanism, and it would not be difficult to show that Schleiermacher helped to create it; and from then on Schleiermacher's theology is part of the situation into which every theological student enters even if it is never expounded to him. But the recognition of Schleiermacher comes very late in the story.

The reason why, in these circumstances, the risk of imposing a false pattern on the history of the doctrine of authority has to be taken is that Schleiermacher disclosed a problem, and propounded a solution to that problem, which, once disclosed and propounded, no Christian theologian,

---

[1] An exception must be made in the case of E. B. Pusey, who heard Schleiermacher lecture in Berlin in 1825. He liked his piety and distrusted his pantheistic tendencies. But it is very doubtful if Pusey's thought was consciously affected in any way.

even if he lived on the other side of the German Ocean and never opened a book of German theology (on principle, or because he did not understand the language, or for both reasons), could henceforward neglect. The Oxford Movement, in an important sense, is a protest against the disclosure of the problem, and, in an even more important sense, a reaction against its Schleiermacherian solution. *Essays and Reviews* acknowledges the problem, but proclaims an alternative solution. *Lux Mundi* sought to combine the *Essays and Reviews* solution with the dogmatic teaching of the Church, but could not deny the problem or altogether avoid the Schleiermacherian approach to it. Since its time the battle has swung from one side to the other, and sometimes a truce has been attempted; but the battlefield is the one that Schleiermacher indicated, and in our time the issue seems almost to have been settled in Schleiermacher's favour.

It may well be, of course, that if Schleiermacher had not made his disclosure and offered his solution, someone else would have done so. It may well be that the disclosure and the solution were implicit in English (and other) theology, and that all that Schleiermacher did was to make them explicit in Germany. In either of these cases 'Schleiermacher' is just a convenient name for a particular moment in the development of Christian thought, and we are in some danger of creating a 'Schleiermacher mythology' if we claim too much for him personally. But it would be a very useful mythology anyhow, and Schleiermacher, on any view, gives the clearest available account of the way of thinking that is associated with his name.

To justify these statements we must begin by going back behind Schleiermacher. The Enlightenment in Germany had taken up and developed certain ideas inherent in many of the Renaissance thinkers, but inhibited for two centuries by the outburst and success of the Reformation: notably the all-sufficiency of human reason, and the superiority of ethics to doctrinal formulation[1] (the same process of thought

---

[1] Leonardo may count as the embodiment of the former idea; Erasmus (see his *Enchiridion Militis Christiani*) as the literary exponent of the latter. Neither of them, of course, was a rationalist in any modern sense.

was followed by the English Deists and Rationalists, but we are here chiefly concerned with Germany). Lessing, for instance, had maintained on rational grounds that 'accidental historical truths can never become proofs for necessary truths of reason', and had gone on from this to show that religious truth cannot be established by anything that Christ did or suffered. Christianity, in fact, was the religion preached and practised by Jesus, not the religion (still less the theology) that has grown up round the person of Jesus. It was the best form of natural religion so far discovered, but would in due course give place to the religion of reason which had yet to be brought to light. This religion would have 'the proof of the spirit and the power', that is, it would ring true to human reason and experience, as Christianity at present does only imperfectly.

Karl Barth, in his penetrating study of the fable which occurs in *Nathan der Weise*,[1] suggests that the fable accurately expresses Lessing's religious views. The fable is about a father who, according to an ancient custom in his family, has to give a certain ring to the son he loves most; the ring has the power of making its owner beloved by God and man. He does not wish to single out one of his three sons in this way, for he loves them all equally. He therefore has two exact replicas of the ring made, gives one of the rings to each of his sons, and dies. Each son thinks that the other two have bogus rings, and they take the matter to court. The judge does not presume to decide which is the real ring; he orders each son to live as if he had the true ring, that is, virtuously, saying that in a myriad years' time a judge will arise who knows which is the true ring. Barth interprets this to mean to Lessing's mind that we are all to live faithfully according to the religion which is ours; in the distant future it will be known which is the true religion.[2]

Such a view as Lessing's not only denies the possibility of revelation in any sense in which it has been understood in Christian history, or rather, reduces all claimants to revelation to the same level and refuses to judge between them. It also tends to atheism. For reason and experience are, on this

---

[1] Act III, scene 7   [2] *From Rousseau to Ritschl* pp. 140ff.

view, the final arbiters of truth; and reason and experience cannot by themselves establish the existence of God. All religions are only relatively true, and all one day will be superseded. Men were bound to conclude that the ultimate religion of reason, possessing the 'spirit and the power', might very well dispense with the notion of God altogether. Indeed, it may be that those who nowadays proclaim the death of God are only drawing the logical consequence from the reasoning of Lessing.

Immanuel Kant might well have followed the path which led to atheism, and reached it very quickly. He was no less a man of the Englightenment than Lessing. By massive argument he demolished one by one the classical proofs for the existence of God,[1] and showed that to believe in God landed the believer in an 'antinomy of pure reason' from which reason could provide no escape. But he did not draw the atheistic conclusion. On the contrary, he was sure that Christianity was the true form of natural religion. The means by which he reinstated the God whom he had dethroned is well known. He argued that the 'categorical imperative' which bid us do this or that at any cost and at any risk, without any regard for consequences, requires us as human beings, endowed with reason, to believe in God as the lawgiver who issues the imperatives. But he did not feel able to say much more about God than that he is the supreme lawgiver, and that the teaching of Jesus lays down for all men the laws which he has enacted. To be a Christian, to believe in God, means to him no more than to obey the laws whose origin we infer to be divine. Religion, as it is usually understood, virtually disappears (Kant could never bring himself to go to church), theology is attenuated, ethics is supreme. It does not even really need the prop of theism; for we know the moral law for certain and cannot escape it; the existence and nature of God are only an inference from that.

One way of saving religion from the men of reason was suggested by Hegel. He adopted the beautifully simple expedient of identifying reason with its object, thought with being, and (in effect) God with man. Man is indeed 'finite Spirit', but he is ultimately identical with 'infinite spirit'. For

[1] *Critique of Pure Reason* pp. 495–524.

39

his thoughts and deeds are the medium through which infinite spirit attains self-consciousness. Man's thoughts are taken up into the thought of Absolute Mind, and when contradiction after contradiction has been reconciled by the process of thesis answered by antithesis, and the resolution of both by synthesis, till there are no contradictions left to be reconciled, Absolute Mind will be all in all. Thus the difficulty of reason in accepting the idea of God turns out to be simply a problem in process of being solved by the ongoing activity of mind; history, which Lessing thought to be irrelevant to eternal truth, turns out to be God's self-realization through the processes of human experience. Believer and unbeliever, historian and scientist, philosopher and theologian, all have an equally honoured place in the triumphal progress of mind, which is also the triumphal progress of reality (except that it is only the philosopher who knows what is going on); and at the end of it all the whole world-process will show itself to have been the total self-manifestation of the Absolute.

No one doubts the immense fascination which this system of ideas had upon some of the best minds of the nineteenth century. Who even today can entirely escape the attraction of the view that evil is unrealized good and error unrealized truth? The history of Hegelianism in Christian theology continues through D. F. Strauss and T. H. Green to the writings of William Temple's middle years.[1] But it is a history which has come to an end. Even those who were carried away by Hegel's transcendentalism had a sneaking suspicion that he was scarcely doing justice to the harsh events of the Passion—to say nothing of the rest of history—or to the facts of evil in human life. And the renewed empiricism of twentieth-century theology and philosophy seems to have given him his final quietus. It seems impossible now to give allegiance to a philosophy which starts from an *a priori* notion of what reality ought to be, adjusts history and experience to fit into that notion, and assumes that what at present seems unadjustable will one day inevitably be adjusted; and it seems impossible that it will ever be possible again.

[1] O. C. Thomas *William Temple's Philosophy of Religion* p. 12

40

When Friedrich Daniel Ernst Schleiermacher took up his position as Reformed preacher at the Charité Institute in Berlin in September 1796, he entered an intellectual atmosphere in which the foundations of Christian theology had been undermined, and it seemed to many to be only a matter of time before the realization of this fact spread far and wide and led to the entire disintegration of the Christian religion. It is not surprising that in such an atmosphere men who retained a loyalty to Christianity, but could not see their way to its intellectual justification, were attracted by the method of reconciling their faith with the best thought of the time that was propounded by Hegel. But the method did not satisfy everyone, and it did not satisfy Schleiermacher. He was a man of the Enlightenment, and felt the full force of its critique of Christian theism and of the doctrines connected with the Incarnation. In his student years at Halle he had mastered the *Critique of Pure Reason*, and saw no good reason for pushing its conclusions on one side. He was strongly influenced for many years–perhaps always–by the idealism of J. G. Fichte, who held that one universal reason dwelt in all men, and that the reason of individual men was the universal reason embodied.

But there was another side to his thinking, and it came directly from the religion of the Moravians, from whom he received much of his education, in Upper Lusatia and Barby.[1] He valued their insights into the nature of Christian truth very highly indeed; he held their religious feelings to be absolutely genuine and their acts of worship to be evocative of true piety. In due course he came to find their discipline too restrictive and their theology too narrow, and left them. For a while he found himself more and more alienated from them as he absorbed the spirit of the Enlightenment. But when he had come through to his own personal understanding of the essence of Christianity, he began to look back on them once again as his greatly valued instructors and pastors. He thought of himself

---

[1] The *Oxford Dictionary of the Christian Church* states (*s.v.* Schleiermacher) that Schleiermacher's parents were *converted* to the Herrnhuter Brethren (i.e. the Moravians); but the evidence is not given.

at that time as, in his own words, a 'Moravian again of a higher order'.[1]

In the 'Wednesday Club' in Berlin, which he joined soon after his appointment to the Charité, he met the leaders of the 'Romantic' circle, all of them profoundly influenced by Goethe, and by his *Wilhelm Meister* in particular. Schlegel and Novalis were his friends, and from them he learned fully, what he had begun to learn from Goethe's writings in the Moravian seminary in Barby, the immense capacity of man and the glory of nature. These lessons were fused with his Moravian education to produce a profound conviction of the value of the individual and of individual insights into the nature of things.

No man alive, therefore, was more thoroughly immersed in the confused currents of thought that were then flowing through the cultured circles of Berlin. Zealous above all things to preserve the power and life and truth of the Christian religion, but at the same time almost equally zealous to make them intelligible and acceptable to the men who derived their intellectual stimulus and their philosophy of life from the Enlightenment, he published, in 1799, at the instance of Schlegel, his *Speeches on Religion to its Cultured Despisers*.[2] The *Speeches* are deliberately apologetic, and his substantial account of the Christian Faith appears more clearly in *The Christian Faith* (1821-2) than in the *Speeches*, but the *Speeches* give us most of what we need for our purpose of discovering Schleiermacher's approach to the problem of authority.

We notice, therefore, first of all, that Schleiermacher is willing to start exactly where the 'cultured despisers' are, and to take nothing for granted. He recognizes their doubts and difficulties about the way in which Christianity is normally presented, defended and expounded, and he addresses himself quite explicitly to the 'sons of Germany', that is, to those of his contemporaries who are most likely and most able to

---

[1] Barth (*From Rousseau to Ritschl* pp. 306–54) does not appear to attach much importance to Moravian influence on Schleiermacher; see, however, John Oman's Introduction to *On Religion* (pp. xiv–xv).

[2] quoted hereafter from Oman's translation (1893)

pick holes in what he says. His reasons for addressing himself to the Germans are not very flattering to members of other nations:

> Those proud Islanders [*sc.* the English] whom many unduly honour, know no watchword but *gain* and *enjoyment*. Their zeal for knowledge is only a sham fight, their worldly wisdom a false jewel, skilfully and deceptively composed, and their sacred freedom itself too often and too easily serves self-interest. They are never in earnest with anything that goes beyond palpable utility. . . . Similarly they know nothing of religion, save that all preach devotion to ancient usages and defend its institutions, regarding them as a protection wisely cherished by the constitution against the natural enemy of the state.[1]

As to the French–

> On them, one who honours religion can hardly endure to look, for in every act and almost in every word, they tread its holiest ordinances under foot. The barbarous indifference of the millions of the people, and the witty frivolity with which individual brilliant spirits behold the sublimest fact of history that is not only taking place before their eyes, but has them all in its grasp, . . . witnesses clearly enough how little they are capable of a holy awe or a true adoration.[2]

Only among the Germans–

> Neither wise moderation, nor quiet contemplation is wanting; there, therefore, religion must find a refuge from the coarse barbarism and the cold worldly mind of the age.[3]

But whatever his reasons for writing directly for the Germans, he knew very well that by so doing he was exposing himself to the most searching and intelligent criticism that he was

---

[1] *On Religion* p. 9f. In his subsequent 'Explanations of the First Speech' Schleiermacher apologizes for his attack on the English by saying (p. 23) that it was launched 'at a time when it seemed necessary to protest strongly against the prevailing Anglomania'. But he does not retract much of his earlier judgement, though he admits that since it was expressed the popular English interest in missions and the spread of the Bible has made it somewhat less tenable.

[2] ibid., p. 10. He makes no subsequent apology to the French.

[3] ibid., p. 10f.

likely to get anywhere, and he wrote, accordingly, with those attitudes clearly in his mind which he knew them to take.

Next, we must notice, and never for a moment forget, his explicit distinction of religion from science and morality, his refusal to identify religion with theology, and his repudiation of theology as something which stands in its own right:

> In order to make quite clear to you what is the original and characteristic possession of religion, it resigns, at once, all claims on anything that belongs either to science or morality. Whether it has been borrowed or bestowed it is now returned.[1]

That is to say, science can give to religion nothing that it wants or needs to have:

> Though you pass from the laws [sc. of science] to the Universal Lawgiver, in whom is the unity of all things; though you allege that nature cannot be comprehended without God, I would still maintain that religion has nothing to do with this knowledge, and that, quite apart from it, its nature can be known.[2]

Science has no light, then, to throw on the nature or existence of God; its methods are of no value when we are considering the truths of religion. It is, of course, an eminently important study for its own purposes, but for the purposes of religion it is worthless. And why?

> It is true that religion is essentially contemplative. . . .
> But this contemplation is not turned, as your knowledge of nature is, to the existence of a finite thing, combined with and opposed to another finite thing.[3]

Science is concerned, in fact, with the physical universe and not with God.

Ethics is in a similar, though not the same, case:

> What is the object of your ethics, of your science of action? Does it not seek to distinguish precisely each part of human doing and producing, and at the same time to combine them into a whole, according to actual relations? But the pious man confesses that, as pious, he knows nothing about it. . . . Only one thing he seeks out and detects, action from God, God's activity among men.[4]

[1] ibid., p. 35   [2] loc. cit.   [3] ibid., p. 36   [4] ibid., p. 36f.

Here we have the acknowledgment of ethics as a science, and a proper subject of human inquiry; but it is a study of the relations between human ethical judgements and the attempt to build them up into a consistent system. Religion, as such, dispenses with all this; it speaks directly on the action of God in human life and on his commandments to men. There is, however, a concession which is not made to science:

If your ethics are right, and his [*sc.* the pious man's] piety as well, he will not, it is true, acknowledge any action as excellent which is not embraced in your system.[1]

That is, a certain harmony may be expected between the findings of ethics and the divine commands to the believer; but it is still true that the construction of an ethical system is not the business of religion, and the harmony which we find between religion and an ethical system is not of great significance to the religious man. After all, there may well be ethical systems which are not harmonious with the actions required by religion (though perhaps Schleiermacher would not take this possibility very seriously), and certainly their existence would not make a ha'p'orth of difference to the religious man. Schleiermacher points out that we expect of women the most refined ethical feeling; we do *not* expect of them any understanding of ethical systems.[2]

'Ideas and principles are all foreign to religion'[3]–and thus theology is not religion. Schleiermacher believes this to follow from the very nature of religion. Theology may well be a description of religion, but it is not religion itself. It is natural, he thinks, that religion should pass into theology, because every man, as a feeling person, becomes an object to himself, and begins to contemplate his own feeling.[4] So theology comes to birth, and a coherent system of ideas and principles begins to emerge. It is quite in order to call them religious ideas and principles, so long as it is remembered that this is the scientific treatment of religion, and not religion itself. And the description of religion can never be equal to the thing described, which is religion.[5]

And since theology is not religion, it is useless if it attempts

---

[1] ibid., p. 37   [2] loc. cit.   [3] ibid., p. 46   [4] loc. cit.
[5] ibid., p. 47

to stand by itself and win credence on its own authority. 'Religion cannot and will not originate in the pure impulse to know.' Therefore what we may know and believe about the nature of things, as a result of our speculations and inquiries, is far beneath the sphere of religion:[1]

Make sure of this, that no man is pious, however perfectly he understands these principles and conceptions [sc. those arrived at by the description of religion], however much he believes he possesses them in clearest consciousness, who cannot show that they have originated in himself and, being the outcome of his own feeling, are peculiar to himself.[2]

This last sentence will be seen to be extremely significant when we take up the attitude of Schleiermacher to the question of authority; but it is already clear that it rules out any theology which is based on pure thought or *a priori* speculation. And it would not be an exaggeration to say that there are some theological systems which Schleiermacher regards as being a thousand miles removed from religion—and he would not limit this condemnation to the 'marvellous and complex genealogies of the gods' drawn up by the Greeks, which are 'vain mythology, and, in respect of science, ruinous mysticism'.[3]

If, then, religion is distinct from science and ethics and theology, what is it? There are many definitions of religion in Schleiermacher's writings, and not least in the *Speeches*. It is certain that the nature of religion was the great interest of all his thinking, and since there have been so many travesties of his view of religion,[4] and so many partial accounts of it, it is as well to let him speak for himself:

The contemplation of the pious is the immediate consciousness of the universal existence of all finite things, in and through the Infinite, and of all temporal things in and through the Eternal. Religion is to seek this and find it in

---

[1] ibid., p. 48   [2] ibid., p. 47.   [3] ibid., p. 49

[4] as, for example, in G. Faber *Oxford Apostles* (Pelican edition), where it is stated (p. 138) that Schleiermacher reconciled the contradiction in himself, which consisted in his being a 'devout rationalist', by 'an exaltation of feeling above thought'. He did not exalt feeling above thought, but indicated the proper place of each.

all growth and change, in all doing and suffering. It is to have life and to know life in immediate feeling, only as such an existence in the Infinite and Eternal. Where this is found religion is satisfied, where it hides itself there is for her unrest and anguish, extremity and death. Wherefore it is a life in the infinite nature of the Whole, in the One and in the All, in God, having and possessing all things in God, and God in all. Yet religion is not knowledge and science, either of the world or of God. Without being knowledge, it recognizes knowledge and science. In itself it is an affection, a revelation of the Infinite in the finite, God being seen in it and it in God.[1]

Again:

Your feeling is piety, in so far as it expresses . . . the being and life common to you and to the All. Your feeling is piety in so far as it is the result of the operation of God in you by means of the operation of the world upon you. This series is not made up either of perceptions or of objects of perception, either of works or operations or of different spheres of operation, but purely of sensations and the influence of all that lives and moves around, which accompanies them and conditions them. These feelings are exclusively the elements of religion, and none are excluded.[2]

But these two definitions are not wholly adequate to Schleiermacher's conception of religion, for they suggest that feeling, arising out of our perceptions of the world around us, but transcending them, is the only constituent of true religion. He gave a place to intuition also, and indeed places the very heart of religion in the unitive moment of feeling and intuition. Intuition, in Schleiermacher's language, seems to be the immediate reception of what is presented to us, which is the Infinite in the Finite, and feeling is the response that our whole nature makes to it. The union of the two is fleeting, it is as

fleeing and transparent as the vapour which the dew breathes on blossom and fruit, it is bashful and tender as a maiden's kiss, it is holy and fruitful as a bridal embrace.

And when the moment of the perfect union of feeling and

[1] *On Religion* p. 36   [2] ibid., p. 45f.

intuition–a moment which is raised above all error and misunderstanding–is past, what remains is the consciousness of what has been, and the knowledge that feeling and intuition are one, though now again they are severed into two.[1]

There is a sense in which Schleiermacher has nothing more to say about the nature of religion than this, though, of course, he illustrates and amplifies his view of it in many ways, and in later writings more fully defines it as 'the feeling of absolute dependence'.[2] Indeed, it may be said that to accept this last definition as Schleiermacher's most characteristic and accurate one would be a mistake, for it draws overmuch attention to the passive side of religion. Schleiermacher had no wish to exalt the passive over the active elements in the religious life, and certainly no intention of withdrawing religious people from the aesthetic and intellectual culture of the time in which they lived.[3]

But if we accept his account of religion, even if we do it only for the sake of argument, we bring ourselves face to face at once with the questions which Schleiermacher imagines his readers as posing:

> Whence do those dogmas and doctrines come that many consider the essence of religion? Where do they properly belong? And how do they stand related to what is essential in religion?

The answers arise immediately, as Schleiermacher points out, from what has already been said about the nature of religion itself:

> They are all the result of . . . contemplation of feeling, of . . . reflection and comparison . . . The conceptions that underlie these propositions [*sc.* the propositions of theology] are, like your conceptions from experience, nothing but general expressions for definite feelings.[4]

The doctrines which he has in mind in this passage turn out to be those which concern miracles, inspiration, revelation and belief, and he leaves the task of dealing with the specifi-

---

[1] ibid., p. 43f.

[2] *The Christian Faith* Introduction, p. 132

[3] Barth (*From Rousseau to Ritschl* p. 317f.) rightly takes issue with Brunner on this point.

[4] *On Religion* p. 87

cally Christian doctrines under this head until he gives them exhaustive treatment in *The Christian Faith*. But it is the doctrines treated here which are most germane to our inquiry into the approach of Schleiermacher to the problem of authority.

He sweeps aside nearly all that has previously been written and taught on the subject of miracles, on the ground that it results from a meaningless and irreligious investigation of such questions as: How much need we believe about the miraculous and retain our reputation as reasonable men? What miracles can we dispense with, and how many must we keep? Such questions, he thinks, miss the whole point. For to the religious man every event is a miracle, for every event is a sign of the Infinite, every event is a work of God; and religious men use the word 'miracle' to describe it because it indicates their view of the relation between the finite and the Infinite. 'Miracle is simply the religious name for event.'[1] Clearly such a view of miracles entirely by-passes most of the questions that the miracle-narratives in the Bible are usually thought to raise, and among them such a question as: Do we believe in miracles because the authority of the Bible or the Church requires us to do so? This fact is in itself a signal that we have entered a new phase in the history of the problem of authority.

What we are told about revelation is even more to this point. We could parody it by saying that every new idea is an example of revelation, and this is, in fact, almost what Schleiermacher says. He distinguishes between what we learn from others and what comes to us from ourselves; and of what comes to us from ourselves he says: 'Every intuition and every original feeling proceeds from revelation.' But it is not to be thought that he is here referring to any idea on any subject; he has in mind those insights into the Infinite through the finite which are to him the very stuff of religion.[2]

The treatment of inspiration is, to anyone nurtured in traditional notions, even more cavalier. Inspiration is simply the general feeling of true morality and freedom, springing from the heart irrespectively of all 'external occasions' and

---

[1] ibid., p. 88f.   [2] ibid., p. 89

all 'earthly entanglements'. And 'the operation of grace' is a term for describing revelation and inspiration–and indeed the whole life of the religious man as it is made up of intuition and feeling, withdrawing from the world and going into the world, action and culture. 'The whole life of the pious simply form a series of operations of divine grace.'[1]

Belief, in the sense of accepting what someone else has said or done, so far from being, as some have held, the most important part of religion, is its enemy. If anyone wishes for such a thing, he is shown to have no taste for religion in the true sense; and to demand it of others is worse still. We are all to stand on our own feet in all matters of truth, and 'religion is no slavery, no captivity, least of all for your reason'. It is granted that, apart from a few choice souls, all men need a guide into truth and a stimulus to awaken them from spiritual slumber. But this is simply an example of the well-known fact that all human capacities have to be awakened in the first place. But once they are awakened they function and develop on their own. So it is with religious feeling. There has to be a period of being awakened and stimulated by others, but this tutelage is soon unnecessary, and each man comes quickly to see with his own eyes. How despicable to derive religion from others, or from a dead writing![2] Every sacred writing is 'a glorious production, a speaking monument from the heroic time of religion'. But to believe in what these writings say is not religion:

> Not every person has religion who believes in a sacred
> writing, but only the man who has a lively and immediate
> understanding of it, and who, therefore, so far as he him-
> self is concerned, could most easily do without it.[3]

When he has treated these subjects in the manner we have indicated, Schleiermacher claims to 'have spoken thoroughly of the nature of religion'. But he is well aware that others–Christians and non-Christians–will not allow this claim. They will press the questions: Have you not virtually eliminated God from religion by defining it without any reference to him or to any beliefs about him? Have you not eliminated immortality also, since immortality cannot be the object of

<hr/>

[1] ibid., p. 90   [2] ibid., p. 91   [3] loc. cit.

direct religious feeling? And what has become of the Church, if religion is something which a man cannot derive or learn from anyone else, but which springs up within each man's individual soul? And to these questions we must add another which Schleiermacher does not ascribe to his contemporary critics and commentators, but which is just as surely posed by everything which he has said about religion, inspiration, revelation, belief and 'sacred writings': What religious authority remains to us, if everything we know about the Infinite, and the finite in the Infinite, and life, and ethics, and truth, and freedom, and everything else that is of any importance, comes to each of us from within himself?

To the questions about God, immortality and the Church, Schleiermacher gives explicit answers. His answer to the question about authority we have to extract for ourselves from his writings.

God and immortality, as they are found in most statements of doctrine, are ideas, and it is possible to be convinced of the truth of both of them without being in any sense religious. But it is of the very nature of religion, not simply to have a feeling, but to have a feeling of *God*. It is God who is immediately and unmistakably present to us through our religious feeling. 'If you see the world as a Whole, a Universe, can you do it otherwise than in God?' 'Is not God the highest, the only unity?' God is presupposed in every description of religion that he has given, Schleiermacher maintains; nothing that he has said about religion makes any sense unless God is present to the feeling and intuition of every religious man. There are conceptions of God with which his description of religion will not easily square, and this he fully admits; but these are rigid ideas, in no way arising from true religious feeling, but the product of misapplied scientific thinking, or compounded from characteristics arbitrarily attributed to God.[1]

Most people's ideas of immortality are, on Schleiermacher's view, similarly irreligious, stemming from man's inveterate but mistaken desire to continue his own personality. 'Religion earnestly strives to expand the sharply cut outlines of personality.' But in a true awareness of God all that is indi-

[1] ibid., pp. 92ff.

vidual and fleeting disappears, and we already have a taste of immortality; in a perfect relation with God we are one with the Infinite. The immortality for which we should long is not that which succeeds upon life in this world:

> It is the immortality which we can now have in this temporal life; . . . In the midst of finitude to be one with the Infinite and in every moment to be eternal is the immortality of religion.[1]

Schleiermacher is by no means willing to draw the conclusion from his own reasoning that there is no need for the Church. Religion, he says, is social, just as the nature of man is social. When a man has received some illumination, when some new understanding has come to birth in his mind, when he is aware of an experience which brings him in touch with the Infinite, he naturally wishes to communicate it to others. A religious man who kept his religion to himself would be as much a morbid anomaly as an artist or poet who destroyed the products of his imagination or forbade others to see them. What a religious man wishes to communicate to others is not his ideas or his system of ideas. These he will wish to keep to himself, knowing how full of error they are likely to be. It is 'the conscious states and feelings in which originally man feels himself passive' that he wishes to share with others. And the religious impulse which predisposes him to pass on what he has experienced provides also the audience to which he passes them on. Other religious people will be as eager to hear what he has to say as he is to impart it. Religious people will therefore naturally assemble themselves together, and converse with each other, not lightly or casually, not with the interspersion of jokes and witticisms, or with retorts rapidly exchanged, but soberly and seriously, and with the awe and reverence that is appropriate to sacred things:

> Religion . . . withdraws itself from too wide circles to the more familiar conversation of friendship or the dialogue of love, where glance and action are clearer than words, and where a solemn silence also is understood.

This assembly of religious people, 'each full of native force

[1] ibid., p. 101

seeking liberty of utterance and full at the same time of holy desire to apprehend and appropriate what others offer,' is the Church. It is a natural and necessary part of religion. It is not purely ideal, a vision of what might happen if men were better and more spiritual than they are; it is real and actual; it exists, and has always existed, never numerous, but always alive and powerful, the true Church triumphant, the Church which has vanquished all opposition, whose training is complete. Within its organic structure there will be some who are further advanced than others in the religious life, and these will be marked out from the rest for a priestly function. But this does not mean that there is a distinction of persons between some who are priests and others who are not. All are priests–in so far as they are capable of drawing others to the point of religious insight which they have reached themselves. All are laymen, in so far as they follow the direction of others to religious heights which they have themselves not yet achieved. Some who have reached the heights of religion may, for a time at least, exercise a priestly function of leadership which others do not at that time possess. But this is a distinction of function and office, not of person.

What is *called* the Church in human society is not truly the Church at all. Least of all is an 'Established' Church the true Church. It is a collection, not of religious men, but of those who are seeking for religion–a mere counterpart of the true Church. It is this bogus Church which is guilty of the pride, the wild proselytization and the bitter divisions with which the enemies and despisers of Christianity tax the Church, and of which the true Church is not guilty.[1]

The true Church is one. But the unity of the Church does not preclude a plurality of religions–in fact, it will encourage it, for 'no man can perfectly possess all religion'. The various religions within the one Church are to be distinguished from one another, not by the 'quantity of religious matter' (i.e., the number of ideas and views and doctrines and rites and ceremonies) which they exhibit, but by the quality of their relationships to the 'Higher Being'. In spite of the evils sometimes in history attached to positive religions, religions with

[1] ibid., pp. 148–58

53

a defined attitude to God and man, positive religions are superior to natural religions, which leave everything vague; for the positive religions, with all their faults, exhibit such wonderful variety and vitality. And of all the positive religions which have so far appeared, Christianity, properly understood, is the greatest; yet it is not opposed to the rise of new forms of true religion.[1]

In a recent book of great value,[2] David Jenkins has pointed out that Schleiermacher as an apologist is the direct precursor of the existentialist theologians, such as Tillich and Bultmann, who put more stress on a man's awareness of God and its results for him than on the God of whom man is aware; and the indirect precursor of those who hold that since God is known only in our awareness of him there is no ground for believing in his objective existence. The defence of religion by Schleiermacher, in other words, is in great danger of being 'the beginning of the end of Theism'. For Schleiermacher rejects the claim of reason, as used in science and morality, to make a contribution to the knowledge of God; he does not turn to revelation as an alternative source of knowledge; and falls back on immediate feeling. There is, for him, no continuity whatever between the activity of reason in establishing the truths of science and ethics and the direct consciousness of God which comes through feeling. But feeling, plainly, cannot demonstrate, or make probable, the existence of a God who is other than our feelings of him and 'is there' whether we have a feeling of him or not. Schleiermacher himself, of course, believes strongly in the existence of an 'objective', 'transcendent' God–so much so that he is never concerned to prove his existence. In his account of religion, therefore, he takes the existence of God for granted; but taking the existence of God for granted is exactly what modern man will not do. Schleiermacher will not permit him the use of science or ethics in his quest for God, and leaves him only with feeling as the means of knowing God. But feeling may slip away and disappear, and God disappears with it. The existentialist theologians like Schleiermacher, retain belief in an 'objective' God, but also, like

[1] ibid., pp. 212–53   [2] *Guide to the Debate about God* (1966)

Schleiermacher, say little about his transcendence, nor is it easy to see how, on their presuppositions, God can be said to exist apart from our awareness of him.[1] Bultmann seems prepared to jettison history also as a manifestation of God, and his description of the resurrection of Jesus, which is really a description of the religious experience of the apostles, bears a strong family resemblance to what Schleiermacher teaches about immortality. Religion and God are within ourselves.

This, then, seems to be Schleiermacher's place in the history of the 'debate about God'. We have to indicate his place in the history of the doctrine of authority, and we have already foreshadowed what we shall find. We have said that he disclosed a problem and propounded a solution.[2] What is the problem? The existing, institutional Church is not the true Church; it is full of error and misunderstanding, of ambition, pride and strife–yet it is the only preserver of Christian doctrine through the ages. Where, then, shall we find Christian truth? Revelation comes solely from within ourselves—what we hear from others is not revelation. But how can we trust ourselves when we know that the 'revelation' received by others is different from ours? To believe in what we find in sacred writings is not religion–it may even be the enemy of religion. So the Bible has nothing authoritative to say–it is just a 'speaking monument from the heroic time of religion'. How shall we discover the authentic voice of Christianity? To believe what others tell us about God is the sign of utter irreligion. If we cannot believe what is handed down to us by tradition or Scripture or Church, what is there left for us to trust?

The problem, then, in a word, is this: On what authority do we believe, or may we believe, what in fact (if we are Christians) we do believe? Is there any authority at all? And this problem has been sharpened since the time of Schleiermacher by every discovery about the actual history of the Church and the processes of tradition, every critical inquiry into the historicity and reliability of Scripture, every psychological and sociological analysis of the working of the human mind. Unless we are able to return to the position which

---

[1] ibid., pp. 25–50   [2] p. 36 above

Schleiermacher abandoned at the start, and hold that
science and morality provide, singly or together, a source of
religious truth–and there seems no immediate prospect of
this–, the problem in this form still exists for us.

And the solution? The one which Schleiermacher propounded follows at once from the words which we quoted[1]
in order to indicate his attitude to theology:

> Make sure of this, that no man is pious, however perfectly
> he understands these principles and conceptions [as we
> saw before, this really means, 'however good a theologian
> he may be'], however much he believes he possesses them
> in clearest consciousness, who cannot show that they have
> originated in himself and, being the outcome of his own
> feeling, are peculiar to himself.

Schleiermacher holds, in fact, that there is no source of truth
except inward feeling, and inward feeling, moreover, which
is peculiar to the man who has it. There is no religious
authority available to man but that–if indeed authority is the
right word to use in this context. And we must go further,
when we remember the relation which he believes to exist
between religious feelings and the doctrines which arise
from contemplation of such feelings.[2] Doctrines are valuable,
even necessary, and Schleiermacher devoted some of the best
years of his life to expounding them in *The Christian Faith*. But
they are wholly derivative, and their authority is secondary.
Moreover, we know that in the one Church–in this case, the
true Church–there will be many different and conflicting
doctrines,[3] and in many cases one doctrine will be in no way
superior to another that contradicts it, nor the other to it.
*So the only 'authority' that we can possibly trust is that of inward
feeling, and the authority of inward feeling is unassailable.*

Schleiermacher has posed the problem in such a form that
we cannot evade it. Has he also provided us with the only
possible solution? And is it a solution at all? Now that
Schleiermacher has written, is there any escape from sub-
jectivism?

---

[1] on p. 46 above   [2] see pp. 48ff.   [3] p. 53 above

Chapter Three

THE GRAMMAR OF INFALLIBILITY

It is impossible to write about John Henry Newman without doing him an injustice. How can any author, by mere words, reconcile Newman the austerely devout exponent of the spiritual life, Newman the lucid expositor of Catholic doctrine, Newman the writer of balanced, impeccable, Ciceronian English, Newman the cool analyst of motives and arguments, Newman the unconsciously unscrupulous controversialist, Newman the manipulator of university politics, Newman the astute propagandist, and Newman the faithful son of Mother Church? Protestants of an earlier generation would have said that it is exactly this combination of qualities that makes a typical Roman Catholic intellectual; but this attempted 'reconciliation' does not correspond any more exactly to the facts of history and psychology than Denifle's dismissal of Martin Luther as a creature of ungoverned lusts who attacked the Church for the sake of his own sensual satisfaction. Nevertheless, the difficulty of accurately assessing Newman's complex character need not prevent us from gaining some understanding of his teaching on authority, and the purpose of this chapter is to make this possible. And if we start by reminding ourselves of his confession to E. B. Pusey that he believed he had an innate tendency towards universal scepticism,[1] and of his assertion in another connexion that from the age of fifteen he knew of no Christianity that was not dogmatic,[2] these passages are cited, not as keys to his

[1] Wilfrid Ward *The Life of John Henry Cardinal Newman* (Longmans, London 1912), i, 31; I owe this reference to David A. Pailin of the University of Manchester.

[2] *Apologia pro Vita sua* (Fontana edition, from which all quotations will be made), p. 56

character and outlook, but as throwing light on the particular matter under discussion.

Newman has set down for us, carefully and elaborately, the way in which his thoughts on the subject developed and ultimately reached their final form, in his *Apologia pro Vita Sua*. We need to be fully aware of the circumstances which called forth this remarkable work. In January 1864 a review by Charles Kingsley[1] in *Macmillan's Magazine* contained these words:

> Truth, for its own sake, had never been a virtue with the Roman clergy. Father Newman informs us that it need not, and on the whole ought not to be; that cunning is the weapon which Heaven has given to the saints wherewith to withstand the brute male force of the wicked world which marries and is given in marriage.[2] Whether his notion be doctrinally correct or not, it is at least historically so.

Newman protested to the publisher, and later published in a pamphlet the correspondence which ensued between Kingsley, the publisher, and himself. Kingsley replied with another pamphlet, entitled, *What, then, does Dr. Newman mean?* As a full-scale reply to all that Kingsley had written, Newman composed his *Apologia*, a history of his religious opinions down to his reception into the Roman Catholic Church on 9th October 1945.[3]

When a man, even with an extremely retentive memory and a relentless power of self-analysis, recalls his own intellectual and spiritual history between two dates of which the later one is nearly twenty years in the past (and this is what Newman does), he is likely, not (probably) to omit any really significant happening, but certainly at some points to falsify the order of events, and, still more, to smooth down and tidy up some of the roughnesses and incongruities which strew the course of actual history and are a perpetual offence to the logical mind. Moreover, in this case the autobiography is written with a consciously defensive and polemical *intent*, and

[1] of Froude's *History of England* vols vii & viii   [2] *Apologia* p. 13
[3] The original review, the subsequent correspondence, and Kingsley's pamphlet are printed on pages 13–65 of the Fontana edition of the *Apologia*.

we rate human nature too highly if we suppose that Newman was entirely uninfluenced by the desire to place his own actions and notions in a favourable light. But even when we have made due allowance for the operation of these factors, the *Apologia* still answers satisfactorily any test of substantial accuracy to which we are able to subject it. Some of the statements which Newman makes about people other than himself may be open to question; what he says about himself we are entitled to accept with the minimum of doubt.

He tells us that the first creed that he embraced was the creed of Calvinism, and that this took place when he was fifteen years of age. Some of this creed remained with him throughout his later development, but that part of it which asserts the doctrine of double predestination dropped off him when he was about twenty-one. This was due to the influence of Edward Hawkins (then Vicar of St Mary's in Oxford, later Provost of Oriel College); and it was Hawkins also who set him decisively on a path which he was to follow for the rest of his life when he preached in St Mary's in 1818 a University Sermon on 'Tradition'. Newman thought the sermon excessively long when he heard it, but on reading it over afterwards he became entirely convinced by Hawkins's argument that Scripture

> was never intended to teach a doctrine, but only to prove it, and that, if we would learn doctrine, we must have recourse to the formularies of the Church; for instance to the Catechism, and to the Creeds.[1]

At about the same time Newman took his first look at Butler's *Analogy*. He was greatly impressed by its

> inculcation of a visible Church, the oracle of truth and a pattern of sanctity, of the duties of external religion, and of the historical character of Revelation.

But chiefly he acquired from Butler a great respect for the idea of an analogy between the higher and lower aspects of God's creation, and (most significantly of all for our purpose) an intense interest in the problem of 'the logical cogency of Faith'—an interest aroused by Butler's view of probability as the guide of life.[2]

[1] *Apologia* p. 101f.   [2] ibid., p. 102f.

It was John Keble's *Christian Year* (1827) that, after an interval of years, revived Newman's interest in the way in which we are intellectually convinced of the truth of the Faith. By this time Newman was aware of a difficulty in Butler's position. It seemed to him to destroy the possibility of that absolute certainty which many people require for their faith to be effective; for it caused them to regard every conclusion as doubtful, and every truth as an opinion; and 'who can really pray to a Being, about whose existence he is seriously in doubt?' Keble seemed to him at the time to resolve this problem 'by ascribing the firmness of assent which we give to religious doctrine, not to the probabilities which introduced it, but to the living power of faith and love which accepted it'. 'It is faith and love which give to probability a force which it has not in itself.' Now

faith and love are directed towards an Object; in the vision of that Object they live; it is that Object, received in faith and love, which renders it reasonable to take probability as sufficient for internal conviction. Thus the argument from Probability, in the matter of religion, became an argument from Personality, which in fact is one form of the argument from Authority.

This, as Newman rightly interprets Keble, means that Christians know that the truths which they have embraced are true from their relationship with God, and not from rational arguments which are of their nature inconclusive; as the friends of God they know by faith, and love his will and his truth.[1]

Yet Newman did not think that this 'beautiful and religious' teaching of Keble really went to the heart of the matter. For it 'did not even profess to be logical'. So, without disputing the value of Keble's insight, Newman continued his own reflection on the matter for many years to come, and eventually set out his considered views in his *University Sermons*, his *Essay on Ecclesiastical Miracles*, and his *Essay on the Development of Doctrine*. This considered view we shall have occasion to scrutinize in due course; it does not belong to the stage of Newman's intellectual development which we have so far reached in the *Apologia*. But it may be useful to say at

[1] ibid., p. 108f.

this point that Newman came to distinguish 'certitude' and 'certainty', 'certitude' being a habit of mind, 'certainty' a property of propositions, and to hold that the certitude which we may come to possess is due to 'an assemblage of concurring and converging probabilities'.[1] And this brief summary enables us to make a comment on Newman's later doctrine which is relevant here: it is not really developed out of Keble's views at all, but more or less directly from Butler. In fact, it seems that, far from building a 'personal' doctrine of authority–that is, a doctrine of authority as grounded in personal relationship to God–on the foundation provided by Keble, he turned away from it and insisted on a rational, 'logical' approach. Keble, by the genuineness and simplicity of his personal religion, had brought him within hailing distance of a view of authority which rested on the religious sentiments of faith and love–even within the same spiritual hemisphere as Schleiermacher; but when he had given this view a formal salute, he turned away and made off in a different direction.

The next milepost we should notice on the road which he had chosen was his discovery that 'Antiquity was the true exponent of the doctrines of Christianity and the basis of the Church of England'. This discovery he traced to his study of the works of Bishop Bull,[2] who persuaded him of the greatness of the School of Alexandria in pre-Nicene times. The thought of Origen and Dionysius especially attracted him by its view of 'the exterior world, physical and historical' as 'but the manifestations of realities greater than itself'; and he found himself also in tune with the notion that the great pagan Greek writers were under a divine dispensation which enabled them to set forth an 'outward framework, which concealed yet suggested the Living Truth'—a framework not intended to be permanent, and now dissolved 'under the beams of the Sun of Justice'. Many minds in addition to Newman's have been captivated by the idea of Greek thought as *praeparatio evangelica*. In Newman's case his semi-

---

[1] ibid., p. 110f.
[2] 1634–1710; Bishop of St David's (1705). Probably the work of Bull which chiefly helped him was *Defensio Fidei Nicaenae* (1685).

romantic attachment to pagan antiquity made the thought of the Alexandrians, who almost welcomed Greek philosophy into the Christian fold, particularly congenial to him. It also prepared him to recognize Athanasius as the champion of Christian orthodoxy *par excellence*, and the battle with the Arians as one of the two or three crucial points of Church history.[1]

While Newman was writing his work on the Arian controversy, *The Arians of the Fourth Century*, to which his enthusiasm for pre-Nicene Alexandria had impelled him, the Reform Movement was gaining strength in England and proceeding to its climax in the passing of the Reform Bill of 1832. Newman recognized the events of this time–together with the overthrow of the Bourbons in France, of which he strongly disapproved–as 'great events'. But it seems that their significance for him lay, not in any contribution they may have made to the righting of wrongs and the spread of social justice, but in the fact that 'Lord Grey had told the Bishops to set their house in order, and some of the Prelates had been insulted and threatened in the streets of London'.[2] The vital question, he says, for him was: 'How were we to keep the Church from being liberalized?' But the Evangelicals, who had been introduced 'into places of influence and trust', were almost as much a menace from inside the Church as the reforming Whigs were from the outside, for they held such views as that 'belief in the Apostolical succession had gone out with the non-jurors' and were, in general, playing into the hands of the Liberals. At such a time as that, the Early Church's unquenchable enthusiasm for the truth greatly inspirited him; he did not yet think of leaving the Church of England, however, for he

> ever kept before [him] that there was something greater than the Established Church, and that that was the Church Catholic and Apostolic, set up from the beginning, of which she was but the local presence and the organ.[3]

His fears (which for others were hopes) that Parliament would do what the Bishops had failed to do, and set the house

---

[1] *Apologia* pp. 114–16

[2] He could have added that the house of the Bishop of Bristol was actually burned down.   [3] *Apologia* p. 118f.

of the Church in order, were abundantly justified by the Irish Church Act of 1833, which (apart from bringing a much needed reform to the Church of Ireland) incited Keble to preach his Assize Sermon, caused the foundation of the Association of the Friends of the Church, and launched the *Tracts for the Times*. Newman tells us the principles by which he was motivated when he took on and continued the editorship of the *Tracts*. The first and fundamental one was the 'principle of dogma'—in direct opposition to liberalism, which was antidogmatic. By this principle he meant that Christianity consists of certain definite religious teachings, and ceases to be Christianity if any of these teachings are withdrawn from it. His second principle was based on the first, and was that 'there was a visible Church, with sacraments and rites which are the channels of invisible grace'. At this point Newman's Platonic Philosophy, of course, chimed in with the Alexandrian theology which he had embraced; as material things are the outward manifestations of deeper reality, so the visible Church and its sacraments are the outward manifestations and channels of the grace which is unseen and eternal. He was sure that this was the doctrine of Scripture (this was before the discovery by scholars that the Hebrew thought-world is dominant in the Bible), of the Early Church and of the Church of England; and he included the episcopal system as an integral part of the visible Church.

The third principle was the need to protest against the errors of Rome. In his Roman days, Newman, of course, was obliged to think again very carefully about his attitude to Rome in 1833, and concludes that while he was still convinced intellectually that Rome was Antichrist, yet he was already moved by affection towards her—largely because of the influence of Hurrell Froude upon him—, so that when he protested against her, he felt as a man feels when he is compelled by his conscience to give evidence in court against a friend. He was certainly convinced that to profess Catholic doctrines, and to give the widest possible publicity to the writings and teachings of the Fathers, in no way conflicted with adherence to the teachings of the Church of England.[1]

[1] ibid., pp. 132ff.

The third principle was still uppermost in his mind while he was writing, from 1834 to 1836, *The Prophetical Office of the Church viewed relatively to Romanism and Popular Protestantism*. Its chief purpose were to compare the Anglican and Roman systems of Christian doctrine, and to begin the erection of a 'recognized Anglican theology as the *Via Media* between Geneva and Rome'. In the fulfilment of the first purpose Newman admits that he was fiercely polemical, and it is hard to resist the conclusion that the ferocity was in part due to the developing clash between his affection for Rome and his now precarious intellectual conviction that Rome was in error. So far as the construction of an Anglican theology was concerned, Newman knew, he tells us, that his work was bound to be tentative and provisional, for no one had attempted such a thing before, and the theological scene of the Anglican Church was simply strewn with fragments of truth, emanating from many different sources and never seriously treated as being integral to each other. One thing was, however, clear to him from the beginning of his project, that the *Via Media*, whatever else it might involve, must certainly include the fundamental principles–of dogma, the ecclesiastical and sacramental system, and opposition to Rome–on the basis of which the *Tracts for the Times* were being written. He thinks it worth while to point out that he had an additional, personal motive for writing this book. Up to then he had never set out 'a basis in reason' for his beliefs, and he held it to be an act of cowardice to refrain from doing so any longer. Looking back on the book in later years, he saw that the 'basis in reason' which he propounded in 1836 was for him no permanent resting place; but at least he had tried to set down what seemed to him to be the true basis at the time.[1]

The ultimate basis of religious belief was the chief subject adumbrated in the *University Sermons*, preached in 1839 and published in 1843. He regarded the treatment which he there gave to faith and reason as merely the tentative commencement of a grave and necessary work', and passed them over quickly in the *Apologia*. Dr Owen Chadwick, however, holds that 'these sermons represent his most delicate thought upon

[1] ibid., pp. 143ff.

the relation between faith and reason';[1] and we shall come back to them later when we turn to the *Grammar of Assent,* to which they form a useful preface. The *Apologia* hastens on to the crisis of 1841, when *Tract 90* appeared. It was soon known to be Newman's work. The Tract appeared to most intelligent Englishmen–and still does to those of them who read it –as a wanton exercise in dishonesty, designed to smooth the author's path to Rome. But according to the author the intention was very different and perfectly honourable. He and his friends–and still more his enemies–were puzzled as to how they could reconcile the views which they were expressing in the *Tracts* with the Articles of the Church of England, and not least with the detailed and comprehensive denunciation of Romish doctrines and practices which the articles contain. By 1841 Newman, who had been brooding on this problem for many years, thought that he knew the answer, and that it would help other people who were in the state of bewilderment which had just left him if he set his answer down. He had decided that the phrase 'Roman teaching' had three possible meanings. It could mean the Catholic teaching of the early centuries, it could mean the formal dogmas of Rome promulgated at the Council of Trent, it could mean popular beliefs and usages allowed by Rome to flourish, but never officially approved by her, and best described as 'dominant errors'. The Articles, he maintained in *Tract 90,* certainly did not condemn Roman teaching in the first sense; they certainly did condemn it in the third sense; while they condemned some, and did not condemn others, of the formal dogmas referred to when the phrase was used in the second sense. On this principle of interpretation Newman comments on all the Articles which were usually held to condemn the teaching of the Roman Church.[2]

This is not the place to discuss the question whether the method employed in *Tract 90* was really as ingenuous as Newman in the *Apologia* makes it out to be–whether, for instance, he was justified, on his own principles, in taking 'Romish' in the Articles to mean 'corrupt-Roman', and not just as a slightly insulting word for 'Roman'. But we ought

[1] in *The Mind of the Oxford Movement* p. 71   [2] *Apologia* pp. 154ff.

to notice the admission which he makes in the *Apologia* that one of his motives in writing *Tract 90* was 'the desire to ascertain the ultimate points of contrariety between the Roman and Anglican creeds, and to make them as few as possible';[1] for this desire shews clearly the way in which his mind was moving, and may well have been instrumental in producing the examples of unconscious duplicity which many readers have detected in the Tract. Nor can we forbear to comment that the whole tenor of the Tract, and of the defence of it which Newman gives in the *Apologia*, suggests that Newman went to the Articles with the preconceived view, which he was determined to establish, that they are at most points perfectly consistent with real Roman doctrine, and that he framed his interpretation of them accordingly.

But there was more to the crisis of 1841 than the arguments with which Newman persuaded himself and tried to persuade others that the Articles, though not the product of a Catholic age, were yet Catholic if properly understood. The *Apologia* indicates that a much more momentous struggle in Newman's mind had started in 1839 and was still going on. In the course of the Long Vacation of 1839 Newman applied himself to a course of reading on the Monophysites,[2] without any thought of their relevance to the issue between Canterbury and Rome; that issue had been away from the centre of his thoughts for two years. But as he read about the Monophysites he found himself more and more identifying them with the members of the Anglican communion. He does not tell us what it was about them that so strongly reminded him of his fellow Anglicans, or about their organization that seemed similar to that of the Church of England. The similarity was presumably not in their doctrinal position; there seems to be no trace in the Church of England of the view that in Christ before the Incarnation there were two natures, and after the Incarnation only one. It must have lain for him in their determination to maintain their eccen-

---

[1] ibid., p. 155

[2] Newman confused the followers of Eutyches, the Alexandrian archimandrite who evoked the *Tome* of Leo, with the Monophysites, who repudiated both the teaching of Eutyches and the Definition of Chalcedon.

tric and heretical views against the declared opposition of the Roman See, and in the verdict which history has passed on them as the followers of a delusion. But as the similarity grew on him more and more he became 'seriously alarmed'. From the Monophysites he turned his attention to the controversy between the Donatists and St Augustine, and was relieved to find no similarity between the Anglicans and the Donatists. But in the treatise by Bishop Wiseman on the Donatists which he was reading, a sentence of Augustine was quoted: *securus judicat orbis terrarum* ('the judgement of the world is secure'). And this sentence he immediately understood to apply not only to the controversy with the Donatists, but also to the controversy with the Monophysites, and therefore to the controversy between Rome and the Church of England, and in fact to every controversy between Rome and any other Christian communion–and to settle the issue at once in every case in Rome's favour. 'By those great words of the ancient Father . . . the theory of the *Via Media* was absolutely pulverized.'[1]

For the time being this devastating discovery receded from the centre of his mind, but he found himself forced to consider it further, until he eventually concluded that the principle of dogma and the sacramental system were better preserved in the Church of Rome than in the Church of England. This meant the collapse of two of the pillars on which the argument of the *Prophetical Office* had rested; the only one of the three that remained was anti-Romanism. This pillar seemed at first capable of standing upright, and Newman felt himself able, in good conscience, to bring positive and definite charges against the corruptions and intolerance of Rome. But he was greatly troubled by the fact, as it seemed to him to be, that the Church of England had paid little or no attention to doctrine. 'Lutherans had a sort of theology, so had Calvinists; I had none' (if Newman had acquired even a slight acquaintance with Lutheran theology in its complexity and comprehensiveness, he would have been even more disturbed by the contrast between it and the theology of the Church of England). Moreover, he felt himself more

---

[1] *Apologia* pp. 182ff.

and more unwilling–no doubt because of the growing attraction which Rome was exerting upon him–to press home the charges that his conscience allowed him to bring against her. By 1840 he was wondering whether the Church of England had the note of catholicity, though he was sure that it had other notes of the true Church. When he retired to Littlemore in that year it had become a matter of life and death to him to be able to prove to himself that 'the doctrine of the Old Church must live and speak in Anglican formularies, in the 39 Articles'. If he could not do that, his whole basis of reason for remaining in the Church of England would be removed.[1] Hence the writing of *Tract 90*.

It is evident that the Tract, whatever its merits or demerits as an exposition of the 39 Articles, is to be thought of by the historian primarily as the expression of Newman's intellectual and spiritual position at the time of writing–a position in which he was confirmed, shortly after the publication of the Tract, by the discovery, from the further reading of Church history, that the Anglicans were not only Monophysites, but semi-Arians into the bargain! 'The pure Arians were the Protestants, the semi-Arians were the Anglicans, and . . . Rome now was what it was then' (the strong suspicion that Pope Liberius, under duress, flirted with Arianism, seems not to have deterred him). 'The ghost', as Newman truly records, 'had come a second time'. And there is no doubt that he was indeed haunted at the time: haunted by the fear that the Church of England was schismatic, even heretical; haunted by doubts about its apostolicity and sacramental system; haunted by the consciousness of its indifference to doctrine. And events in the world of reality did nothing to exorcize his demonic enemies. One after another the bishops, as if by prior agreement, mentioned *Tract 90* in their diocesan charges with condemnation–the bishops, who on Newman's view, were the appointed guardians of the Faith–,and so made it impossible for the interpretation of the Articles which Newman had propounded to be accepted by the Church of England. And then, to cap everything, came the affair of the Jerusalem Bishopric.

[1] ibid., pp. 187, 189–91, 196f.

The British Government and the king of Prussia agreed together to consecrate a Protestant bishop for the Holy City. The idea was supported by the Archbishop of Canterbury, Howley, and (apparently) by all the English bishops; and Michael Solomon Alexander was duly consecrated in November 1841. The reasons for this curious proceeding were many and complex. There were only six Anglicans in Jerusalem, and their pastoral needs did not form a large element in the situation. Many English Evangelicals hoped for the evangelization of Palestine. The Prussian king, engaged on the forcible unification of Lutheran and Reformed churchmen in his dominions, wished to introduce bishops in the historic succession to the united Church.[1] One of the functions of the new bishop, as laid down by the Act of Parliament which authorized the scheme, was to

exercise . . . spiritual jurisdiction over the ministers of British congregations of the United Church of England and Ireland, and over such other Protestant Congregations, as may be desirous of placing themselves under his . . . authority.

It was the mention of 'such other Protestant Congregations' that exacerbated Newman beyond endurance (quite a number of his fellow Tractarians approved of the Jerusalem Bishopric scheme, in spite of the presence of this clause in the Act). These 'other Protestant Congregations' consisted of Lutherans and Calvinists. And these Lutherans and Calvinists were going to receive communion from the bishop! And the bishop, very likely, was intending 'to make converts from the orthodox Greeks and the schismatical Oriental bodies'! The Anglican Church 'actually was courting an intercommunion with Protestant Prussia and the heresy of the Orientals'. Never had Newman's irreconcilable hatred of Protestantism come so furiously to the surface; and the coincidence in time of this utter betrayal of Anglican principles by the Archbishop of Canterbury with the climax of Newman's doubts about the apostolicity of the Church of England was probably the precipitating cause of his departure into the Roman communion.[2]

[1] O. Chadwick *The Victorian Church* Vol. 1, pp. 189f. gives the political reasons also.
[2] *Apologia* pp. 204ff.

But it was not yet all over bar the shouting. Newman was no longer able to hold the view that antiquity, in the shape of Apostolic Succession, together with adherence to the Creeds, guaranteed the place of the Church of England in the One, Holy, Catholic and Apostolic Church, without union with the Roman See. But he was still sure that the Church of England had *one* Note of the Church, the Note of Sanctity, in as full a measure as the Church of Rome,

> or, at least, . . . that we had it in such a sufficient sense as to reconcile us to our position, and to supply full evidence, and a clear direction, on the point of practical duty.

And he still condemned the Roman Church on the charge of political vices. But he knew that the *Via Media* theory could not be resurrected; the best that could be hoped for the Church of England was that it could be allotted the status of Samaria in relation to Israel.[1] The reading of St Alfonso da Liguori's Sermons convinced him that Italian Romanism was not as superstitious as he had thought, though he could not yet reconcile himself to the devotion to the Blessed Virgin and the Saints which it encouraged (and in fact he admits that he never entirely did so).[2] Re-consideration, however, of the idea of the Blessed Virgin led him to the thought that it was *magnified* in Rome, magnified in the sense in which what is seen through a telescope is magnified. This conception might well apply, he went on to think, to all Roman ideas and practices. Rome, perhaps, was the telescope through which 'pale, faint, distant Apostolic Christianity' could be seen, larger than life, no doubt, but essentially the same. This was the germ of the idea of the development of Christian Doctrine which Newman now proceeded to work out.[3]

His full treatment of this matter we shall consider a little later. Here we notice that the formation of this notion was the penultimate step to the elaboration of the full argument that justified and required his secession to Rome. He does not give the connexion very carefully, but this is the argument: I decided that my belief in God is grounded in my belief in my own existence; for 'I feel it impossible to believe in my own existence . . . without believing also in the existence of

[1] pp. 207ff.   [2] ibid., p. 244f.   [3] ibid., p. 246

Him, who lives as a Personal, All-seeing, All-judging Being in my conscience'. Now to believe in God involves me in Catholic doctrine, for the principle of development shows that under the guidance of the Spirit the Church has been led, logically and irresistibly, from primitive belief in God to the acceptance of the full range of Tridentine doctrine. Therefore only two possibilities are open to me: Atheism or Catholicity—there is no middle point. I am not an atheist; therefore I am a Catholic.[1]

So much for the logic of it. But there was the question of religious faith, as well as that of rational argument. Catholicism is logically required by belief in God, Newman was now claiming. But how did a man become sure of it, or, in Newman's terminology, attain *certitude* of it? By the effect on the mind of the accumulation of probabilities. 'I say, that I believed in a God on a ground of probability, that I believed in Christianity on a probability, and that I believed in Catholicism on a probability', and that all three were about the same kind of probability, 'a cumulative, a transcendent probability, but still probability. Three probabilities add up to a transcendent probability, and provide the certitude that is required.[2]

So Newman became a Catholic, some way into 1844; now he thought not only 'that the Anglican Church was formally in the wrong', but that Rome was 'formally in the right'. Now he 'had nothing more to learn'.[3]

It begins to be evident that the strength of the case for Newman's view of religious authority hinges on his ability to substantiate his contentions on two subjects: the relation of certainty to certitude, and the 'development of Christian doctrine'. If we consider his case *without* these two contentions, what he says amounts to little more than this: Christianity consists in a number of coherent propositions, known as its dogmas. One of these dogmas is that there is a visible, sacramental institution, known as the Church. There are many bodies, including the Church of England, the Church of Rome, and the Monophysite Oriental Churches, which

[1] ibid., p. 247 [2] ibid., p. 247f. [3] ibid., p. 248

claim to be the Church, or at least to be part of the Church. But Rome is universal, whereas the others are local. It is the *universal* Church which has authority. Therefore the Roman Church has authority, and its doctrines are true.

Now, this argument lacks plausibility unless it can be shown that (a) Christianity does really consist in a number of consistent propositions (in the *Apologia* Newman seems simply to *assume* this); (b) there is good reason to believe in the truth of these propositions once we know what they are; and (c) the doctrines of Rome are in fact these propositions. Newman sets out to show (b) in the *Grammar of Assent* (1870), and (c) in the *Essay on the Development of Christian Doctrine* (1845). To these works we now turn, and will take them in their logical rather than their chronological order.

There are, according to Newman, two kinds of assent in matters of religious faith. There is simple, or material, assent: that is to say, implicit acceptance without argument of what is taught. There is also complex assent, which is the same as certitude. Simple assent, if it is genuine, develops into complex assent when it is under the fire of questioning. Once a man has reached complex assent or certitude, he may be troubled by questions of theology, but his troubling is only superficial and he is no longer in danger of being fundamentally disturbed.[1]

Now, certitude is always certitude of *truths*. One cannot be certain, in this sense of 'certain', of what is in fact untrue. Therefore it is permanent and indefectible. Does this mean, Newman asks, that certitude implies infallibility? No, for I may well have certitude of what happened yesterday, but I am not therefore infallible. Certitude is directed towards one particular proposition. So I can be certain that the Church is infallible without being infallible myself. Certitude is at most infallibility on one particular point, and promises nothing as to the truth of any proposition other than the one with which it is immediately concerned. The situation may arise in which it is shown that one of my certitudes is mistaken—I may receive and admit further evidence which causes me to revise my opinion and to come to a different certitude.

[1] *An Essay in Aid of a Grammar of Assent*, pp. 203–13

But what has happened is that I was not in fact certain in the first place, and the necessity of changing my mind does not call in question my capacity for certitude, or the possibility of certitude in general.[1]

I have certitude, says Newman, of the truths taught by the Roman Church. It is objected that not everyone accepts these truths. So how can I be said to be certain of them? But surely it is perfectly possible to be certain of truths which others have not yet reached; for instance, of scientific truths which have not yet penetrated to the general public; and this is the case with Catholic truths. It is further objected that people sometimes lose their certitudes, and that various ceritudes conflict with each other: that is, people go from one point of view to another, and when they do this they part with the certitude they once had about their earlier point of view; and the certitudes of the adherents of different religions differ from and contradict one another. But what people drop are not really their certitudes, but the beliefs which they erroneously supposed to follow from their certitudes, and now see not to follow from them. When certitudes appear to conflict it will usually be found that the non-Catholic 'certitude' (for instance, a Protestant one) is not really a certitude, but a prejudice–however tenaciously it may be held. So we need not hesitate to assert that indefectibility is an attribute and criterion of certitude.[2]

Having indicated the nature of inference, and then of natural religion, Newman concludes his argument by undertaking to prove that Christianity, i.e. the doctrines of Catholic Christianity, is a tissue of probabilities so related to one another as to lead to the certitude of which he is speaking; for it is the accumulation of probabilities that leads to certitude. If a man begins by accepting natural religion, and works on the accepted principles of logic, as Newman has set them out, he will find that the existence of conscience leads him from probability to probability until he is certain of the doctrines of the Catholic Church. Conscience will lead to Providence, and Providence to Revelation, and Revelation to the Roman Church, and so on until the process is complete.[3]

[1] ibid., pp. 218–32   [2] ibid., pp. 232–51   [3] ibid., pp. 404–85

No one will want to deny the profundity of psychological insight which characterizes much of the *Grammar of Assent*, and it is this which has given it the position which it holds in the theological literature of the nineteenth century. But its arguments do not improve on the carefully made and upheld distinction between faith and reason which appears in the *University Sermons* of 1839–between faith, which is an instrument of knowledge and action, unknown to the world before the coming of Christianity, not grounded on reason, but approved by reason; and reason, which is the faculty of gaining knowledge without direct perception, either simply by direct inference, or more subtly by development, analysis, criticism, proof, system, rules and laws.[1] And, taken as arguments, they have difficulty in standing up at all.

In the first place, it is not at all clear, nor is it satisfactorily shown by Newman, that certitude has anything to do with the truth or otherwise of the proposition about which a man is certain. It may be true, psychologically, that in fact we become certain about a proposition to which converging or accumulating probabilities point. But if each is *only* a probability, the convergence or accumulation of many such gives no sure indication of its truth. And if all we have is certitude, without relation to truth, how can it be said that certitude is always of *truths*?

Newman rightly urges that if we are certain of some particular proposition, or are even infallible about it, it does not follow from this that we are infallible *simpliciter*. But if this is so, how can I be certain that the Church is infallible *simpliciter*? All I can be certain of is that the Church is infallible *in this particular instance*. It by no means follows from this, as Newman has himself virtually conceded, that it is infallible *simpliciter*. But can I not be certain at a particular time that the Church is always infallible? Hardly, for to be always infallible means to be infallible in the future as well as in the present and the past, and how can I be certain *now* that the Church will make no mistakes in the future?

Newman is right, of course, in saying that it is possible to

[1] see the important extracts in O. Chadwick *The Mind of the Oxford Movement*, pp. 71ff.

be certain about truths which are not yet universally accepted, and the fact that they are not universally accepted is no argument against their truth. But is it not dangerous to maintain that people change their beliefs and not their certitudes, when they themselves have claimed to be certain in the past? May it not be that their present 'certitude' is only a belief wrongly drawn from their certitude? Nor can we easily accept the contention that Protestant 'certitudes' are really prejudices, and Catholic 'certitudes' are really certitudes. What is the criterion of a certitude? That it is of truth? But the question of truth is precisely what we are discussing. Permanence and indefectibility? But there is no evidence that Protestant certitudes are any less permanent and indefectible than Catholic ones. Newman really must not argue from his own case to a general principle! All that we have left is 'strength of conviction', and this will not help us in the least to decide between conflicting candidates for truth in religion.

There is no doubt that the *Essay on the Development of Christian Doctrine* still exercises a very powerful influence on Roman Catholic thought. In fact, its influence is probably more powerful now than at any other time since its appearance. At first it was not welcomed by many Roman theologians as a constructive contribution either to the history of doctrine or to the elucidation of Roman teaching on authority, but it has gradually won its way against opposition. Thirty years ago it was still probably usual in the Roman schools of theology to explain the fact that there are doctrines laid down by the Roman Church, for instance by the Council of Trent, which are not to be found in Scripture, by saying that the Risen Christ imparted them to the Church, in the persons of the Apostles, during the forty days between his Resurrection and his Ascension, with instructions to pass them on to their successors as a 'secret tradition' until such times as the Holy Spirit ordered them to be disclosed, one by one, to the faithful. The theory of Newman, that the Incarnate Christ and the Holy Spirit disclosed all doctrines *in embryo* to the Apostles and Apostolic writers of the New Testament, and that the so-called additions to Scriptural

75

doctrines are really only logical and inevitable developments from what was disclosed at the beginning, was certainly mentioned by Roman teachers, and held by some; but this was all. Nowadays the naïveté of the 'forty days' theory has sent it into the background, and Newman's view is much more widely accepted than it was. The attempt of the *Essay* to show that the doctrines now taught by Rome are in essence the same as those taught by the New Testament is, therefore, worthy of serious consideration.

It runs like this: Christianity is a fact of history, not just the private view of a number of people, nor an amalgam of various differing beliefs. 'It has an objective existence, and has thrown itself upon the great concourse of men'. Therefore, until evidence to the contrary is forthcoming–and none so far is–we are justified in assuming that Christianity has remained through the centuries what it was at the start, and that the external unity of name, profession and communion which it presents argues a real continuity of doctrine. There is, of course, the possibility that it has changed so much during the centuries that it is no longer what it began by being, but this possibility is so abstract that we need not stop to consider it. Nor need we listen to the people who argue that the beliefs of Christians now are so mutually contradictory, and that its history has followed so many divergent paths, that we are compelled to go right back to the Bible to discover what Christianity really is. The study of history will certainly not reveal Protestantism as the Christianity of history, and therefore we do not need to go back to the Bible. (The point of this argument, which is perhaps not very clear, seems to be that we shall find *so little* Protestantism in Christian history that it is unnecessary to talk of the beliefs of Christians as mutually contradictory; recourse to anything except history is also, therefore, unnecessary.)[1]

But it has to be admitted that there are apparent inconsistencies between the Christianity of the New Testament and the Christianity of today. Several theories have been adduced to account for this. The first is that Christianity is for ever

[1] *An Essay on the Development of Christian Doctrine* (New Ark Library edition, from which all quotations will be made), pp. 3ff.

changing according to the time and place in which it is found–so that there is no *authentic* Christianity at all. We can rule out this theory because it implies that there is no such thing as revealed truth and that Christianity has no supernatural origin. The second is the much more plausible, typically Anglican, theory, that we must use as the criterion of authentic Christianity the famous Vincentian Canon: *quod semper, quod ubique, quod ab omnibus creditum est* ('what has been held always, everywhere and by all'). This would enable us to accept as authentic everything that was believed by the Fathers, and invite us to 'lop off' everything in doctrine and practice that did not receive the sanction of the patristic Church. For after the time of the Fathers the Church was divided, and nothing since then has the sanction of the Universal Church. But there are great difficulties about this. If we take some of the great doctrines of the Faith, such as the doctrine of the Trinity, we shall find that it has not been believed *semper*, nor, therefore, *ubique* nor *ab omnibus*. For the doctrine was gradually developed during the ante-Nicene period, and some of the early Fathers state it in nothing like a complete form; and some of them, like Tertullian, are heterodox on the Person of Christ, while Origen is highly suspect. Then in relation to the Real Presence in the Eucharist, it is true that some of the Fathers hold the full-orbed view which the Church has accepted, but there are others who hold a different view. The Vincentian Canon must be regarded as theoretically valid, and very useful for the age in which it was enunciated, but impossible of application today.

The third theory is that of the *disciplina arcani*, which is that certain parts of the ceremonial and teaching of Christianity, though revealed to the Church from the beginning, were deliberately, by divine order, kept dark during the period of the persecutions when it would have been dangerous to the life of the Church to reveal them. It may be admitted that certain things were kept in reserve during the time of persecution, for obvious reasons, but the theory does not explain more than a few of the facts. Many of the variations which cause our original problem continued long after the persecutions had ceased, and long after there was need of any kind to conceal any part of the practice or dogma of the Church.[1]

The problem is solved by the doctrine of *development*. The development of ideas, institutions and practices is to be found in all areas of human life. It is natural, it is legitimate, it is to be expected, and examples of it can be given from politics, logic, history and ethics.[2] There is an antecedent probability that religious ideas also will develop, and the ideas of Christianity in particular. It is, in fact, generally agreed that there are developments of Christian doctrine within Scripture itself, and that Scripture does not give answers to all the questions of theology, but rather in many cases provides the seed out of which the answers can be developed. The Parables of the Mustard Seed and the Leaven give Scriptural warrant for holding that this is so.[3]

The question, of course, is: Granted the probability of development, how are we going to distinguish between true development and false? The doctors of the Church are very useful in this regard, and we must give them due honour. But they are not sufficient for our purpose. We need an external, infallible authority. For Christianity is an objective doctrine; not just a human discovery, like those which occur in the sciences, but a revelation which comes to us as a revelation. Therefore it needs not only to be true, but to be accredited as true, and for this accreditation an external authority is needed, and the external authority needs to be infallible. Now it is objected to this, *ab initio*, that if we accept an infallible authority, we accept it on the ground of probability, and it is absurd to accept infallibility on the ground of probability. But it is not absurd. We can perfectly well be certain, on the ground of probability, that an authority is infallible, without being infallible ourselves.[4] It is further objected that an infallible authority destroys our personal judgement. This is not so; we can reject an infallible authority's pronouncements, if we wish to do so. Nor is the objection valid which is urged by Butler from the Analogy of Nature, that this Ana-

---

[1] ibid., pp. 7ff.   [2] ibid., pp. 25ff.   [3] ibid., pp. 41ff.
[4] see the discussion of this view as it is argued in the *Grammar of Assent* p. 72 above

logy gives no good reason for expecting an external author-ity, which may be necessary at the outset of a religion, to continue. For this objection proves too much: the Analogy, strictly considered, does not lead us to expect a revelation at all. It is rather to be maintained that a revelation, once given, creates the expectation that it will be continued.[1]

Now, Catholics and Protestants agree that the fact of revelation in Scripture requires the continuance of revelation from the past into the present–and this cannot be provided by Scripture (history shows that when, as in the Reformation, it was used for this purpose, the results were disastrous). The need is met by the Church, the pillar and ground of the truth, as Scripture itself calls her. The divided state of opinion about the Faith requires not only an external authority–provided by the Church–but also an infallible one; for Chris-tianity is both social and dogmatic, and it cannot truly be these things unless its teaching is infallibly guaranteed.[2]

So far, all we have done is to establish the antecedent prob-ability of the hypothesis that there is an infallible authority to distinguish between true development and false. Now we look at history, and find that the developments of doctrine in Rome spring logically from the original ideas of Christianity and logically cohere among themselves. To establish this point the best method is to start off with a *prima facie* belief that it is sound, rather than with a doubt whether it is sound, and then to see if the facts fit the theory that it is. And we may set down the 'notes of a genuine development' like this: (a) There must be the preservation of the same *type* within the development, as in the case of physical growth. (b) There must be continuity of principles (as in grammar and philo-sophy), and no logical inconsistency. (c) There must be, at each stage of the development, the power of assimilation to the environment. (d) There must be logical sequence. (e) There must be, at each stage, anticipation of what the future may bring forth (as Luther should have anticipated the cor-ruptions to which his views would lead). (f) There must be, at each stage, a conservative attitude to the past. (g) There

[1] *Development of Christian Doctrine* pp. 55ff.
[2] ibid., pp. 64ff.

must be persistent vigour throughout the whole development (whereas heresies flourish for a while and die).[1]

We need not expound the argument of the book further. The rest of it gives the historical examples which Newman believes to prove his main contentions. In sum, he urges: I have shown the inherent probability that the doctrines of Christianity have developed. I have shown that the power of deciding which developments are legitimate and which are not is likely to be vested in an infallible authority. I have indicated the notes of true development. The facts of Christian history bear out the contentions that Christian doctrines *have* developed, that Rome provides the necessary infallible authority for deciding between true and false development, since it employs the proper criteria of a true development, and therefore that the doctrine taught and the practices enjoined by the Roman Church are the true developments of Biblical teaching.

At one major point of his argument Newman has triumphantly succeeded. He has demonstrated, beyond a cavil, that the doctrines of Christianity as they are received today are the results of a long development. It is not really possible to find it in the New Testament the full statement of what the Church of Jesus Christ believes; and if anyone thinks that he has done so, what in fact he has done is to read into the New Testament the teaching which he has accepted from other sources–Calvinism, or Lutheranism, or Methodism, or Anglicanism, as the case may be. The appeal, 'Back to the Bible', turns out in all cases to mean, not really 'Back to the Bible', but 'Back to the interpretation which I propose to put on the Bible'. Newman can be said also to have shown that the process of development is legitimate and, indeed, inevitable; and that many doctrines which are accepted by the whole of Christendom, such as the doctrines of the Trinity and of the *Homoousion*, are, in fact, legitimate developments–as indeed is conceded by those who accept them without admitting that they hold a doctrine of development.

But has he demonstrated, or even made plausible, his notion that Roman Christianity is the true and authentic

<hr />

[1] ibid., pp. 73ff., 125ff.

development of original Christianity? This is highly dubious. If we leave aside, as not germane to the argument, the insistent impression that Newman presupposes at every point the inerrancy of Rome (which is the very thing that he is setting out to prove); if we accept, for the sake of argument, the contention that probabilities can establish infallibility, although we have found it to be very unconvincing; certain fatal objections still present themselves:

(a) The form of the argument is *a priori*. 'It is inherently probable that this and this and this and this is so; let us see whether they are so.' Who or what has indicated what is inherently probable? The human intellect? (But has it?) The nature of things? (Who knows whether it has or it has not?) And while this uncertainty persists, as it must always persist, how can we be sure that in any argument from 'inherent probability' the one who propounds it has not carefully chosen the premisses which will bear out his conclusions?

(b) All the way through there is the hidden assumption, which we have noticed before in Newman's writings, that Christianity consists in a number of propositions or dogmas. Surely need this assumption to be proved before we can agree that a certain set of propositions constitutes authentic Christianity.

(c) Newman has what can only be called a 'romantic' view of the Fathers. He is prepared to admit that they did not all possess Christian truth in its entirety, and even that they conflicted at some points among themselves. But he argues far too facilely to the conclusion that they rightly interpreted the teachings of the Apostles. A very strong case can be made out for the view that at some points, for instance in the understanding of grace, most of them perverted the teaching of Paul; and that by interpreting Christian theology in the terms of post-Platonic philosophy they did what was no doubt necessary in the interests of Christian communication in their own times, but at the same time reduced, or even perverted, Christianity to what could be said through the terminology that they had adopted–that a New Testament doctrine of the Christ, for instance, cannot really be stated in the language of 'essence' and 'nature'. (But then, of course, Newman himself accepted post-Platonic philosophy.)

(d) Lutherans, Calvinists, Anglicans and many others, with learning equal to that of Newman, have shown that the dogmatic system which they prefer is the true development from New Testament Christianity, and is indeed authentic Christianity. And who shall say which of the schools of thought has proved its point? Fortunately, the advent of the Ecumenical Movement has shown the inadequacy and folly of such attempts, and set us out on more profitable lines of inquiry. But the case stands against Newman. It could even be added that a Marxist of learning, and some sympathy with Christianity, would not have all the difficulty in the world in showing, by methods to those of Newman, that Marxist Communism is a legitimate development of New Testament Communism—once granted that some selected body possesses infallible authority.

Thus, Newman has given us no good reason for believing the statements of the Roman Church, nor has he shown that they are essentially the same as those of New Testament Christianity. And the assumption that Christianity consists of propositions remains totally unexamined. We are driven back on the argument from the dogma of the visible Church, and the universality of Rome.[1] These will scarcely suffice to uphold the infallibility of Rome. The challenge of Schleiermacher remains unmet.

---

[1] see pp. 71f. above. Of the three points made there, we have seen that the 'principle of dogma' is quite unsupported.

Chapter Four

THE VIA MEDIA DEFENDED

While Newman was making his 'attempt at commencing a system on the Anglican idea, and based upon Anglican authorities'—an attempt which issued in *The Prophetical Office of the Church*, published in 1837—'Mr. Palmer', he tells us, 'was projecting a work of a similar nature in his own way.'[1] The 'Mr. Palmer' here mentioned was the Rev. William Palmer, Fellow of Worcester College, Oxford, from 1831 to his death in 1885. This William Palmer is to be distinguished from another William Palmer, a younger contemporary, also the Fellow of an Oxford college (Magdalen), and also a supporter of the Oxford Movement. The Magdalen Palmer gave his support rather from the outside, toyed with the idea of joining the Orthodox Church but was deterred by that Church's insistence on re-baptism, and eventually went to Rome instead in 1855. The Worcester Palmer was associated with the Tractarians from the beginning, having attracted their favourable attention by his *Origines Liturgicae*, a history of the English liturgy which came out in 1832. He toured the country to obtain support for the Association of the Friends of the Church, but was for the most part occupied in academic studies, largely historical and liturgical. He was very troubled by the drift of some of the Tractarians towards Rome, and in 1846 issued a reply to Newman's *Development of Christian Doctrine*. He had previously approved of the establishment of the Jerusalem bishopric, which Newman had bitterly opposed, partly because he had a greater understanding of Lutheranism than Newman, and was (as we shall see) prepared to grant it the right to

[1] *Apologia* p. 144

exist and flourish where circumstances demanded. Thus he represents another side of the Oxford Movement than the one to which Newman in his Anglican days adhered, and never gave up his unyielding opposition to the Papal claims. He was rigid in many ways, and this was certainly one of them.

Newman said of *A Treatise on the Church of Christ*, the book which was almost contemporary to his own *Prophetical Office*, that it was

> one which no Anglican could write but himself [Palmer]– in no sense . . . a tentative work. The ground of controversy was cut into squares, and then every objection had its answer. This is the proper method to adopt in teaching authoritatively young men;[1] and the work in fact was intended for students in theology.[2]

The book (in two volumes) is indeed a massive work, excellently organized and meticulously argued; it proceeds from point to point and from argument to argument with inexorable lucidity and conclusiveness. And if the author is 'high and dry' in his approach, lacking the warmth and intensity which, although controlled and suppressed, are on every page of Newman, and if he has not that personal experience of pastoral situations without which (probably) no theology should be written, his clarity, conscientiousness and argumentive power are beyond question.

If we are to appreciate his arguments and conclusions in the matters which most concern us, we must carefully note the stages by which he reaches the 'base' from which he goes on to those arguments and conclusions. We should do a theologian of his type much less than justice, and William Palmer himself no justice at all, if we were to jump at once to consider his conception of the authority of the Church as he sets it out in the course of the second volume of the *Treatise*; we must first examine the way in which his conception of the Church itself is built up, and this will involve us in a brief scrutiny of the first volume. While we are carrying this out, it will no doubt become clear why Palmer is usually regarded as one of the best and clearest expositors of the 'Branch' theory of

[1] Is it?   [2] *Apologia* p. 145

the Church, though we have no particular reason for pausing on this aspect of thought.

Palmer's first objective is to prove by Scripture, and by the opinions and practices of the Fathers, the Reformers (and sometimes even the Dissenters), and the Anglican theologians, four things about the Church: (a) It is perpetual. (b) It is visible. (c) Salvation is found in it alone. (d) Its notes are oneness, holiness, catholicity and apostolicity. He does not need at this point to say more about the perpetuity and visibility of the Church, and its position as the sole vehicle of salvation (this will come later), but he at once draws attention to the fact that among the notes of the Church 'general Truth of doctrine' is *not* included; this is so, he argues, because in any actual case of a doctrinal issue it would be difficult, and take a very long time, to investigate all Christian truths in the manner that would be required:

Each society pretends its own soundness in these respects, and sustains its own views by scriptural and other arguments; and the critical investigation of *all* the doctrines and duties of Christianity in controversy would be impossible to the infinite majority of men. It would demand, at all events, too lengthened a process; and as men are, in general, always obliged either to follow the doctrine of their church, or to be uncertain on many points; it is impossible that they should *discover* the true church, by investigating all those doctrines which, through their ignorance, they are obliged by the arrangements of Divine Providence to receive on her testimony.[1]

In other words, a man looking for the true Church would have no difficulty in observing oneness, holiness, catholicity and apostolicity where they are present, but could not be expected to recognize truth of doctrine. Palmer goes on to modify this slightly by pointing out that, of course, any society that rejects any article of the Creed, or refuses to administer any one sacrament, is 'plainly no part of the Church'.[2]

Among the notes of the Church the note of oneness, or unity, is the one that engages Palmer's most prolonged atten-

A Treatise on the Church of Christ (3rd edition), i, 19   [2] ibid., i, 3–21.

tion, as we should expect. It is the duty of Christians, as members of the one Church, to be in communion with each other, not only in inward matters of charity and brotherhood, but also in outward matters of mutual help in the form of money and encouragement, of admission to fellowship in worship of those commended by other parts of the Church, and especially in breaking together the One Bread of the Sacrament of the Eucharist.[1]

From the duty of communion in all matters with the Church follows the wrongness of voluntary separation from the Church. Men have often sought to justify such a separation, not rarely on the ground that the external body of the Church includes evil men and doctrinal error, and that it is necessary to separate oneself from 'the unclean thing'; but they have failed to realize that the Church is a mixed, not a perfect, body, and that the presence of those who live unholy lives and of those who hold doctrinal error within its number is to be expected. The enormity of schism—that is, separation voluntarily and deliberately undertaken, from the Church—is unanimously attested by the New Testament, the Fathers, the Reformers, by such nonconformists as Richard Baxter and John Owen, and by the Councils and theologians of the British Churches.[2] It may, of course, be necessary for the Church to separate from its number those who are guilty of sins against charity but who do not wish to be separate from the Church. But this should be done always with the greatest possible care and the greatest possible respect for the principles of justice: the facts of the case should be meticulously examined, and the judgement should be virtually universal before the sentence of excommunication is pronounced, so that a man may well be condemned by a particular Church, but acquitted by the Church Universal (the difficulties involved in the procedure imagined do not seem to be in Palmer's mind, and the whole passage does greater credit to his charity than to his awareness of the practicalities of the situation in a divided Church).[3]

The cases of a whole array of excommunicated heretics and schismatics—Arians, Novatianists, Donatists, Pelagians,

<hr>

[1] ibid., i, 34–8   [2] ibid., i, 38–50   [3] ibid., i, 51–4

Monothelites, etc.–are thus covered.[1] But what shall we make of those cases in which the external communion of the Catholic Church itself has been interrupted? Roman theologians, such as Bellarmine, maintain that such interruptions have never in fact occurred, for the Catholic Church can never exist except as perfectly *one* in external communion. This is, however, an untenable position. Scripture tells us plainly that the Church will contain evil men as well as good; and that even the good men in the Church are not free from the human frailties of error and ignorance. This being so, it is absurd to suppose that the work of evil men, or the error and ignorance of good men, has never led to divisions of the sort in which the blame is equally divided between the participants, and it is impossible to say that either is formally guilty of schism. This is borne out by Scripture, which in no place promises the perpetual absence of division, but rather by its inclusion of exhortations to prayer for unity, suggests that divisions will occur. The same applies to the writings of the Fathers. Cyprian, with his statement that 'unity cannot be severed; nor the one body by laceration be divided', is adduced as a witness to the contrary; but he is saying, in this and other similar passages, not that there cannot be estrangement between Churches in various parts of the world, but that the Church in one locality cannot be divided (and here we agree with him, says Palmer). Augustine is claimed to have denied the possibility of the interruption of communion by his statement, against the Donatists, that those who do not communicate with the universal Church 'thus diffused' (i.e. scattered over the earth) do not communicate with Christ. But all he is saying here is that those who *reject* the communion of the whole Church, on the ground that it is apostate, or are excluded from it by excommunication, are not members of the body of Christ.

Neither Scripture, then, nor the testimony of the Fathers asserts the impossibility of breaks in communion within the Church of Christ. And history contains many examples of such breaks. Leaving aside for the moment the final division between East and West in the eleventh century, and the

[1] ibid., i, 54

Reformation, we can point to the division between Hilary of Arles and Leo, in the fifth century, many divisions between the Pope and the Oriental Bishops before the final break, and the Great Schism in the Western Church which continued from 1379 to 1417, when there was one Pope in Avignon and another in Rome. Roman theologians, as a matter of fact, have been in many cases aware of the fact which Bellarmine denies; one of them (Nicole)[1] says, for instance:

> We do not pretend that the actual unity which consists in the effective union of all the Church is essential to the Church, because this union may be troubled by divisions and contests which God permits.

Rome has, in fact, no real answer to the contention that breaks in communion within the Church not only are possible, but have actually happened.[2]

But under what conditions is an interruption in communion permissible? There is no doubt that voluntary separation from the communion of the whole Church is always wrong; there is no doubt that it is legitimate, or rather necessary, to cut off heretics, idolaters, and such-like, from the Church. But these heretics, idolaters and others, may be bishops, or other dignitaries of the Church. It is, therefore, legitimate, necessary, even at times a sacred duty, to separate oneself from bishops (and, by consequence, from those parts of the Church over which the culpable bishops hold jurisdiction). This right must, however, not be abused, and this duty must not be carried out lightly or irresponsibly, for it is no small thing to separate oneself from one's fellow Christians, however great their offences. History abounds in instances of the misapplication of the sound principle that in the cases mentioned separation is legitimate, and these misapplications have been the partial or whole cause of further schisms and other incalculable evils. We must make absolutely sure that the heresies and idolatries of those from whom it is proposed to separate are notorious and certain, and that the

---

[1] presumably Pierre Nicole (1625–95), a friend of A. Arnauld, translator into Latin of Pascal's *Provincial Letters* and a moderate Jansenist until late in his life; in his later years also an anti-Quietist and supporter of Bossuet

[2] Palmer, op. cit., i, 54–64

accused are given full opportunity of self-vindication and explanation before judgement is given and sentence is passed. Above all, it must be completely certain that those who perform the act of separation have no intention whatever of separating from the whole Church, but only from heretical or idolatrous persons.[1]

We must take breath at this point in Palmer's argument. It has become more and more manifest, surely, as the argument has proceeded, that he is preparing the ground, assiduously and thoroughly, for the defence of the Church of England against the charge that she has voluntarily separated herself from the Catholic Church, and for the assertion that the separation that she has carried through has been from heretical bishops, archbishops and Popes. It is no less clear that he has at the same time prepared the ground for the conclusion that dissenting bodies in England and the Church of Scotland are not parts of the Catholic Church, since they have voluntarily separated themselves from it. When the conclusion of an argument begins to loom up almost as soon as the premisses are stated, the edge of the conclusion when we reach it tends to be blunted. And when a man sets out to establish, by elaborate argument, a position which we know him to be bound to defend, we are sometimes visited by the suspicion that the whole process is a rationalization, not an argument. But we are not entitled to discredit this reasoning on such grounds as these. The strength of his argument may be so great that even the statement of the premisses points irresistibly to the conclusion, as the summit of a snow-capped mountain may draw on the climber irresistibly from the moment he sets foot outside his hotel; and the stages of the argument may in actual fact be the ones by which its expounder himself reached the conclusion towards which he marches so triumphantly. But we *are* entitled to scrutinize the argument, from the premisses to the conclusion, with extreme care, lest our suspicions turn out to be justified after all.

Under such scrutiny in this case certain weaknesses appear. Palmer's case for the perpetuity and visibility of the Church,

[1] ibid., i, 64–9

for his contention that salvation is found in the Church alone, and for the notes of the Church which he gives, rests on a consensus of Scripture, the Fathers, the Reformers, the Dissenters, and the Anglican Divines. It is hard to see what place the Dissenters have in such company, in view of what Palmer elsewhere says about them. But we may leave this point aside. The qualities which Palmer claims for the Church are proved to belong to the Church by the testimony of what is in fact the Church in a large number of its manifestations. But why should we believe the testimony of the Church unless its authority is already established, which in fact it is not? Palmer comes on to establish this authority at a later stage of his main argument, but only, it seems, after assuming the authority of the Church from the outset. This is an example of what may be called the haunting circularity of most arguments about authority–to prove the authority of a person, thing or institution, it is necessary to assume the authority of the source from which the premises are derived, and this source often turns out to be the person, thing or institution whose authority it is proposed to prove. We shall have to return to this point.

Then, it is by no means clear that Palmer has really done justice to the Roman claim that breaks in communion within the Catholic Church are impossible, since the Catholic Church is by definition one and indivisible. The Scriptural evidence, from the proneness of man to divisiveness, can be interpreted in either direction, for the good reason that the Scriptural writers were not aware of the problem in the terms in which it was presented and formulated by later generations. And it is certainly open to Rome to interpret the historical examples, which Palmer alleges to be cases of division *within* the Church, as cases of division *from* the Church, since the Papacy is held by Rome to be the guarantee of the presence of the Church. This applies even to the Great Schism of the Papacy itself, for on the Roman view either the Avignon Pope or the Roman Pope was the true Pope and the guarantee of the Church's presence–even if it is very difficult to determine which of the two Popes actually filled the bill.

There is, of course, a strong argument, derived from many general considerations, such as the persistence of true doctrine and true sanctity and effective sacraments in the 'separated' portions of Christendom, for Palmer's view that there have been, and still are, interruptions of communion *within* the Catholic Church. But Palmer's argument for his own view is very vulnerable.

He must, however, certainly maintain the possibility of interruptions of communion within the Church if he is to prepare us for the assertion that the break between the Church of England and the Church of Rome is such an interruption. But if we turn to what he has to say about the Dissenters and, later, about the Church of Scotland, against both of which kinds of Christian he seems to cherish a quite unreasonable bitterness, we are bound to ask: In what sense is it true to say that the Church of England only separated itself within the Catholic Church, from heretical and idolatrous bishops, archbishops and Pope, whereas the Dissenters and the Church of Scotland separated themselves–and did so voluntarily–from the Catholic Church? A twofold answer would, no doubt, have seemed obvious to Palmer: (a) They have set up separate altars in the places where the Catholic Church is present and operative. (b) They have denied articles of the Creed, such as the clause about the oneness, holiness, apostolicity and catholicity of the Church, and have gone out of the Catholic Church asserting that it is not they, but the Catholic Church which is heretical–and that, in fact, the Church was in continuous error until they appeared.[1] In such an answer the first part depends on the second, and to the second part the Dissenters and the Presbyterians would certainly answer in their turn that they are part of the Catholic Church precisely because they have preserved the true doctrine of the Church, whereas the episcopalians have denied it. In other words, they have a different concept of the Catholic Church. They may be right; they may be wrong. But Palmer is surely not justified in ruling them out of court by a *fiat* which assumes his own orthodoxy and their error. The setting up of separate altars arises from the conviction that the episco-

[1] cf. ibid., i, 306–9

palians are in error, and even Palmer agrees that where the Catholic Church is in error separate altars may legitimately be set up.

Palmer includes the Wesleyan Methodists among the Dissenters,[1] and applies what he says about the Dissenters as much to them as to Independents and Presbyterians (and Quakers, Swedenborgians, Socinians, Jumpers, the followers of Joanna Southcott etc. Here he commits a serious historical blunder. The Wesleyans do not rank with historic Dissent in respect either of origin or of principles, though their worship and some of their practices were assimilated to it to some extent in the nineteenth century. It is a matter of continuing uncertainty among historians whether they separated voluntarily from the Church of England or were excluded from it; their doctrine of the Church is nearer to that of historic Anglicanism, though not of Anglo-Catholicism, than to that of Independency, and they have never repudiated episcopacy though they do not hold it to be essential to the existence of the Church.

We may now return to the main stream of Palmer's argument, and follow it for a while without so much cavilling. The whole system and body of the Christian religion, he says, is necessarily free from the slightest admixture of error or falsehood, because it comes from Christ himself; and heresy, which is the pertinacious denial of some truth certainly revealed, excludes a man from salvation, as is seen from the fact that heretics have always been cut off from the Church by Fathers, Reformers and Anglicans. The Church must have power to exclude heretics, and in fact has such power. But not all errors are heresies; they may only be mistaken opinions, even if they are held to be articles of faith when they are not. The whole universal Church could not, of course, teach such errors as true doctrine, but there is no promise that the Catholic Church in its historical existence will be perfectly agreed on doctrine, even though when it judges collectively it cannot err. There must be some means provided in the Church for preserving or restoring unity in believing the truth, and therefore any society which is prevented by its

[1] explicitly, ibid., i, 306

principles from sustaining unity in the truth cannot be part of the Catholic Church; and any society which separates itself, or is solemnly cut off, from the great body of the Catholic Church on any question of the faith is not part of the Catholic Church.[1]

The sanctity of the Church does not mean that all its members must be holy, nor does its catholicity mean that it must be *called* Catholic. Its apostolicity does mean that it must be derived from the Apostles by 'spiritual propagation' or union; and this applies to the ministry of the Church in particular. The argument for the Apostolic Succession is this: The Christian Ministry is admitted by all to be essential to the Church. It must for ever exist, for if it be acknowledged at any time to have ceased to exist, we have no means of telling that it exists now. The essence of the Ministry is divine commission. For this commission an inward sense of call is not sufficient, nor is popular election (for there have been periods in history when this has been entirely lacking). Commission by the Apostles and their successors is the only other possibility; and the apostolic mode of ordination by the imposition of hands is the only mode which has always existed in the Church. Therefore succession from the Apostles by the laying on of hands is the only right way of continuing the Ministry of the Catholic Church.[2]

We must next ask—and Palmer does so at considerable length—whether the various communions which make up Christendom are parts of the Catholic Church; and the way to do this is to see whether they have the notes of the Church. The case of the Eastern Churches is not difficult to determine. They maintain principles which lead to unity of communion and faith, they inculcate holiness, they are plainly catholic. They never separated themselves from communion with the great body of the Catholic Church, for there are as many of them as there are of those from whom they were separated by the schism of East and West. The blame for this schism does not rest exclusively with either party, but equally with both. The effect of the schism was not to separate either party absolutely from the Catholic Church, for neither act of ex-

[1] ibid., i, 71–98   [2] ibid., i, 132–44

communication was known to or approved by the majority of the excommunicating Church. The Eastern Churches were not schismastic, in spite of Rome's charge against them to this effect, because their attitude was justified by the overweening pride of the Popes. They were certainly not heretical. We must conclude that they are, and always have been, part of the Catholic Church.[1]

The British Churches (that is, the British *episcopal* Churches, as is clear from the context) preserve unity among themselves and condemn schism roundly; they desire to be in communion with the rest of the Church, and they have never been excommunicated by any part of it, except by the Roman Church, which was itself corrupt at the time of the excommunication (and non-communion with Rome, as history shows, does not necessarily mean schism). They continue the unity of the faith, and their principles are calculated to preserve them in this (for instance, Article 20 lays it down that the Church has authority in controversies of faith). Differences in their Articles from the Decrees of the Council of Trent do not prove that they are in heresy, for the Council of Trent was not sound in the faith. They are holy–as witness their many saints. They are catholic–though they do not, of course, constitute the whole of the Catholic Church–for they receive the faith of the Catholic Church, and have not been cut off from it. They are apostolical, for they are derived from the Churches founded by the Apostles; and their ministry, in spite of all the cavils of Rome, is derived from the Apostles. Therefore they are true Churches of Christ, and parts of the Catholic Church; and they are fourteen centuries old.[2]

We come to Rome, for Palmer the crucial case. There is no dispute about the place of the Roman Church in the Catholic Church up to the time of the Reformation. All Christians acknowledge it, and Luther and Calvin in the Reformation period itself do not deny it. It is, however, maintained by some, including Jewel and other Anglicans, that after the Reformation Rome ceased to be part of the Catholic Church, in view of the fact that many errors,

[1] ibid., i, 145–68   [2] ibid., i, 174–94

heresies and idolatries exist in Rome, and have the sanction of authority. With some misgivings, it must be regarded as safer to admit that Rome has remained part of the Church. The error prevalent in Rome that she is the divinely ordered centre of unity accounts for the survival of many of her other errors, and we cannot really hold her guilty of 'pertinacious opposition to the evident truth'. The members of the Roman Church have been 'prevented by so many excusable circumstances from seeing the right way, that we ought not to judge too harshly; to exclude from the church of Christ so vast a multitude of believers, so many nations, and such a crowd of ancient churches is very difficult'. After all, these Churches are very ancient, they preserve unity of communion between themselves; they have never been excommunicated by the majority of the Catholic Church, and 'if they have unjustly expelled some from their communion, it can be shown that it was under the influence of preconceived opinions, or from ignorance'; they have a zeal for unity, they admit the authority of the Universal Church, they receive the apostolical faith, their doctrines have not been formally condemned by the Universal Church, they inculcate holiness, and they have a ministry descended from the Apostles.

What we must deny to Rome is a monopoly of the 'efficacious principles of unity'–for the papal authority has, in fact, divided the Church, and there are Jansenists in Rome to this day; or of sanctity–for there are many saints outside the Roman Communion; or of catholicity; for in early days Rome herself admitted that she was only part of the Church; or of apostolicity–for other Churches have an apostolic origin, and an apostolic ministry as truly as she has. We can, however, justify the presence of Roman Churches in the areas covered by other parts of the Catholic Church when it is required by language difficulties and is agreed to by the authorities of the Church of the land. Such Churches are schismatical if they have deliberately separated from the Church of the land, as happened in England in the reign of Elizabeth I.[1]

The case of the Continental Reformed Churches is very

[1] ibid., i, 212–36

different. But we should not regard them as schismatical, in spite of all the charges laid against them by Rome. Martin Luther did not separate from the Church; he was expelled from it. He constantly appealed to a General Council, as is the right of every Catholic Christian, and this was constantly denied to him. Zwingli did not separate from the Church; he also was expelled, though he differs from Luther in not having appealed to a General Council.[1] The principles of Luther, Zwingli and Calvin were not subversive of unity, for they respected Councils and tradition. They were opposed to the unbounded liberty of private judgement, which is so fruitful a source of heresy.[2] The great deficiency of the Continental Reformed Churches is their lack of an apostolical ministry (except in the case of Sweden). But this was forced upon them by the exigencies of the times. We may regret that the institution of a non-apostolic ministry, which was intended to be temporary–to last only until such time as the restoration of true episcopacy became feasible–has taken on the appearance of permanence, and is actually defended as Biblical, and we may hope that it will soon be replaced by the ministry which is of divine ordering. But meanwhile we have no right to regard these Churches as schismatical. They are parts of the Catholic Church, and, 'material as are the deficiencies under which they labour, those defects will be either excused, or extraordinarily supplied by the Author of all Grace'.[3]

The charity which Palmer extends to Rome and the Continental Protestants fails him when he comes to English Dissenters (among whom, as we have seen, he unhistorically includes the Wesleyans). In a few pages he dismisses them as guilty of schism and heresy, denies (quite properly) the claim made by some of them to *be* the Catholic Church, and goes on roundly to assert that they are not part of the Catholic Church at all. He finishes his discussion of the question thus:

As every officer of a voluntary association or club derives

---

[1] Palmer appears to regard Calvin as a follower of Zwingli, since he does not mention him explicitly at this point.

[2] It is pleasant to find an 'Anglo-Catholic' avoiding the constant 'Catholic' mistake of supposing that the supremacy of private judgement was a principle of the Reformation.   [3] ibid., i, 292–302

his commission entirely from those who create him, so the dissenting minister is commissioned to preach the Gospel, not by God, but by man. He is the minister of man only; and therefore the dissenting communities being destitute of a true ministry, which is essential to the church, are not churches of Christ. I shall add nothing more in a case so easy and clear.[1]

We must certainly pause at this point, and look for a moment at Palmer's bad-tempered attack on the Dissenters. Earlier in the book he has drawn up a formidable list of the 'idolatries and heresies which are held without censure in the Roman communion'. They include the contention that 'latria', the worship paid to the divine nature, is also due to images, relics, the Bible and the Blessed Virgin, and divine honours to all the saints and angels; the claim that the Virgin is superior to her Son, and is the source of all grace; the teachings that after justification a sinner is still subject to the wrath and vengeance of God and that the righteous suffer the tortures of hell-fire after death; and the notion that the sacrifice of Christ on the cross is repeated or continued in the eucharist. He will not admit the defence that these errors have not been laid down *de fide* by Trent or any other Council as excusing the Roman Church from guilt or as preserving its members from dangers to their salvation.[2] The Dissenters, on the other hand, are charged with the heresies of holding principles which involve separation from every other part of the Church, of denying the place of all human authority in the Church, and of believing that the Church is a 'voluntary society of professing saints'.

But whereas the heresies and idolatries (surely a serious matter!) sanctioned by the Church of Rome do not disqualify it from membership of the Church of Christ, the heresies of the Nonconformists do. Two grounds are given for this discrimination: the heresies of Rome have never been asserted by a Council, whereas the 'principles' of the Nonconformists are inherent in Nonconformity. But this is not a very strong point, for the principles of the Nonconformists, though much written about by Nonconformists, have no

<hr />

[1] ibid., i, 305–17   [2] ibid., i, 272–4

more the approval of a Council than the heresies found in the Roman Communion–for the simple reason that the Nonconformists do not believe in Councils anyway. The other ground is that Dissenting principles in themselves involve separation from every other part of the Church–and Palmer has prepared the way for this objection to Dissenters already.[1] But surely it is arbitrary to rule that toleration of the paying of divine honours to one who is not divine, and even to material objects, does not put a body of people outside the Church, while the holding of a particular principle of separation does exactly that (we have seen that the ascription of this principle to the Nonconformists may well be unjust, but this does not affect the present issue). This 'short way with Dissenters', so lamentably characteristic of the Oxford Movement, and, for several generations, those influenced by it, seems to spring from largely non-theological causes, one of them being the smouldering resentment of the fact that other institutions calling themselves Christian had set themselves up in opposition to the Church of England, and had won large successes among the people of the country (the Wesleyans were especially guilty of this), and another being the uneasy consciousness that the Church of England could be said to have itself committed, in the time of Henry VIII, the crime which it now laid at the door of the Dissenters. Palmer, indeed, argues that it is absurd to compare the separation of the Church of England from Rome with the separation of the Dissenters from the Church of England, but his argument presupposes that the claims of the Roman Pontiff to authority over England were false, while the claim of the Church of England to be the true Church of the land, though the Dissenters said it was not, was true. But these are the very matters at issue between Rome, Anglicanism and Dissent.[2] One of the advantages of living in the second half of the twentieth century is that we have at least got beyond this kind of dispute.

---

[1] see p. 88 above

[2] ibid., i, 317f.; cf. W. C. Sellar & R. J. Yeatman *1066 and All That* (Methuen, London 1930), p. 55: 'The Pope . . . seceded with all his followers from the Church of England.'

Palmer concludes his first volume by showing that the Church of England was not founded at the Reformation by separation from the Catholic Church and that its faith was not invented or changed by Henry VIII or any sovereign, but that it is in fact the Catholic Church in these islands.[1] This involves a severe castigation of the Church of Scotland, which is apparently as truant and delinquent as the Dissenters; its ministers are incompetent to administer the Sacraments–in fact, it does not even know whether it intends to ordain presbyters or bishops.[2]

In the course of his vindication of the Church of England Palmer states the principles of the English Reformation as being these: (a) 'the authority of provincial or national churches to correct doctrine and discipline without the necessity of waiting for the Pope or the Universal Church. (b) 'The supremacy and sufficiency of Scripture', combined with reverence for the catholic tradition–as against any Church which asserts the right to add doctrines to the Faith which are not contained in Scripture.[3] In his second volume Palmer goes on to vindicate the second principle at considerable length. In fact, there is a sense in which the whole of the first volume is an elaborately laid foundation for the building of a doctrine of authority, and this is why we have summarized it and commented on it.

Palmer proceeds at once to defend Article Six:

Holy Scripture containeth all things necessary to salvation: so that whatsoever is not read therein, nor may be proved thereby, is not to be required of any man, that it should be believed as an article of the Faith, or be thought requisite or necessary to salvation.

He points out that this does not mean that men may not be asked to acknowledge certain truths which are not matters of faith; and he answers the objection that the doctrine of the inspiration and canonicity of Scripture, which is apparently to be believed as necessary to salvation, is not in Scripture but proved from tradition, by saying that as soon as the Author of Scripture was known, its inspiration and canonicity followed without the need of special revelation

[1] ibid., i, 325–444 [2] ibid., i, 437–44 [3] ibid., i, 376–85

(this would be sound, surely, only if we had some means of knowing that God *is* the Author of Scripture).

Palmer's principal opponents on this issue are to be found in Rome, and it is with the Roman defence of tradition that Palmer now proceeds to contend. To the statement that only a part of the Word of God is in Scripture, while the rest is in unwritten tradition, he replies that since God wrote the Scriptures in order to preserve revealed doctrines, he would scarcely have omitted any that needed to be preserved. If some doctrine is to be found only in tradition, why is it that not all doctrine is to be found there? This arrangement would have saved us from all the inconveniences that arise from the interpretation and misinterpretation of Scripture! If we consider, in the light of these facts, the nature and purpose of Scripture, it is evident that it is perfect in the sense of containing all doctrines necessary to salvation, even though it is not possible to prove this contention from Scripture itself. The Romanists can object, if they like, that the patriarchs had to make do with tradition since they had no Bible, and so did the Church until the New Testament was written; but it does not follow that the arrangements necessary at some points in history apply for all time.[1]

From confuting the Romanists Palmer turns to deal with the extreme Protestants. He argues that what may be proved by Scripture can legitimately become an article of Faith. To deny this, and to affirm that all inferences from Scripture and all interpretations of the sacred text are matters of opinion only, suggests that there is no important difference between orthodoxy and heresy—since in a dispute about doctrine the disagreement is always, in fact, about the inferences to be drawn from Scripture, and if all inferences are matters of opinion only, the disagreement is trivial. We should rather say that Scripture may supply such premises that the conclusion is, in effect, manifestly taught by Scripture also. This is where the doctrinal tradition of the Church comes into the picture. Its function is to confirm the true meaning of Scripture, in the sense of interpreting Scripture as a whole, and to rule out heretical meanings. And there is, by divine grace, a

---

[1] ibid., ii, 3–25

universal tradition, taught by those who were themselves taught by the Apostles; and this universal tradition is divinely, infallibly true. It is to be found in the creeds and professions of faith acknowledged by the Universal Church (remember that Palmer has carefully told us where we can find the Universal Church); in the creeds and liturgies of particular Churches, as evidence of their belief far back into the past; in the attestations of particular fathers and councils of bishops; in many ancient customs and rites; and even in the objections of infidels and sectaries through their statements of the beliefs which they reject.

To seek to controvert this view by appealing to the frailty of all human testimony leads in the end to the denial of all knowledge about anything which we do not personally perceive with our senses. And the sectarians who deny this view do so in the interests of their own private notions. The parrot-cry, 'The Bible alone is the religion of Protestants', is simply bad history, for the Reformers had a great respect for catholic tradition. Both Rome and the Church of England appeal to tradition, with different results. But the differences are due to the fact that the Church of England appeals to early tradition, Rome to later tradition. We infer from this that both have support from tradition, and that the differences between them do not concern things necessary for salvation.

There is, of course, a famous Puritan argument that nothing which is not in Scripture is a legitimate tradition. Hooker has confuted this by agreeing that general principles as to rites and discipline are laid down in Scripture, and that anything contrary to these must be ruled out, and then going on to show that Scripture does not contain express mention of everything lawful; for (a) Scripture itself does not assert that it does; (b) Scripture, on the contrary, does say that where there is no law, there is no transgression—so that what is not contrary to divine law is lawful; (c) Scripture lays down general principles for the guidance of the Church in external matters, and so allows the Church to regulate external matters in detail; (d) all Churches, whether they admit it or not, have in fact practised things which are not laid down in Scripture.[1]

[1] ibid., ii, 26–52

The validity of the principle that Scripture contains all necessary doctrines and that the Universal Church infallibly interprets Scripture is illustrated by the way in which faith is produced in men and women. Faith is aroused by the teaching of the Church, which is carried out, not only by its ministers, but by all who teach the young. Ordinary Christians engaged in teaching cannot be expected to carry out a minute examination of Scripture; they have to rely on the teaching of the Church. Some would argue that faith founded on the testimony of fallible men is insecure, and that we therefore need an infallible Church or an infallible Bible at every point. But, in experience, what happens is that a man believes ultimately because God has spoken, but receives God's message through fallible teachers—the pastors and members of the existing Church. His faith comes to him *through* fallible people, but behind them stands the infallible Word of God, the true meaning of Scripture established by the consent of all the ages and the irrefragable judgement of the Universal Church.

Romanists try to argue that the *existing* Church is infallible. But they argue in a circle. They assume the infallible authority of the Church in order to prove that the Bible is true; and then prove from the Bible that the authority of the Church is infallible.[1]

We can therefore proceed to the conclusion that the judgements, not of the existing Church in any place or time, but of the Universal Church, properly arrived at, are absolutely binding on all Christians from the moment of their full manifestation. We have seen that Christ has authorized such judgements; we know from the Bible that the Church cannot fail or become apostate; it is incredible that any individual could judge better than the Universal Church, and it would be fatal to the whole Church and the whole Gospel if he could; and we plainly cannot trust the sects for the purpose, for the division into sects is an evil thing, springing from the deep-seated disease of 'private judgement'—the one thing that all the sects have in common—though God has, of course, authorized individuals to judge in controversial matters, to

[1] ibid., ii, 57–63

a limited and provisional extent, until such time as the Universal Church determines the issue.

The judgements of the Universal Church are irreformable and unalterable. For every individual Christian must submit to them, and has no right ever to raise the question of their correctness. One age of the Church has no greater access to the truth of God than any other; judgements reached by the Universal Church in any age have exactly the same status as those reached in any other age, and therefore the judgements of one age cannot supersede or overrule those of another. Moreover, the Church could not reverse or alter its judgements without admitting that, although she has called on the divine aid and used all appropriate means of reaching divine truth, she has been mistaken; and to believe that the Church, relying on the help of the Holy spirit, can err, is contrary to faith and would open a floodgate of doubts about the reliability, and even the existence, of the Church. And, finally, Christ has guaranteed the inerrancy of the Church's judgements by his promises to it, and by his establishment of it as the 'pillar and ground of the truth'.[1]

We have now reached the climax of Palmer's argument about authority. We have not by any means reached the end of his book, or of his discussion of various other views of authority. But what follows the positive statement of his own doctrine is largely taken up with a careful refutation of Roman views about Oecumenical Councils and the infallibility of the Pope. He points out that there is some dispute among Roman theologians about the number of Oecumenical Councils that have been held, some giving the number as eighteen, some restricting it to nine or ten. He quotes Bossuet's judgement that the criterion by which an Oecumenical Council is to be recognized is its acceptance by the whole Church, and adopts this, as against a contrary Roman judgement that any Council whose findings have been accepted by the Pope is oecumenical. On this basis he decides that there have been six Oecumenical Councils: Nicaea, Constantinople I, Ephesus, Chalcedon, Constantinople II and Constantinople III. The Council of Trent cannot be put in

[1] ibid., ii, 82–6

this class, for its judgements do not express the mind of all parts of the Catholic Church, and it was rejected by considerable parts of the Church; as a matter of fact, it simply expressed the mind of the Pope and those present.[1] As to the Thirty-Nine Articles of the Church of England, not all of these are articles of faith, though some of them are; the rest are 'pious opinions'. Anglican clergy are rightly required to subscribe both to those which are articles of faith, and to those which are 'pious opinions', subscription to the latter being desirable for the sake of the peace of the Church. (He does not give any machinery for deciding which of the Articles belong to each of the two categories; and it could surely be urged that to require subscription *ex animo* to 'opinions' is an unfortunate repression of the liberty of opinion. But he does not treat these questions.)

He does, however, give indications as to how the Articles are to be interpreted; in the circumstances of his time such guidance was plainly necessary. The sense of the Articles to be accepted, he says, is not that of the writers, for we do not even know who they were, but of those who imposed subscription to them, that is, of the authorities of the Church of England. In any cases of obscurity, we should use the other formularies of the Church of England and its formularies of worship in order to determine the issue; and in cases of real, continuing doubt, we should adopt the sense most harmonious with Scriptural and Catholic doctrine.[2]

Palmer leads up to his treatment of Papal infallibility by acknowledging that the Apostle Peter himself was the first in faith of the Apostles, and first in evangelical success. But he will not grant him primacy over the other Apostles in the matter of jurisdiction and disciplinary authority; in this respect all the Apostles were on an equal footing. Nor was his personal pre-eminence in faith and the Gospel transmitted to his successors in the See of Rome. The pre-eminence of that See in later times was due to historical causes, not divine instigation. The Pope, therefore, has no jurisdiction over other bishops *jure divino*—still less, temporal jurisdiction over the whole world, as the medieval Popes and their successors

[1] ibid., ii, 112–87   [2] ibid., ii, 194–221

have claimed to have. The Pope is not the fountain of ecclesiastical jurisdiction, nor is he the centre of Catholic unity.[1]

After these preparations, the doctrine of Papal infallibility is easily confuted. No argument to it can be supported by Peter's pre-eminence among the Apostles, for this was not transmitted. The promises of divine support in the preservation and proclamation of the truth were made to the whole Church, not to Rome only, nor to its bishop. In early times Papal decrees were never esteemed infallible, but were judged by the Universal Church. The *Tome* of Leo was judged by the Council of Chalcedon, and found to be true. The decrees of Vigilius, Honorius I and others, were judged by the Church at large and found to be false.[2]

Of course, the Roman See has great authority as a metropolitan See, and therewith a special responsibility to resist evil and error and encourage unity. But the patriarchate of Rome does not extend beyond Italy and the adjoining islands, and the transgression by the Popes of their proper authority has led to great evil in the Church. It has been argued in recent times, says Palmer, that the Church must have a centre, must be monarchical and must be infallible, if it is to fulfil its divinely given function. But there is no need for it to have a visible centre, since Christ is its Head; and Peter and his successors for many centuries did not claim infallibility. Nor will the theory that the doctrine of Papal Infallibility is legitimately developed from a germ or seed in Holy Scripture meet the case. For we have no right to assume *a priori* that God's decrees work by development; nor, in this case, have we any proof of the original institution of that which has now developed.[3]

As we try to assess Palmer's massive argument, we are compelled at the very outset to point out that it all proceeds on a certain complex assumption, which can be set out as follows: The Christian Faith consists of a body of propositional truths which have been revealed by God to men

[1] ibid., ii, 369–401, 408–12
[2] ibid., ii, 406f.; cf. R. E. Davies *Why I am a Protestant* pp. 61–4
[3] ibid., ii, 414–51

through Jesus Christ and the Holy Spirit. The Church is a visible institution set up with two functions, one of them to preserve and communicate this body of truths to mankind, the other to provide sacramental means by which men can be enabled to live the new life bestowed by Jesus Christ and finally to enter the divine presence and receive the vision of God. If we make this assumption, all that remains is to identify the Church among bodies of people which claim to be the Church, and to recognize the machinery by which the truths are communicated and the life conveyed. This is, in effect, what Palmer sets out to do, and, within the limits of his assumption, does it admirably and persuasively.

But is the assumption legitimate? Does the primary record of the origins of the Christian Faith, and of the personality and teaching of its Founder (which is what the New Testament is recognized on all hands to be) support the notion that the essence of Christianity lies in a system of truths? Does it not rather suggest that this essence lies in personal trust in Jesus Christ and self-commitment to what he was and did and taught; and that the propositional truths which go under the general name of 'Christian doctrine', are secondary, derived from the process of theologizing which must necessarily start and continue when intelligent people become Christians, but always under the judgement of Christ himself as he is known to us through the Gospels? If the answer to the second question be in the affirmative (though, of course, it raises its own difficulties, which must later be discussed), no system of doctrine, nor any body of persons which propounds one, can be called infallible in any sense whatever, and Palmer's whole enterprise collapses.

But even if we grant that assumption, can the resultant argument reach a solid conclusion? Does not the 'haunting circularity', to which we have already referred, appear again? If Christianity is a system of propositions, on what grounds do we accept the proposition whose acceptance will, no doubt, logically involve the acceptance of all the others? This proposition will normally be: the Church (or the Bible, or the Pope) is to be trusted. But why should anyone believe this until he is already persuaded that the system of thought

106

of which this forms a part is itself to be trusted? So round and round we go!

It will come as no surprise, therefore, to discover that Palmer's own argument is circular. He starts the whole process by appealing to Scripture, the Fathers, the Reformers, and the Anglican theologians, to prove that the Church is perpetual, visible and the bearer of salvation. Then, on this basis, with great elaboration, he goes on to show that the Universal Church is infallible in its judgements. But the Universal Church turns out, in the course of the discussion, to consist substantially of the New Testament Church, the Church of the Fathers, the Churches of the Reformers and the Church of England, together with the Church of Rome, which is held to be often in error, and the Oriental Churches, which are not held to contribute very much beyond what the Fathers had already said. So we have a careful proof of the authority of those persons and bodies to whose authority appeal was made at the beginning of the argument.

And if this is thought not to be completely fair, since the Universal Church is more than a conglomeration of the bodies which constitute it, and its judgements more than the opinions of those who lead the thoughts of those bodies, it has to be asked: Where in this case is the Universal Church to be found, and where are its judgements recorded? The answer to both these questions has to be: Since the adjournment of the Second Council of Constantinople in 553, nowhere. And though we live in a time when the assembling of a truly 'Oecumenical' Council is once again beginning to look just feasible, many centuries will have passed, if and when it meets, during which the Christian world has lacked the infallible authority which it is alleged to need for the interpretation of Scripture. A doctrine of authority, according to which infallible authority rests in a body which does not now exist, would be of little practical use, even if it were theoretically defensible.

Does not Schleiermacher still hold the field?

Chapter Five

REVOLT AND RETRENCHMENT

Until *Honest to God* appeared, it was virtually impossible for a man of the mid-twentieth century to imagine the tumult and turmoil that were caused among the public at large by the publication in 1860 of *Essays and Reviews*. How could matters of purely theological interest flutter any dovecotes whatever, except for those in remote cathedral closes? The very word 'theological' was now a synonym for 'obscure, intelligible only to experts', and when Conservatives were able to dismiss the disputes in the Labour Party in the 1950s about Clause Four as 'theological', they felt that they had uttered a shattering condemnation of their complete irrelevance. But when in 1963 a small paperback, heralded by an article on the front page of *The Observer*, and written by a bishop, came into the bookshops, a furore broke out which has many features in common with the excitement caused by the symposium of the Seven Oxford Men.

Of course, there are differences as well as similarities. The *Essays and Reviews* are long and leisurely pronouncements in the manner of the times; their arguments are deployed with a careful eye for consistency and precision. *Honest to God* comes straight from a man's questioning and unsatisfied mind, and the radical statements of one page are often contradicted by the conventional sentiments of the next. The themes of *Essays and Reviews* are the traditional ones of Bible and revelation and the historical element in the Faith; Bishop Robinson is concerned with the meaning of the word 'God', with ethics and personal relations and the meaning of prayer. And there were no heresy trials in 1963 or later.

But the similarities are considerable. Both books were

written by men of standing in the Church, so that people could say: 'If so-and-so, who speaks with the authority of his office in the Church, thinks this, then perhaps I can think it too.' Both books on the one hand gave a feeling of immense liberation to many people who were profoundly dissatisfied with what they believed they were expected to believe, and on the other hand appeared to people of conservative frame of mind to undermine the very foundations of Christianity. Both books showed that the public, whether or not it honours churches and chapels of the land by its actual presence, is in fact deeply concerned about those matters which form the incentive to religion and the content of theology. And both books, no doubt, were feverishly and at length discussed by many people who had not read them or had not understood them.

The sensation produced by *Essays and Reviews* did not immediately follow the publication of the book, even though it was released into an intellectual atmosphere already rendered turbulent by Darwin's *Origin of Species*, which had come out less than two years earlier. In fact, it was not until Frederic Harrison, who was already moving in the direction of Positivism, drew attention to it by a review, in which he said (somewhat extravagantly) that it made mincemeat of orthodox Christianity, leaving a 'revised Atonement, a transcendental Fall, a practical Salvation and an idealized Damnation', and called on its authors and supporters to be brave and honest, and join the forces of positivistic enlightenment[1] that Bishop Wilberforce of Oxford thought it sufficiently important to denounce it in the *Quarterly*. After that, condemnations flowed thick and fast. The bishops declared it to be heretical, and the Archbishop of Canterbury ratified this judgement by publishing it as an encyclical. While its synodical condemnation by the Lower House of Convocation was under discussion, several of the authors were personally attacked. The men picked on for this purpose were Benjamin Jowett, Henry Bristow Wilson and Rowland Williams.

[1] In the same way Professor Antony Flew, in *The Observer*, claimed that the author of *Honest to God* was trying to 'eat his cake and have it', and urged him, in effect, to come clean and join the atheists.

Jowett was arraigned before the Court of the University of Oxford for heresy, but the case was ruled out of order. Wilson and Williams were brought before the Court of Arches on the same charge, found guilty and sentenced to deprivation for a year. But, on appeal, the Judicial Committee of the Privy Council reversed the verdict,[1] and the two men retired into obscurity, much damaged in health. Eleven thousand Anglican clergymen, in protest against the book's denial of received doctrine, publicly declared their unswerving belief in the inspiration of the Scriptures and the eternity of punishment for the wicked; synodical condemnation of the book duly followed in 1864.

The authors, in their preface, are careful to point out that each of them was responsible for his own article only, and that they had written 'in entire independence of each other, and without concert or comparison'. Some of them, indeed, did not know what the articles written by others contained until they saw them in print, and there was no editor. This method, or lack of method, of writing had serious personal consequences, since each author felt himself bound in loyalty to the others not to criticize views with which he would not have associated himself if he had been asked to do so—though one of them, Frederick Temple, did say many years later that there were views expressed in the book which he did not hold or approve. It also has awkward consequences for the reader, for he is prevented from reading the book as a coherent whole, and is at a loss to know whether he should attempt to harmonize the notions on one subject which he finds in one chapter with those on another which he finds in another chapter. In spite of this, there is, on the subject of our particular interest, that of authority, a unity of approach which will show itself as our analysis of the volume proceeds.

The first essay, by Frederick Temple, at the time of publication Headmaster of Rugby School, seemed the least shocking of all those in the book, and did not prevent its author from

---

[1] see Peter Hinchliff *The One-Sided Reciprocity* pp. 163ff. for a discussion of the significance of this event

rising steadily through the bishopric of Exeter to the archiepiscopal see of Canterbury. The Essay traces the stages of a child's education into the freedom of man's estate, and claims that the world has gone through the same stages, so that now it can be said that 'we are now men, governed by principles, if governed at all, and cannot rely any longer on the impulses of youth or the discipline of childhood'. The education by reason of which man has now 'come of age' was mostly provided in the early stages by the Old Testament; but considerable help was also afforded by the literature of Greece and Rome, especially in intellectual and political matters. The New Testament inaugurated the last era of the world's education. The Hebrews had 'disciplined the human conscience, Rome the human will, Greece the reason and taste, Asia the spiritual inclination [by which he means the recourse to the contemplative life in oriental countries wearied of perpetual war and conquest]'. Then came Christ 'in the "fulness of time", for which all history had been preparing, to which all history since has been looking back'. The Gospels and the Epistles record his greatness and his message, but since the finishing of the New Testament there have been no direct or infallible messages from God, and the Church has been left to work out, with the help of the Holy Spirit, 'the principles of its own action'. The Fathers, rather unwisely, set about doing this by striving to answer all the questions, including the unanswerable ones; the Creeds formulated answers for the whole Church, and the Councils of the Church made the mistake of thinking and saying that the doctrines of the Creeds were true, not only in relation to the various heresies which had evoked them, but for all time and in all places. In fact, they embodied, but did not define, the truth, though definition was what they set out to provide; and much of what was laid down by the Councils is demonstrably antiquated and irrelevant.

Then came the invasion and occupation of the Roman Empire by the wild and vigorous nations which we are pleased to call the 'barbarians'. The Church set about the task of domesticating and educating them, and did so by falling back on rites and ceremonies, and by insisting on the outward observance of legal prescriptions. These methods really belong to an earlier stage in human development, and the Dark and Middle Ages mark a period of retrogression in human affairs; but this was no doubt necessary, since the exhausted Roman Empire had no other means of teaching discipline to the undisciplined. It might have been expected that the Reformation would bring in a new age of theological formulation, to make up for the lack of intellectual progress during the preceding centuries. But this is not what happened; in fact, the Reformation introduced a quite new principle, that of toleration, and toleration

implies in reality a confession that there are insoluble problems upon which even revelation throws but little light. Its tendency is to modify the early dogmatism by substituting the spirit for the letter, and practical religion for precise definitions of truth.

Toleration led to the emancipation of the human mind from dogmatic presuppositions, and the progress of science which it made possible has had an influence, sometimes unwished for, on 'our determinations of religious truth'. Thus men have found that there are more things in heaven and earth than are dreamt of in patristic theology. In the turmoil of ideas which now assaulted the Church it was necessary for it to have 'a firm spot in which she might stand', and she found it in the Bible. The Bible, fortunately, is not drawn up in 'precise statements of faith, or detailed precepts of conduct'; if it had been, the Church would have been forced back into the bondage of legal and dogmatic constraint. But it is history, and

even the doctrinal parts of it are cast in a historical form, and are best studied by considering them as records of the time at which they were written, and as conveying to us the highest and greatest religious life of that time.

Temple proceeds:

hence we use the Bible–some consciously, some unconsciously–not to override, but to evoke the voice of conscience.

And here, it is clear, we reach the nub of the argument. For 'conscience' now comes to the very centre of the stage.

When conscience and the Bible appear to differ, the pious Christian immediately concludes that he has not really understood the Bible.

Temple concedes that the interpretation of the Bible differs somewhat from age to age–it has been held to teach purgatory, to condemn Galileo, to rule out the scientific study of geology. But

The current is all one way–it evidently points to the identification of the Bible with the voice of conscience. The Bible, in fact, is hindered by its form from exercising a despotism over the human spirit; if it could do that, it would become an outer law at once; but its form is so admirably adapted to our need that it wins from us all the reverence of a supreme authority, and yet imposes on us no yoke of subjection. This it does by virtue of the principle of private judgment, which puts conscience between us and the Bible, making conscience the supreme interpreter, whom it may be a duty to enlighten, but whom it can never be a duty to disobey.

Since the Reformation, and the setting up of the authority of the Bible, there have been tendencies to try to copy too exactly the institutions and ideas of an earlier age in the development of the human race, and these are regrettable. But the growth of toleration has for the most part checked this tendency, and so long as the pursuit of truth is allowed to flourish unrestricted, and the critical study of the Bible is heartily encouraged by the Church, we shall fully enter upon our maturity.[1]

Fortunately the strength of Temple's argument does not depend on his historical accuracy. No responsible historian would now dismiss the Middle Ages as a period of fettered dogmatism, or ascribe the emergence of tolerance directly to the Reformation. Nor can it be said with any accuracy that the understanding of the supreme role of conscience or of private judgement was taught by the Reformers in England or on the Continent. Tolerance, the claims of conscience and the principle of private judgement were virtually unknown to Luther and Calvin, and completely so to Henry VIII.

[1] *Essays and Reviews* pp. 1-49

They emerged in the situation created by the Reformation, under intellectual as well as religious pressure, and they cannot be credited to the Reformation itself.

But Temple's main contentions are unimpaired by this. He affirms that the supremacy of the Bible discloses and reinforces the supremacy of conscience, that the deliverances of the Bible are the same in content as those of conscience, so that if there appears to be a discrepancy we assume that our interpretation of Scripture is wrong (the possibility that our interpretation of conscience is wrong is not mentioned at this point, though later on the need to enlighten the conscience is acknowledged), and that the further study of the Bible will further increase the domain of conscience. In other words the Bible and conscience are equated in content and authority, and the difficulty created by the fact that the Bible is an *external* authority is obviated by saying that the teaching of the Bible is the highest teaching available at the time of its writing, and by the suggestion that it must therefore be subordinated to conscience. For this really is what the equation of Bible and conscience amounts to: the ultimate supremacy of conscience, masked by the normal agreement of the Bible with it.

This, one would have thought, was a novel and fairly subversive view in an England where the necessity for an objective authority had not been seriously disputed for a long time. Perhaps its enormity was concealed by the reverent language which Temple always employs about the Bible, and still more by the greater radicalism of those whose writings came later in the same volume. For our age, the *naïveté* with which the infallibility of conscience is proclaimed is tempered by the pronouncement that

> he is guilty of high treason against the faith who fears the result of any investigation, whether philosophical, or scientific, or historical. . . . Even the mistakes of careful and reverent students are more valuable now than truth held in unthinking acquiescence. The substance of the teaching which we derive from the Bible will not really be affected by anything of this sort. While its hold upon the minds of believers, and its power to stir the depths of the spirit of man, however much weakened at first, must be immeasur-

ably strengthened in the end, by clearing away any blunders which may have been fastened upon it by human interpretation.[1]

The second contribution to *Essays and Reviews* is an encomium, in the form of a review, of the various books on Biblical subjects written by Christian Carl Josias von Bunsen, known as Chevalier Bunsen, or Baron Bunsen. His profession was diplomacy, and he was Prussian ambassador in London from 1841 to 1854. He was widely regarded as an exceptionally able negotiator, and before coming to London he had carried out some very delicate work on behalf of his government in its relations with the Holy See. But his consuming interest was theology, and he was able to complete an immense amount of research on the problems of early history. His Biblical works are voluminous,[2] and nowadays are never read, but they excited in their time the warm admiration of men with liberal views. He was able to combine the main concerns of his life, diplomacy and theology, when he helped to bring into being the Jerusalem Bishopric (1841) which so deeply upset Newman and his friends.[3]

Rowland Williams, Vice-Principal and Professor of Hebrew in St David's College, Lampeter, and at the same time Vicar of Broad Chalke, Wiltshire (to which he withdrew after his condemnation for heresy, and subsequent vindication by the Privy Council), sums up his commendation of Bunsen in the words:

> Bunsen's enduring glory is neither to have paltered with his conscience nor shrunk from the difficulties of the problem; but to have brought a vast erudition, in the light of a Christian conscience, to unroll tangled records, tracing frankly the Spirit of God elsewhere, but honouring chiefly the traditions of His Hebrew sanctuary.

He goes on to show how Bunsen applies scientific methods to

---

[1] ibid., p. 47f.

[2] such as *Egypt's Place in Universal History* (five volumes: Longmans, London 1848–67). *God in History* (three volumes: Longmans, London 1868–70). Bunsen's *Bible for the People* appeared (1858–70) in nine volumes! He also wrote earlier books on some of the Fathers.

[3] see p. 69 above

the Old Testament, and how he traces out the way in which
men's ideas of God developed according to

> principles of reason and right, to which our heart per-
> petually responds, and our response to which is a truer
> sign of faith than such deference to a supposed external
> authority as would quench these principles themselves.

The tradition of scholarship which Bunsen inherits and en-
riches has thrown a blinding light, according to Williams, on
the utterances and writings of the prophets, for it makes
them intelligible in their own historical context, and yet witnesses to the divine government of the world. Christ appears
as the moral Saviour of mankind. Justification is interpreted
as peace of mind and the sense of divine approval which
comes from trust in a righteous God (the 'fiction' of merit by
transfer being expressly repudiated), regeneration as the
awakening of spiritual forces in the soul, resurrection as
spiritual quickening, propitiation as the recovery of the peace
which we cannot have while we are divided from God by
sin, Gehenna as the fires of remorse.

Williams is not unwilling to see errors and defects in Bunsen's writings, and certainly does not accept all his detailed
views about Biblical authorship. It is his spirit and attitude
which win his vast esteem, and he brings his paean of praise
to its climax by quoting Bunsen's, 'How long shall we bear
this fiction of an *external* revelation?', acknowledging that
some will think such words 'too vehement for good taste', and
continuing:

> Others will think burning words needed by the disease of
> our time. They will not quarrel on points of taste with a
> man who in our darkest perplexity has reared again the
> banner of truth, and uttered thoughts which give courage
> to the weak, and sight to the blind.[1]

The author of these words was among the most vulnerable
of the contributors to *Essays and Reviews* because of his com-
parative obscurity, and this is no doubt one reason why he
was singled out as an object of attack. But it is possible to see
why his review of Bunsen was particularly offensive to the
orthodox. He praises a man who has not only thrown into

[1] *Essays and Reviews* pp. 50–93

doubt the authority of the Bible, and by implication all other external authorities, but has also moralized salvation and internalized the Resurrection. It was grossly unfair to charge him with holding all the views which he ascribes to his hero, since he carefully says from time to time that he does not agree with Bunsen on every point, but he must certainly have created the general impression that he held Bunsen to be on the right lines on most major points. For our particular purpose, however, the most significant part about Williams's article is his constant appeal from external authority to reason and conscience (the word 'conscience' comes into his sentences with very great frequency)–here he is entirely at one with Bunsen–and he is in fact reiterating in a more obtrusive form the emphasis which we have already found in Frederick Temple.

The next chapter in the book did not create a furore of the same sort as the others aroused, perhaps because the author was neither a professional theologian, nor an instructor of the young in theological matters, but Savilian Professor of Geometry in the University of Oxford, Baden Powell; in any case he was out of the effective reach of ecclesiastical censure. He wrote, 'On the Study of the Evidences of Christianity', and paid most of his attention to the question of miracles. He began by deploring the confusions and corruptions that usually seep into discussions of the evidences of Christianity, with those who claim to stand on the ground of reason appealing to moral sense, and those who claim to appeal to moral sense in fact resting their case on reason. But the really serious trouble, he thinks, lay far deeper. All systems of religious belief so far enunciated have been based on the idea of a 'positive external Divine revelation of some kind'. Rome has adduced the 'living voice of the Church', and claimed infallibility for it; Anglican divines have produced a modified form of the same claim by speaking much of the authority of the Church without claiming infallibility for it; most Protestants have given the same place to the Bible as Roman Catholics give to the Church, and have asserted that it is infallible, as containing the 'finally closed' and 'permanently recorded' Divine Word.

Baden Powell proceeds to trace the history of Christian apologetics. Its early practitioners, he says, argued for the general truth and validity of the Christian Faith by the methods customary in their age, which have no lasting historical significance. But the notion of the Church's authority took over in subsequent ages, and it came to be regarded as superfluous and impious to discuss, still more to question, the evidences for the Faith. Criticism, in fact, ceased until the fifteenth century, when the excessive subtleties of the Schoolmen aroused a certain number of protests. It was the Reformation which really brought the question of evidences out into the open again, and Protestantism more and more demanded definition, argument and proof, not the bare assertions of authoritative bodies. In the seventeenth and eighteenth centuries the Deists, who used rational arguments to disprove the distinctive claims of Christianity, were countered by other rational arguments—and a chief argument among these was from miracles. Miracles, it was contended, were attested by eye-witnesses, and therefore have sound historical evidence on their side; moreover, the divine omnipotence accounted for the occurrence of events which seem contrary to the order of things. And miracles proved the doctrines of Christianity to be true. Some appeal was sometimes made to the intrinsic excellence of Christian moral teaching and the doctrines with which they were combined, but this was a subordinate argument.

But this type of apologetic will not work any longer, and the approach of Archdeacon Paley is already giving way to that of Bishop Butler. The argument *from* miracles is being weakened by the growing weakness of the argument *for* miracles. Science can now explain events which once seemed to require a miraculous explanation; and it has to be said that belief in the miracles of sacred history, on which we are bidden not to lay impious hands, depends on the view which is taken of God. Does the Christian view of God really encourage us to believe that he would suspend the laws of nature? Even if there were no difficulty in believing in the historicity of the miracle-narratives, it is now plain that Jesus himself did not stress the evidential value of his works of healing and other mighty deeds; he referred to them 'as only secondary and subsidiary to the higher evidence of his character and doctrine'. Some have suggested that miracles were useful as evidence only in the first age of Christianity, or are useful only to the simple-minded. In recognition of these facts, Christians of many schools of thought have come to discredit their evidential value altogether. The Tractarians rely on the authority of the Church, the Evangelicals on 'spiritual impressions', not reason at all; and S. T. Coleridge has persuaded many people that Christianity must be its own evidence. Even strong believers in miracles nowadays play down their evidential value. Thus we are moving into an age in which intrinsic evidence is the only kind which is seriously considered; anything external is ruled out as evidence from the start.

This is a development heartily to be welcomed, for all attempts to prove miracles *as miracles* can now be seen to fail, for the very good reason that the accumulating discoveries of science all tend in the direction of establishing universal causation according to law. It is now apparent, Baden Powell concludes, that

'the *reason* of the hope that is in us' is not restricted to *external* signs, nor to any one kind of evidence, but consists of such assurance as may be most satisfactory to each earnest individual inquirer's own mind.[1]

Baden Powell has brought us by a different route to the point to which we have already been guided by Temple and Williams—the virtual supremacy of individual conscience, or rather, of conscience informed by reason. It is true that the 'mind of the earnest individual inquirer' takes the place of 'conscience' in the verbal formulation of the position reached, but no real distinction is discernible, and the point of view is very much the same in all the three writers we have yet examined, so far as their approach to the problem of authority is concerned.

The subject of H. B. Wilson's chapter, 'The National Church', does not impinge so directly upon our problem as those of the earlier chapters in the book, but his attitude to it

[1] ibid., pp. 94–144

becomes very clear before the end. He takes as his point of departure a recent controversy in the Church of Geneva between those who maintained that Constantine had introduced a pagan principle into the Church by allaying it with the State, thus producing 'multitidinism', and those who asserted that 'multitudinism' was essentially Christian, and that Constantine was completely justified in producing it.

Wilson makes it clear that he is in favour of 'multitudinism', and defends his view at some length. Religion, he points out, is decaying in England; this is shown by the fact that only 42 per cent of the population attended Church on the Census Sunday in 1851. This decay is the result of dissatisfaction with the Church's teaching. This dissatisfaction is often dismissed 'as a disease contracted by means of German inoculation'. But the real causes of it are the growth of our knowledge of the world and its inhabitants, and the questions which are thus raised in the minds of all thoughtful men –questions such as, 'What is the fate of those millions of mankind who have never heard of Jesus Christ?'; 'What has become of the promise of Scripture that the Gospel will be preached in all the world, when we know that the Christians amount to no more than a quarter of the total population of the earth?' These and similar questions cannot be sidetracked; we have, in fact, to admit that Christian doctrines concerning salvation are for the most part applicable only to those to whom the preaching of Christ comes, that the promise of the universal preaching of the Gospel was 'limited to the understanding of the times' when it was made, and that we must draw our conclusions about the fate of the heathen from our own moral instincts rather than from the express assertions of Scripture. And we are comforted in these reflexions by the knowledge that Jesus himself indicated that 'the conditions of men in another world will be determined by their moral characters in this, and not by their hereditary or traditional creeds'. Now this priority of life over doctrine is characteristic of the Early Church as a whole, before doctrine was hardened into a test of Christian discipleship. Thus men of dubious doctrines were retained in the Church in early times. But not only so. We also find that men whose lives were immoral were indeed admonished, and even avoided, but not excommunicated or refused the title of 'brother' or 'Christian'.

Thus, the Church of apostolic times was multitudinist. What Constantine did was to make it *national* also, on the analogy of the Jewish and heathen 'churches'. The beneficial effect of his work was limited by the introduction of doctrinal limitation at the same time, with the effect of expelling from the Church those whose views were thought to be unorthodox; and also by the necessity of requiring personal conversion in those who came over from paganism to the Church. But individual conversions are not an essential or permanent element in Christianity, though they belong to certain stages in its history. And the excommunication of heretics is contrary to the true nature of the Church.

The Church of Christ, then, is multitudinist and national in every land in which it is found. It is the task of this Church to assist the spiritual progress of the nation and all its citizens, and it cannot expect all those for whom it cares to be at the same stage of development. So it should not define its teaching too narrowly, or confine its teachers within limits too close. On the contrary it should avail itself of the unfettered powers of reason, and not least of the present opportunity for the frank criticism of Scripture. The Sixth Article of the Church of England does not say that the Bible is supernaturally dictated, nor does it attempt to define inspiration; and it would be wholly wrong to force the Article into line with the Confessions of the Protestant Churches of the Continent. Nor does the Article command us to believe everything in the Bible at equal peril, nor does it state that the Word of God is co-extensive with Scripture; nor does it rule out the literal, the allegorical, the poetical, or the legendary understanding of the stories of the serpent, the ass that talked, the corporeal assumption of Elijah into heaven, or other remarkable events. A man may accept the Article, and be free in his judgement on miracles and the authorship of Biblical books. Scripturalism [that is, what we should call Fundamentalism] has done great harm to our children. The conflicts and contradictions which occur in Scripture between the teaching of the Synoptic Gospels and the Fourth Gospel, and at other points in the Bible, are real conflicts and contradictions, not to be reconciled by theological ingenuity; and there must be freedom to accept one or other view on the issues raised.

Thus it is certain that the national, multitudinist Church must allow freedom and difference of opinion. Certain restraints are due to be removed. The requirement of subscription to the Articles by the clergy of the Church needs to be looked into. It is in general true that the clergy are free in their opinions, but not in their expression. But the legal obligation of those who subscribe to the Articles, and thus seem to limit themselves in the expression of their views, is not at all clear from the perusal of the Canons of 1603, or indeed from any subsequent writing. It may not amount to more than the acceptance of the Articles as the formal law to which the subscriber is in some sense subject. Certainly there is much flexibility in the way in which subscription is in practice interpreted. It is not practicable to alter the Articles, to make it easier to subscribe to them. The best course is to abolish the necessity of subscription, but to leave the Articles protected against direct contradiction or impugning, by penalizing those clergymen who indulge in this.

This relaxation would abolish the invidious distinction between clergy and laity in the matter of doctrine, and with it the imposition of an oath which often proves impossible to keep. It is no solution to keep subscription and tell those who do not wish to subscribe that they can join one of the sects. For this would be to erect barriers in front of those who have full right, as citizens of the country, to enjoy the benefits conferred by membership of the National Church. Indeed, the endowment of the National Church is not justly used unless it is distributed among the whole nation, not among half of the nation only, as at present. The National Church has responsibility for the moral progress of the whole nation, and for the discharge of this responsibility it needs to recruit members and teachers from the whole nation. It is true that the existence of Dissent has, politically speaking, enabled ill humour to evaporate harmlessly. But it is a very great pity that many intellectual people stay out of the National

Church because of its real or supposed dogmatism. The Bible, surely, is patient at many points of either a literal or an ideological [i.e. allegorical] interpretation–and both should be allowed within the Church, for it is the meaning, and the meaning only, which matters. The same applies to the Sacraments, and to the ecclesiastical hierarchy. To impose, or expect, speculative or historical unanimity of belief at these points would stifle Christian life. The National Church is there for all, and its task is to care for all, in whatever state of spiritual development they are to be found, and whatever stage they may have reached before they die.[1]

Wilson could be said to have flung wide open the doors of the Church to orthodox and heretic, saint and sinner, and everyone in between; to agnostic and reprobate; and, virtually, to 'heathen, Turk and Jew'. He stops short only of admitting the professed atheist. At least, this is how his essay must have struck many devout Anglicans fearful for the safety and purity of the Church of England. For us, at a sober distance, it is difficult to see what his terms of entry into the national, multitudinous Church would have been if he had drawn them up. We should perhaps not be very far wrong if we suggested that he would have admitted all those who are conscious, however rudimentarily, of 'bearing a part in a great moral order'.[2] And so we are back again at conscience, differently described, as the test of membership of the Church and, indirectly, of the truth of its doctrines.

The chief impression made upon posterity by the author of the next chapter, 'On the Mosaic Cosmogony', C. W. Goodwin, has been that he was the one Cambridge man to share in the writing of *Essays and Review*. But he deserves a better fate than this, for he states a view of the first two chapters of the Book of Genesis that not many scholars nowadays would wholly deny. He remarks that the attempts of theological geologists to square these chapters with modern knowledge are discrepant among themselves, despite the confidence of each of these experts that he has solved the problems involved; and he shows that the scientific accuracy of Moses can be defended only by regarding the chapters which des-

[1] ibid., pp. 145–206   [2] ibid., p. 205

cribe the creation of the world as consisting of a series of elaborate equivocations. It is much more sensible, he contends,
to think of these chapters as an early attempt by a Hebrew
Descartes or Newton to give the most probable account of
the world's origin, and to explain the oracular nature of his
utterances by reminding oneself that science in its modern
form had not arrived to teach him true modesty. The author's
good faith is, of course, beyond dispute, and we can credit
him with having set down for the world one great truth: 'the
unity of the design of the world, and its subordination to one
sole Maker and Lawgiver'.[1]

But Goodwin does not raise the problem of authority except by implying that Christians need not accept the literal
truth of the Pentateuch. Nor is there much to help us in our
quest in the chapter by Mark Pattison on 'Tendencies of
Religious Thought in England, 1688–1750'. Pattison, who by
the time of writing had entirely thrown off the influence of
the Tractarianism into which John Henry Newman had
once led him, is concerned to show that theology developed
considerably during the period under review, and, by implication, that it is always developing; and he pleads for a
method of writing the history of theology which does justice
to the forces exerted upon theology from outside, such as the
growth of political and religious toleration and the extension
of the range of human reason.[2] His thesis and his mode of
presenting it are in line with the general tendency of *Essays
and Reviews*, but his approach is historical rather than theological.

In the Great Hall of St Paul's School on its earlier site in
West London[3] there is a bust of Benjamin Jowett, and it is so
placed that the whole weight of the organ, which is dedicated
to his memory, seems to rest upon it. When he wrote the final
chapter for *Essays and Reviews* he did not yet have the responsibility, which later came to him, of being Master of Balliol—
he was simply Professor of Greek in the University. But it is
apparent that the chief responsibility for *Essays and Reviews*,
the impression it makes and the effect it produced, does rest

[1] ibid., pp. 207–53   [2] ibid., pp. 254–329
[3] The school has now been removed to a site in Mortlake, Surrey.

upon him, and that without his chapter it might have passed comparatively unnoticed. It is therefore somewhat surprising to find how harmless his chapter is when viewed in the light of the present state of Biblical scholarship. There is scarcely one of the positions which he took up, to the fury of Bishop Wilberforce and the Tractarians, which has not long ago been conceded by scholars of all parties except that of the Conservative Evangelicals. Nor does he write in an offensive or provocative manner, but only with the slight acerbity of any Oxford don.

His title is 'On the Interpretation of Scripture', and he begins by showing that while 'all Christians receive the Old and New Testament as sacred writings . . . they are not agreed about the meaning which they attribute to them'. The Bible itself remains the same: 'the commentators seem rather to reflect the changing atmosphere of the world or of the Church'. This is partly due to the controversies in which each side quotes Scripture to prove its case, and the legacy which is thus left to the successors of the original champions, and partly to the development of the human mind. In general, we can trace three kinds of interpretation, the mystical (or allegorical), the logical (under the influence of the prevailing philosophy), and the rhetorical. The last method is especially congenial to preachers, who have a 'tendency to exaggerate or amplify the meaning of simple words for the sake of edification'. This tendency has had a very

> unfortunate effect on the interpretation of Scripture. For the preacher almost necessarily oversteps the limits of actual knowledge, his feelings overflow with the subject; even if he have the power, he has seldom the time for accurate thought or inquiry.

It is very difficult to apply Scripture to the needs of the hearers without impairing the meaning. But, preachers apart, all the resources of scholarship are sometimes directed to upholding a received interpretation, not to discovering the true one.

The real purpose of interpretation is to find the original meaning of the passage under investigation by transferring oneself to the age in which it was written. This means, in effect, 'to read the Scripture like any other book'. To appreciate the importance of doing exactly this, we shall do well to trace the history of the interpretation of Scripture, for such a history

> would present in one view the causes which have darkened the meaning of words in the course of ages; it would clear away the remains of dogmas, systems, controversies, which are encrusted upon them.

It would make it very plain that Biblical criticism has clung more to the past than any other study. And today educated people are asking what the Bible does mean, not what it can be made to mean by ingenious scholars dedicated in advance to a particular point of view.

Unexamined presuppositions, such as that 'The Bible cannot err', or that 'The Creeds are infallible', have been responsible for much of the confusion, and some of it also has been caused by the use of the same word to mean different things. A case in point is the word 'inspiration'. All profess to believe that the Biblical writers are inspired, but they mean very different things by this statement according to the tradition from which they come. The real meaning of inspiration as applied to the Biblical authors cannot be decided in advance. We must examine the Bible itself before we know what is meant by inspiration in this context. We shall soon discover that it has components of many different kinds, and we shall need a doctrine of progressive revelation to cover all the facts. But this is not all. Our notion of inspiration must take account of the well-ascertained facts of history and science. If we find that certain statements in the Bible contradict these facts, it is no use hoping that science or historical research will collapse or go into reverse, and come to support the Bible after all. That road is closed for good and all. It might well be better to wait until knowledge has progressed still further before attempting to define the term 'inspiration'.

Further obstacles have been put in the way of a true understanding of the Bible by those who write Christian apologetics. In the effort to defend the faith they forcibly adapt the Scripture to the doctrines of the Creeds, or violently apply the maxims of Scripture to the needs of their own age.

Neither of these attempts can meet with anything but disaster. The truths and maxims of Scripture refer to the age in which they were propounded. The precepts of the Gospels cannot be made absolute rules for us. What relevance have they for modern politics? People who wish to apply them to modern conditions, and so claim the support of Scripture for what they have decided on other grounds, appropriate some words of Scripture for their own purposes, and neglect others; for instance, they take literally what Jesus says about divorce, and explain away what he says about riches and poverty.

This means that it is impossible to prove doctrines from Scripture. For Scripture contains no system, and must not be interpreted in scholastic or theological terms; those who do this have to resort to the expedient of wrestling words from their context and turning them into technical expressions. The allegorical method of interpretation, for all its long and distinguished history, submits the book to the interpreter's fancy, or to the changing wind of ecclesiastical doctrine. The meaning of the Old Testament is very different according to whether you read it as it stands for itself, or in the light of the New Testament; and the former method is the only legitimate one.

It may well be thought that the exposure of these difficulties in the interpretation of Scripture will confuse and alienate the sensitive, as well as the weaker brother, ' "for whom", nevertheless, in the touching language of St Paul, "Christ died" '. But there is a duty laid upon Christians to speak the truth, as well as a duty (in certain cases) to withhold it. Truth alone makes free, and 'the healthy tone of religion among the poor depends upon freedom of thought and inquiry among the educated'. Besides, these difficulties are already well-known to educated men, though a tactful reticence leads to a conspiracy of silence–and to a 'smouldering scepticism'. But 'Doubt comes in at the window, when Inquiry is denied at the door'. We can no longer ignore the results of criticism, and have no right to ascribe them to unbelief. If we are to reconcile the intellectual man to Christianity we must avoid all suspicion of dishonesty; and by bringing the discrepancies of Scripture out into the open we are taking the first step towards leading the various interpreters to the point of agreement. To commend this method is no kind of insult to the older interpreters; their faith was great, but their resources were limited.

The lessons to be drawn from this can be briefly stated: (1) Interpret the Scripture like any other book–and the respects in which it is unlike any other book will appear during the process. (2) Discover the meaning which every passage had to the original writer or speaker, and avoid mysterious and double meanings. (3) Interpret Scripture from itself. It is not an 'indistinguishable mass', and this principle therefore means that we cannot understand Scripture until we are familiar with it. (4) Study carefully the outward form of Scripture, that is, its language. The Greek of the New Testament is degenerate; it has qualities which made it universal, but at the cost of precision. Its modes of thought and figures of speech require thorough investigation. (5) Do not confuse interpretation with application. Application is, of course, legitimate, but it must always be made in the spirit of the Gospel. Sometimes it is comparatively easy, as in many parts of the New Testament; sometimes it is very difficult, or impossible, as in many parts of the Old Testament which exhibit the state of man's relation to God at the time of writing.

It will naturally be asked what effect modern criticism, and the kind of interpretation here advocated, will have on the theology and life of the future. It can be prophesied that they will enable different sections of Christendom to meet on the common ground of the New Testament. Some of the divisions in Christendom are already passing away with the help of Biblical criticism, for the Bible is becoming a bond of union, not a bone of contention. We can also hope that missions overseas will cease to be denominational, and rest rather on the universal truths of Christianity; and that the Bible will come to play a larger and larger part in liberal education.

A man thinking of being ordained may be troubled by all the questions that we have raised. He may be comforted by the thought that he may not be, himself, the man who has to deal with them. But even if he is, they are not so dire as they have been painted. The faithful and honest treatment of them will remove the old obstacles between religion and science–and surely this is great gain? We may well have to risk opposition by pursuing the studies we have suggested. But the pursuit of truth is never popular; yet the man who pursues truth, at whatever cost to himself, is accepted before God.[1]

This, then, is Jowett's great blast of the trumpet which sent fear into so many timid hearts. Nowadays the Bible is always 'interpreted like any other book'; we do not, indeed, acknowledge that this is all that has to be done about the Bible, and there is a very proper way of interpreting the Old Testament in the light of the New, though not the ham-handed and tendentious way that Jowett rightly condemned. Yet it is clear to all that the *first* thing to do with any passage or book of Scripture is to find out what it originally meant.

So far, then, Jowett is justified. What is not so immediately acceptable, though we may have to come to accept it, is the view of authority which runs through the whole chapter though it is nowhere explicitly stated. Jowett does not use the word 'conscience' so often as many of his collaborators, nor does he so often appeal to reason in plain words. But in practice he takes the label 'authoritative' off the Bible, and submits it ruthlessly and objectively to the bar of human knowledge, reason and conscience. The 'original meaning' of Scripture may many times, especially in the New Testament, emerge unscathed from such an ordeal, and Jowett would certainly claim that human reason and conscience are now enlightened by the spirit of Christ; but many times the original meaning will be found guilty of error, and immediately consigned to the place where that literature is preserved whose importance is limited to the relevance which it has for those who lived in its own time.

It is evident that the authors of *Essays and Reviews* took very seriously, though perhaps without knowing it, the challenge of Schleiermacher. He had said that there was no authority anywhere except in inward feeling, and in the inward feeling

<hr>

[1] *Essays and Reviews* pp. 330–433

of every man; and that no doctrine which was not derived from such feeling had the slightest value. They spoke of conscience and reason rather than of feeling–they were perhaps not men who had much experience of the kind of feeling which Schleiermacher describes–and they did not so much say that doctrines come out of reason and conscience as that, wherever they come from, they must be brought to the test of reason and conscience. But they were at one with him in the basic conviction that external authorities, however high and holy, have no standing except in so far as they justify their declarations to the individual–whether it be to his feelings or to his reason or to his conscience is not of great importance. It is fair enough to retort on both Schleiermacher and on Benjamin Jowett and his friends that they did not take sufficient account of the fact that many generations of Christians had come to the same beliefs and doctrines by reflexion on their experiences, and that this is a *prima facie* argument for the value of the Church as the repository of doctrine and for the authority of the Church as it expounds the gathered wisdom of Christian people. They would have replied, no doubt, that the sameness of belief was imposed by the power of an institution. But this covers only some of the facts, and the case here lies against the individualists. And the difficulty of the individualists, when they are asked to set out a doctrine which will convince the world, is well-known; for why should anyone, still less the world, believe what comes from the experience of one man, when everyone else's experience is likely to be different? Yet *Essays and Reviews* had now assisted Schleiermacher to make it virtually impossible to clamp down upon doubts and critical inquiries by the blank assertion of authority.

Nor did Anglican writers again attempt to do so, once the fury against Jowett and the rest had cooled off. It is true that a somewhat unnatural alliance of Tractarians and Evangelicals did what it could to prevent the appointment of Frederick Temple as Bishop of Exeter. But while the champions of orthodoxy were trying–and failing–to build a bastion against the incoming waters of Biblical criticism at one point or another along the shore, the tide was steadily coming in everywhere else, and twenty-five years after *Essays and Reviews* most of the opinions which its authors had been almost stoned for holding were acknowledged to be sound by the great majority of reasonable men in the Church of England and beyond. It was, in fact, now impossible for the Bible *not* to be read and interpreted 'like any other book', and the results of such reading and interpretation were gradually and steadily accepted–reluctantly, and after a burst of resistance, when they were put forward arrogantly by Colenso, discreetly and devoutly when they were put forward modestly by Westcott and Hort and Lightfoot.

Meanwhile the distressing facts about the social conditions of the industrial areas, to which the eyes of the early Tractarians had been blinded by their intense devotion to the sacraments of the Church, were now apparent to their successors, and the alliance between the Anglo-Catholics and the Christian Socialists, who had at one time suspected each other of adhering to different religions.[1] was in process of being forged. So the intellectual and spiritual atmosphere was very different from that of the late 'fifties when Charles Gore recruited his team for the writing of the book which appeared as *Lux Mundi* in 1889. The first preparations for the book were made between the years 1875 and 1885, when all the authors were teachers of theology in Oxford, and often met together to discuss the new problems of the time. In 1885 they began to disperse to various parishes and to other universities, but their common mind was sufficiently cohesive to express itself in a book which shows a consistent pattern of thought. Gore himself had learned enough from the fate of *Essays and Reviews* to be sure that the failure of the authors to take common responsibility for the book was partly responsible for the troubles in which they landed.

The interests of the authors of *Lux Mundi* were many and varied, partly Biblical, partly theological, partly scientific, partly historical, partly political and social. But they were

---

[1] In March 1864, Pusey declared, in a letter to F. D. Maurice, that they 'worshipped different Gods' (F. Maurice *The Life of Frederick Denison Maurice* Macmillan, London 1884, ii, 468). I owe this reference also to David A. Pailin.

agreed that 'Jesus Christ is still and will continue to be the "Light of the World", for

if men can rid themselves of prejudices and mistakes (for which, it must be said, the Church is often as responsible as they), and will look afresh at what the Christian faith really means, they will find that it is as adequate as ever to interpret life and knowledge in its several departments, and to impart not less intellectual than moral freedom.

They were also agreed 'that if the true meaning of the faith is to be made sufficiently conspicuous it needs disencumbering, reinterpreting, explaining'. And they professed to write 'as servants of the Catholic Creed and Church, aiming only at interpreting the faith' they had 'received', but, on the other hand 'with the conviction that the epoch' in which they lived was 'one of profound transformation, intellectual and social, abounding in new needs, new points of view, new questions'.[1]

Since we are about to consider the doctrine or doctrines of authority which *Lux Mundi* can be shown to state or imply, we are bound to take notice of a disclaimer on this matter which appears in the Preface to the tenth edition of the work. The book, and chiefly certain parts of it, had been criticized on the ground that it did not raise, or dealt inadequately with, the questions which concern the seat and methods of Church authority. The Preface replies to these criticisms by saying that they are based on a misunderstanding of the point of view from which the book was written. This was that there were certain questions arising, for instance, from the development of science and Biblical criticism and the consequent need to give a rational justification for faith in Christ, which had to be dealt with before the question of Church authority was even relevant, and that it was the business of the book to deal with these, and leave the question of Church authority for later discussion and determination.[2] It can be readily agreed that the point of view here described was a fair and proper one for the authors of this work to take. But this need

[1] Charles Gore (ed.) *Lux Mundi: A Series of Studies in the Religion of the Incarnation*, p. vii f.
[2] ibid., p. xiii f.

not deter us from asking whether there is a view of authority in general, though not of the 'seat and methods of Church authority' in particular, which is conveyed by its authors; for, as the Preface to the tenth edition states, they *were* concerned with 'rational justification' for 'faith in Christ', and this concern brings us very near the question of authority as we are considering it.

Most of the chapters, however, as this Preface makes it easy to understand, do not affect our present quest. In fact, there are only three which do. The first is that of R. C. Moberly, who was teaching at Christ Church during the decade of consultation between the future authors of *Lux Mundi*, a country vicar at the time of its publication, and three years later Regius Professor of Pastoral Theology in Oxford. His later works, *Ministerial Priesthood* and *Atonement and Personality*, are more famous, and at the same time more distasteful to Evangelical theologians, than his contribution to *Lux Mundi*. But his chapter in that book is extremely important for the understanding of the whole. Its title is 'The Incarnation as the Basis of Dogma'. It begins by rebutting the argument that dogmatic theology is in principle impossible, since theological truth is of its nature uncertain and indefinite. Moberly points out that the reason given for the impossibility of dogma is itself dogmatic. The Church claims to have both certain and definite knowledge. The only way to test this claim is not to rule it out *a priori*, but to consider the evidence which is produced for it. If the evidence turns out to be insufficient, then the claim must be dropped; if it turns out to be sufficient, then it must be accepted. The question at issue is that of the *truth* of dogma.

He proceeds to claim that the evidence for the truth of Christian dogma is in certain respects parallel to that which is offered for scientific principles, and that the acceptance of Christian dogma is similarly parallel to the acceptance of scientific principles. For instance, in both cases the apprehension of truth is progressive; a man accepts his first set of truths in a somewhat provisional manner, and as his knowledge develops proceeds towards certainty; the proofs which he is invited to consider deepen and strengthen his convictions as he goes on with his work. Then, again, both the scientist and the Christian believer accept a certain amount on authority–the scientist on the authority of the scientific world, the believer on the authority of the Church; yet neither is asked to continue to believe what he has been told on authority unless he is in due course given intelligent and sound evidence for it. We 'take religion on trust' in the first instance, as we take the diagnosis of a doctor; for we know that in some matters this is the wisest thing to do. But we do not rest content with what we are told; rather do we go on with our thinking and experiencing until 'the doctrines of the Church are to [our] entire faculties, mental, moral, and spiritual, proved and known to be true'.

But there are also differences between the acceptance of science and the acceptance of Christian truth. These lie in the subject matter of what is believed, and in what is involved by the truths in question if they are believed. The Creeds are authoritative for the Christian, not because we are told that they have God's authority (for how do we know that they have this?), but because, being persuaded on good evidence that their main substance is sound, we go on to accept them as a whole. Then, the Creeds are much more *final* than science, for science claims to have conquered only a small part of the realm of truth, whereas the Creeds introduce us to a supreme Person, by believing in whom we come to believe in the comprehensive truth about all things, however little we understand it at first. The evidence, too, accepted by science, though it is similar to that which is accepted by religion, is not of exactly the same kind. The proofs of science appeal only to the intellect; the proofs of religion appeal to the whole man. They are not just literary and historical, they are also moral, spiritual and metaphysical; they come from all life as the Christian experiences it, and they appeal to the whole life of man.

We come, then, to the evidences for Christianity. The truths of the faith presented themselves to human consciousness in a historical order–first of all there was the preparation for the coming of Christ, then the actual coming of Christ, consisting in his life and death and resurrection, and then the results of his coming; and all of these are matters of historical inquiry and evidence. But the middle event is all-important; if that fails for lack of evidence, all is lost for the Christian Faith. 'All turns, then, upon a certain passage of history. Is the history, as believed by Christians, true or false?' In other words, did the Incarnation (which for the purpose of this argument includes the Atonement) happen, or did it not? Now the 'heart and core' of the New Testament case for saying that it did happen is the Resurrection. So we must ask whether the Resurrection happened. This is not just a question as to whether a man reappeared after death. 'The inherent character of' the one who is said to have risen, and 'the necessary connection between what He was, and had said and claimed for Himself, on the one hand, and on the other His rising out of death' are 'essential part of that fact of the Resurrection, which comes up for proof or disproof', for 'the Resurrection of the crucified Jesus cannot possibly be a bare or simple fact'. But of course we have to establish the simple fact of his actually having risen from the dead—for if that falls, everything falls with it. No one disputes that Jesus died on the Cross. Did he rise on the third day?

Moberly does not think it part of his task in this chapter to give the evidence for the Resurrection, but only to show how vital that evidence is. So he goes on to assert that if the fact of the Resurrection is accepted, then the doctrines of the Creeds flow naturally from it, and in the first place the Incarnation. For if Jesus rose from the dead, all men are forced to ask who or what was the man who thus rose. It is agreed that he was truly man; on the evidence of the Resurrection, together with other evidence, the Church claims that he is also truly God. And this claim must be either true or false—there is no middle course. The Councils expressed the beliefs to which the Resurrection of Jesus Christ gives rise. They did not discover any new truth; they unfolded what was already revealed. Christians do not believe the doctrines of the Creeds on the authority of the Councils alone; if the Creeds could be shown to be unscriptural, we should have to disbelieve them. But in fact they are scriptural. The doctrines which they propound spring from the Incarnation, and the Incarnation is demonstrated by the Resurrection. Dogma, then, is the self-realizing of the consciousness of the Christian community in respect of the answer to the great question which exceeds in importance every other question: Who do you say that I am?

When this is understood, we can say of the dogmas of Christianity that they are our real certainties–'the immutable principles of Church truth'. There has grown up around these dogmas a mass of theological literature, very valuable and important in its own time and place, but not comparable with the formulated statements of the Creeds. For instance, there have been expositions of the doctrine of the Atonement, and many illustrations have been used in order to make it clearer to human logic. But the Church has found

> that the modes of thought which seemed adequately to explain the doctrine to the conscience of some ages, have not only failed to satisfy, but have actually shocked and offended, others.

But the doctrine itself remains and is fundamental to Christianity. The 'liberalizers' of theology have done good as well as harm in their expositions of doctrines; they have purged the grossness with which some doctrines have been presented by some writers, for instance in the cases of predestination and hell. But they have also tended to neutralize the good which they do 'by overvaluing themselves and forgetting the loveliness and the power of perfect subordination to the Church'.

But 'we must not claim for phrases of earthly coinage a more than earthly and relative completeness. The Creeds are temporary, in that they are a complete and sufficient statement of truth only for time.' They are 'the most perfectly balanced and harmonious expression of the truth' of which we are or will be, in our earthly existence, capable. Yet of course our powers of conception and language are necessarily inadequate to express God's nature; the truths of God are greater than our conception of them on earth can ever be. The Creeds therefore will be superseded in heaven, but not before. In time they can be disproved only by disproving the truth of the historical Incarnation and the revelation which it contains. But nothing short of a divine revelation can do that. Even the damnatory clauses in the Creeds are necessary in order to distinguish truth from error, and to show that if to believe the truth is life, to disbelieve it is death.

Nothing of this is to say that the Creeds, because they are imperfect, earthly expressions of divine truth, are less than, or inconsistent with, real truth; it is not possible to agree with those who say that the Scriptures and the Creeds are not factually or literally or historically true, except in part, but are vivid expressions of spiritual truth. Such a view rests on a preconception of what can or cannot happen, as in the case of the miracles reported in the Gospels, not really on a careful scrutiny of the evidence. We have, indeed, a preconception when we read the Gospels, but we have reached it after a scrutiny of the evidence, not before. To dispose of miracles may lead to dispensing with more of the historical facts of the Gospel. This tendency to a 'spiritual' religion, however lofty its aims, sooner or later loses hold of all reality and ends 'in evanescence'.[1]

The notable feature about this chapter of Moberly's is its duplicity (the word, of course, is not used in a moral sense). On the one hand, in answer to the 'liberalizers' and the 'spiritualizers', and to the whole spirit of *Essays and Reviews*, he exalts the dignity of the Church and the authority of its Councils and Creeds, and 'the loveliness of perfect subordination to her'; on the other hand, in the desire to bring the Church's teaching into greater accord with the spirit of the times, with the critical temper of scholarship and with the desire of many intellectual Christians to subject questions of faith to the light of day, he claims that Christianity is as firmly based on 'evidence' as the findings of the scientists. But–with doleful consequences for the success of his total enterprise–he is forced by his own logic to put his first endeavour at the mercy of the second: the 'authority' of the Church, on his own reasoning, can stand up only if the 'evidence' for its central affirmation, the doctrine of the Incarnation, is sound. And the evidence in question is primarily the historical evidence for the Resurrection of Jesus Christ. The

[1] ibid., pp. 218–72

whole splendid superstructure of Christian doctrine depends on the soundness of one pillar.

And is the pillar sound? Few people, even today, would deny that Christianity is an important sense a historical religion, and that its power to persuade men of its truth depends to some extent on the result of historical inquiries. Perhaps later in this book we shall be able to see how great or small this dependence is, and what are the present results of this dependence. But it was already manifest when Moberly was writing, as it has become much more manifest since, that the historical evidence for the Resurrection of Jesus Christ, understood as his literal, personal (though not necessarily physical) rising from the dead, is not of the sort to satisfy those who are not already committed to, or highly sympathetic with, the Christian position; and that even for many of those who are thus committed and thus sympathetic it is by no means conclusive. It scarcely seems that we can allay the doubts of modern man, Christian or otherwise, about the truth and authority of the Christian revelation by putting all our eggs in this particular basket.

It was Charles Gore's own contribution, on 'The Holy Spirit and Inspiration', that chiefly upset the Tractarians of the old school, and may even have hastened the death of their leader, H. P. Liddon. Gore altered the text of his chapter at several points in succeeding editions of *Lux Mundi* in order to avoid misunderstandings and answer criticisms, and he devotes a large part of the Preface to the tenth edition to dealing with the criticisms which persisted after the alterations had been made. We shall discuss the chapter as it appeared in its final form, but it should be noted that the criticisms which it received largely concerned themselves with Gore's acceptance of the 'analytical' approach to the study of the Old and New Testaments, and with his view that Christ as man was ignorant of the true authorship of certain Old Testament books, and not with his general doctrine of authority, which is our main interest in what he writes.

In fact, he reaches the point of saying what he says about the Bible and its inspiration only after a careful statement of the authority of the Church. It is right, he begins by telling us, for Christianity to appeal to experience, in spite of the abuse of that appeal by 'ungoverned enthusiasm and untrustworthy fanaticism'; for it is in essence a *life*–a life manifested in Christ and shared by his people. We appeal to the life of Christ himself, and to that life continued in the Church. The giver of that life is the Holy Spirit, who is at work in the whole of nature and in all mankind. But mankind in general has not responded to his offer of life, and he has had largely to narrow his work to the Church, which is not, indeed, the exclusive sphere of his operations, but the 'special and covenanted sphere of His regular and uniform operation'. In his work in the Church and Holy Spirit treats man as social, and therefore provides the Church with an order of ministry, and with ' "a pattern of sound words", embodied in Holy Scripture and perpetuated in a teaching Church'. Thus the knowledge of God is not an individual illumination, but the result of incorporation in the Christian community. Yet none the less the Spirit encourages individuality and the development of individual powers, with the result that there is a variety of disposition and character, and of piety, within the Church.

'What is true in the life of religion as a whole is true in the department of the intellect.' There is the authority of the collective society, to which the individual owes his knowledge of the Faith; but this authority nourishes individuality. Each individual Christian is enjoined by Scripture to 'keep the traditions', but not as an external law; for tradition passes into the individual consciousness and imparts freedom, so that there is a place for individual inspiration. But this inspiration originates in the community, and ends there also. This points to a perfectly simple view of authority, expounded by Plato long ago. Authority is the function of the Church as it implants the right ideas and affections in the young, in order that as they develop they may recognize the right reason of things, and welcome truth as a friend. Thus, authority 'is a necessary schooling of the individual temperament'.

It is in this light that we should understand the often emphasized maxim of antiquity: *credo ut intelligam:*

The Creed represents the catholic judgment, the highest knowledge of God . . . granted to man by the Divine Revelation. Let a man put himself to school in the Church with reverence and godly fear, and his own judgment will become enlightened.

The individual has much to do on this showing. He is to help to prevent the tradition of the Church from deteriorating into something else. He is to pay the debt of his education by testing all things. And some specially gifted individuals may be raised up by God to reform the Church and restore the apostolic teaching to it, though they have no function of innovation, but only of restoration. There must be no bar on free inquiry into the truth of Christianity, though Rome endeavours to set one up. If a man, after full inquiry, decides that Christianity is not true, we cannot complain of the method he has used, though we shall have to tell him, even if it irritates him, that he is mistaken.

The Holy Spirit, in addition, consecrates physical nature and spiritual nature, and allows no divorce between them. Thus, he does not constitute the Church as a purely spiritual entity, but as an entity which is both physical and spiritual. But because of our fallen humanity the unity between spirit and flesh is not yet an accomplished fact, but is gradually taking place. So the Old Testament, under the guidance of the Holy Spirit, reveals the nature and purposes of God *gradually*. It is in many ways a very earthy and material book, with its material sacrifices and frequently low standard of morals; finality came with the New Testament. The Church also is imperfect; it is still becoming what it is to be, and we should be patient with her, as the Spirit is.

The inspiration of the Scripture is to be looked at in the light of all this, not in isolation. It contains the indispensable record of historical fact, but it is useless to us unless we are prepared in mind and spirit to believe what it says. That is, we need conceptions of God, of sin, of redemption; and the Holy Spirit keeps these conceptions alive in us. The Church is always assuring us that God's offer in Christ is true, and commends it to reason and conscience. The Creed is a revelation continuously renewed in men's hearts by an organized and systematic operation of the Spirit in the Church, while at the same time it finds its guarantee and security in certain Divine acts of historic occurrence.

So the belief that the Scriptures are inspired is to be 'held in context by the belief in the general action of the Holy Spirit upon the Christian society and the individual soul'.

Gore is now able to tell us in some detail how Scripture should be read and interpreted. The Apostles had a unique authority, but they had it as ministers of a tradition, not absolutely for themselves. Their writings were written in and for the Church, and written for the edification of those within, not for the initiation of those without. We may conclude from this:

(a) The doctrine of the inspiration of Holy Scripture is not a basis of Christian belief but a derivation from it. We believe the facts about Christ on sound, though not infallible, historical grounds. It is only after we have come to believe them that we formulate a doctrine of the Bible's inspiration. (b) Yet it is a doctrine implied by Christian belief, as we see from the fact that the Lord himself, the Apostles and the Church all hold it. (c) The doctrine means that the Jews were selected by God to be 'the sacred school for all the world of the knowledge of God and of the spiritual life' (Gore here quotes from Athanasius, *de Incarnatione* 12): that special men among them were chosen to interpret the divine message; and that these special men were the 'subjects of a movement of the Holy Ghost, so shaping, controlling, and quickening their minds'.

From this point onwards we must deal with the two Testaments separately. In the Old Testament there are degrees of inspiration, and various sorts of inspired literature. The inspiration of the historians consists in their giving the history of their people from the point of view of those who saw in history the activity of God for the salvation of man. The poets were inspired in that they directed their poetic gift to reveal the soul in its relation to God. The Spirit inspired the prophets by deepening and intensifying their faculties, not by superseding them; thus inspired, they did not foretell the future accurately, but they did teach what God was commanding and saying in the age in which they lived. And the

Old Testament presents itself to us as an organic whole which postulates a climax not yet reached.

We see the inspiration of the New Testament correctly if we remember that Christ in the days of his flesh prepared certain men to perpetuate and interpret his message, and the Spirit endowed them with the gifts necessary for ensuring that they represented Christ correctly. This applies both to the Apostles and to their friends who wrote some of the New Testament books.

So far, surely, says Gore, all Christians will agree. But some questions arise. Does the inspiration of the Old Testament guarantee absolute historical accuracy? To this we can say that it is reasonable to suppose that the account is substantially true, though there may be an admixture of the non-historical. But we need not suppose that inspiration means the miraculous communication of facts which cannot otherwise be known, nor the freedom of the authors from all historical processes. We have to allow for the possibility of some idealizing of Hebrew history, and for the prevalence of the dramatic over the historical in Job and Daniel. All these matters are for historical critics to look into; their work is to be welcomed, not prevented, for we are not committed to a dogmatic definition of inspiration.

But what of Christ's use of Scripture? Do we not have to withdraw in his case the concessions which we have made to the critics of the Old Testament? He undoubtedly implies the inspiration of the canonical writings. But his use of Jonah and the narrative of the Flood does not prejudge critical questions. He had no wish to convey critical and literary information. He does not bring to bear 'the unveiled omniscience of the Godhead to anticipate or foreclose a development of natural knowledge'. To assert that he did so is to deny the self-emptying which was involved by the Incarnation. Theology should leave open for free discussion the questions raised by Biblical criticism.[1]

This free and frank acceptance of the methods and results of Biblical criticism by a leading member of the school of thought which regarded itself as the principal guardian of

[1] ibid., pp. 315–62

the Church's traditions, was without question a milestone in the history of the Church of England. It emancipated innumerable minds, and it enabled the Church of England to hold up its head again in an age in which it was coming to be regarded as the last refuge of the obscurantist. Nor should it have shocked Liddon as much as it did. For Gore makes it abundantly clear that the study of Scripture is subject to the authority of the Church in the sense that the Church is and remains the authoritative source of Christian truth, and will continue to expound the eternal doctrines of the Creed as the true interpretation of Scripture, whatever the Biblical critics may say. But what we have to ask is whether the authority of the Church as Gore asserts it is securely founded.

Each man, we are told, is to go to the school of the Church. He is to believe what he is told, but also, as he grows in knowledge and understanding, to test what he is told, to discover its truth for himself. If he does that, he will come to realize for himself what the Church has told him from the beginning, and so the Church's faith will become, in a real and vital sense, his faith. But what if something goes wrong, and he comes to the conclusion that the faith of the Church is false? In that case, says Gore, no one should complain of the fact that the man in question has gone through the process of thinking things out for himself; but his conclusions are certainly erroneous, for the Christian faith is in fact true.

Even if we take this, as we should, in conjunction with what Gore says about the provision by the Holy Spirit of the Church to meet our needs and give us the authority of the collective society, are we not, in the end, being informed that we are to believe what the Church says because what the Church says is true, and that this is all there is to it? And are we not back again in the realm of dogmatism?

We may conclude this chapter briefly by asking whether Walter Lock, in his contribution on 'The Church' extricates us from this very difficult situation. He points out that all human beings require co-operation for the spiritual life, association for the propagation of ideas, and participation with others for worship. In Old Testament times God satisfied this need by giving the Church of the Jews. Now, for the same purposes, we have the Christian Church. The historical continuity of the Church is necessary for the spiritual life of man. In the propagation of ideas the function of the Church is to be the school of truth and to bear witness to what has been given to it. Its authority is guaranteed by its possession of the Episcopate. The higher, more fundamental truths of the faith were given to the Church from the beginning, and these it has always taught authoritatively; the controversies which arose in respect of some of them caused it to formulate them in the form of creeds, and these creeds are the authoritative teaching of the Church. When we are young we believe what the Church teaches because the Church teaches it; later we love the Church and trust it yet more because it has taught us the truth. There are no new truths for the Church to discover and proclaim; the Church is a 'casket' for the preservation of the truths already revealed. Its function in worship is to continue Christ's priestly work, and this it does through its priests; for sacerdotalism is of its very essence.[1]

There is plainly no inquiry here into the nature of the Church's authority, or into the reason for accepting it. We have nothing but simple assertion, followed by the elaboration of what is asserted. We must conclude that Lock takes us no further than Gore; in fact, if the truth must be stated, not so far.

[1] ibid., pp. 364–402

Chapter Six

INSIGHT ABOVE ALL

John Oman (1860–1939) is an undeservedly neglected theologian. As has recently been pointed out in a long and very valuable appraisal of his work,[1] he concerned himself at the beginning of this century with many of the problems which are agitating the Church and its thinkers today, and suggested approaches which, if taken, might have saved the men of today much perplexity about questions such as whether Christianity is still tenable in face of modern science, in what sense we can validly speak of transcendence and the supernatural, and how we can come to the knowledge of ultimate reality. Of his books, the one which penetrates most deeply to the heart of religion is *Grace and Personality* (first published in 1917), and it is to be hoped that the enterprise of Collins in bringing it out twice in a Fontana edition, in 1960 and 1962, has been rewarded, not only by large sales, but by a more widely-spread understanding of Oman's thought. He deals in the book with the problem of reconciling the absolute sovereignty of God with human freedom, and sees the clue in the conception of a 'gracious personal relationship' which God offers to his obedient children; in the course of his exposition he gives an interpretation of the Beatitudes which equals anything else written on the subject. His last book was *Honest Religion*, published posthumously; it anticipates, almost in detail, many of the questions which arise today about the integrity of those who commit themselves to a positive religion, and emphasizes the point, frequently forgotten, that honesty requires, not only the doubting of propositions which have no genuine credentials, but the affirmation of

[1] F. G. Healey *Religion and Reality*

145

those which commend themselves to our understanding and stand up to scrutiny.

It seems that *Vision and Authority* was his 'most popular book'.[1] Oman wrote it when he was minister of Clayport Church, Alnwick, not so very long after he had translated Schleiermacher's *Speeches on Religion,* and when he must have been still strongly under the influence of that work. *Vision and Authority* came out in 1902, went, of course, out of print, and was re-issued in 1928 and 1948. Oman revised it in part for the second edition. He curtailed and changed the first two chapters, and replaced the third chapter by an entirely new one. But he refused to make any radical alterations either in the thought or in the structure. His reasons for this refusal are instructive. It is worth remembering that when he wrote the book he was a youngish man and a parish minister to people of no great learning, and that when he prepared the book for its second edition he had been for twenty-one years Professor of Systematic Theology and Apologetics at Westminster College, Cambridge, and Principal of that College for six years. The first reason he gives for refusing to revise his earlier work is that it was the result of a personal search for truth. This personal search had been virtually forced upon him, he tells us, by the trial of Robertson Smith for heresy in 1877, and still more by the comments of a lawyer friend, who was also an elder of the Kirk, upon the trial: 'Granting that Robertson Smith is right, if it is truth, it is dangerous truth, and he has no right, as a professor of the Church, to upset the Church by declaring it.' Oman adds the acid comment that he found the same attitude to truth as the Scottish elder's in Newman, and that it led the highly sophisticated Newman and his friends to Catholicism. 'But, having had it first presented to me unadorned, I was left no option between facing the search for a truth, which would shine in its own light in face of all inquiry, and complete scepticism.'

The second reason he gives is that the first form of his arguments was determined by the need to present them to ordinary people, and that in this form they had won response. So there was no need to change it now, and certainly no case for

---

[1] Healey, op. cit., p. 11

146

mixing it with a more complex form. It is true, we may remark, that *Vision and Authority* is the simplest in style and presentation of all Oman's books, but that betokens no great simplicity. It is gratifying to note that the book won the response that Oman claims it did from 'ordinary' people.

The third reason is, for our purpose, the most revealing of all:

> At that stage, I had rather seen things by way of intuition than based them on grounds of reason. Since then I hope I have made some progress in the latter task, but I have found little of the intuition to alter. Much of what is here said is not as new as when it first appeared, but it still seems to me as true, and as relevant to the needs of the time. I still see no reliable ground for faith except insight into reality, and no worthy and final goal except freedom in loyalty to its requirements.[1]

We are here bidden to notice, as we study the contentions of *Vision and Authority*, firstly, that Oman never changed his mind on the main issues, though he would have felt able in later years to bring a greater array of rational arguments to the support of his position, and, secondly and more particularly, that he never came to see any other sound basis for religious faith than 'insight into reality'.

Oman begins the build-up of his argument by showing— what no one nowadays at least would dispute—that the present age is one of great perplexity about the ultimate questions of life. He admits that every age is claimed by those who live in it, or at least by those of that number who have some sort of spiritual perception, to be one of exceptional uncertainty, and that our claim for our age may spring from this tendency of seriously-minded people (not many people would admit that today!). But

> in any case there has been an exceptional shaking of the foundations, so that no one seems quite sure what things that cannot be shaken remain. All authority has been questioned, and moral as well as intellectual confusion has ensued.

In such an age the supreme question is the question of

---

[1] *Vision and Authority* (2nd edition), pp. 9–11

authority; and 'the spiritual problem cannot be solved by evading the intellectual', for 'obscurantism is already unbelief'. In such an age, many, probably most, people are in desperate need of security. But we have no right to perpetuate systems of thought simply because they are useful and will give people at least the *feeling* of the security which they need (here we see the impact on Oman of the Scottish lawyer's comment on Robertson Smith). *Not* to inquire upon what basis our belief rests, is to

> go on in life, like skaters on a pond from which the water has been withdrawn, the ice floating upon air, and not on the native element that produced it, pretence seeming as good as the reality, till suddenly the crash comes with swift ruin and confusion.[1]

Oman goes on to welcome the concept of biological evolution as one without which the intellectual needs of our age cannot be satisfied. But he at once repudiates the notion that it is a new concept. The highest religion has always thought of the order of things as being 'first the carnal, then the spiritual'; it has always known that the making of man in the divine image is 'the goal, not the starting-point' of human development, in fact as 'the purpose of experience and the meaning of history'. So, under God, man is working upwards 'from a kingdom of physical laws to a kingdom of holiness and love', from life under the pressure of material necessity to life lived in freedom and aspiration, from a religion of blind faith to one of freedom, holiness, adoration and love.[2]

We tend, he goes on to say, as the universe discloses itself to the men of science as vaster and vaster, and man finds himself to be smaller and smaller in relation to the vastness of the universe, to 'despise the day of small things'. But this is a temptation to be resisted. For we, with all our physical smallness, belong to an 'order of greatness' in virtue of which we can look with confidence into the face of God our Father. For we have learned that the value of a religion is to be measured, not by 'the greatness of its rule and the age and size of its institutions', but 'by the quality of its life and its faith and its hope'. So the real authority of religion has no-

[1] ibid., pp. 19–25   [2] ibid., pp. 26–30

thing to do with the 'power of the papal throne, which has inherited the empire of the Caesars, which, long as it has endured, abides in face of eternity only for a moment', but 'in the fisherman of the Galilean lake with his faith able to embrace the infinite and the eternal and his vision of a kingdom to which there is no limit and no end'.[1]

All men seek to 'inherit the earth', the next chapter points out, and there are various ways of trying to do so. The obvious method is that of acquiring as much of it as possible by conquest or hard cash. But the 'joy of possession' often turns out to be little more than pride in having what others want, and the only certainty which it provides is that 'instead of inheriting the earth, the earth will finally inherit' us. The artist's appreciation of the earth is a far superior mode of inheriting it. Yet it leads to the possession of only half of the earth, for man is nourished by bread just as surely as he is not nourished by bread alone, and he must learn to come to terms with the soil which nourishes him just as surely as he must be lifted above the soil by the artist's joy. The true possession of the earth comes only through spiritual insight into the whole of life. We are bound to begin by distinguishing the secular from the sacred, and by concentrating on certain things, such as faith and hope, as especially sacred because they disclose the ultimate meaning of life. But the distinction between secular and sacred is 'of man's requirements, and not of the nature of things'; as we come to the fullness of our possession of the earth, it is a distinction that is more and more obliterated, for we learn the uses of all things, both those called secular and those called sacred; and we reach

[1] ibid., pp. 31–33; cf. Robert Bridges in *The Testament of Beauty* (Clarendon Press, Oxford 1929):

> So it was when Jesus came in his gentleness
> with his divine compassion and great Gospel of Peace,
> men hail'd him WORD OF GOD, and in the title of Christ
> crown'd him with love beyond all earth-names of renown.
> For He, wandering unarm'd save by the Spirit's flame,
> in few years with few friends founded a world-empire
> wider than Alexander's and more enduring;
> since from his death it took its everlasting life.
> *HIS* kingdom is God's kingdom, and his holy temple
> not in Athens or Rome but in the heart of man.

(I, 771–80)

that fullness, not by material acquisitiveness or poetical appreciation, but by 'the acceptance of life's discipline and the performance of life's duty'.[1]

And what is this 'spiritual insight into reality' of which Oman makes, and will continue throughout the book to make, so much? He devotes the next three chapters to telling us. Spiritual insight is to be most sharply distinguished from the 'faith' of the man who is steeped and stereotyped in creed –who, indeed, is like Nicodemus, and must go right back to the beginning and be born again, if he is to have any chance whatever of entering the Kingdom. It is, essentially, the attitude of a child: the attitude of eager, unclouded speculation, readiness to learn, 'submissiveness to reality, unconsciousness of the dead formulas which cover ignorance, and the conventions which save investigation'. The spiritual man has, moreover, a child's modesty and a child's confidence; and this is the only condition on which infinity can 'condescend to a being who, in a vast universe, draws one breath of life between eternities', the only condition on which 'eternal wisdom' can teach such a being a lesson. Jesus was right to compare the organ of spiritual insight with the physical eye. The physical eye, on first thought, is wholly incapable of discharging the task which is given to it. It is a nerve and not a sinew, a thread and not a cable. It is exceedingly delicate and easily damaged. It is 'so personal and transforming that philosophers have contended for ages, yet are little nearer determining what is outward reality and what is only individual sensation and impression'. Yet, of course, it is this very delicacy and personal quality which give it the power to reveal to us delicate distinctions and designs, and to make us personally aware of the universe around us; and at the same time to put us into communion with others who have the same delicate organ on which to rely. Spiritual insight requires the same delicacy in the organ and the same personal quality in the apprehension. Clearly such insight, like knowledge of every kind, is individual, for we cannot know with any mind, or see with any insight, but our own; thus we are liable at all points to error. But, although it is individual, it is

---

[1] *Vision and Authority* pp. 34–42

not individualistic. For truth is universal, not for one man's reason only. If we know the truth, we know the truth which all men can know, and by knowing it we are brought into the community of those who know it also. So by insight we are not shut up in ourselves; rather, we are led out into agreement with a world of men. Agreement in error is merely a convention, and is soon a cause of dissension; 'but truth is a bond of union, determined in the nature of things'.

This does not mean that the only things that matter are agreement and unity; in fact, the desire for unity may arise from a distrust of man's power to reach the truth. But if all men seek truth, in the knowledge that unity is not the starting-point but the goal, they will come in due course to unity in the truth. Meanwhile we travel on with those who are engaged in the same search, disregarding no discovery of the past and no previous experience of mankind, but being careful to distinguish right from wrong, and valuable experiences from those of the other sort, aware that only those who are adaptable, sympathetic, loyal to their convictions and humble in service are able to keep their spiritual vision fresh.[1]

Oman closes the first main section of his book by indicating the possible causes of failure in the spiritual search to which we are committed–lack of earnestness, disloyalty to the truth which we already acknowledge, and self-satisfaction (which is far worse than the sins of the flesh, and may bring it about that the prostitute enters the Kingdom of God before the priest); and then by speaking of the unity of experience and the task of the prophet. The reason why much is revealed to babes which is hidden from the wise and prudent is not that wisdom and prudence are bad things, but that without humility they are worthless, and many who are wise and prudent lack humility. True humility includes that faith in the indivisible unity of life which leads to unremitting inquiry into the truth. The wise and prudent, lacking this humility, often advise us to retreat into the safe shelter of a Church which has settled all problems, has received an infallible doctrine, and assures us of a mystical salvation. But how do we know that it can really fulfil the promise which it makes? How do

[1] ibid., pp. 43–61

151

we know that the harbourage which it offers is safe, except by intellectual inquiry into its credentials–which is the one thing we are not allowed to undertake? Some, indeed, encourage us to flee into the harbour offered by an infallible Church on the ground of 'any port in a storm'; but 'an appeal to timidity is the opposite of an appeal to faith: nor was panic ever a good pilot'. To take the course thus commended is a sign of unbelief, not of faith. And to teach, as some do, 'that the sole spiritual purpose of intellectual perplexity is to terrify men from all exercise of the intellect, is to set God's creation at variance with God Himself'. Advance in science is the friend, not the enemy, of religion, and intellectual inquiry cannot be put into a separate department from religious faith. But when we realize that truth is one, because God is one, we have faith in the unity of experience, and can go on from height to height of knowledge and faith. But we need a prophet to tell us again that God is one, the origin and end of all things, and that all is one in him. Then we shall learn the deep truth of the doctrine of the survival of the fittest. It is true that it is the fittest who survive, but the fittest are those who are spiritually fittest, the holy and the loving; for it is they whose fitness truly corresponds to the whole environment of a just and ordered world.[1]

So far Oman has spoken of the *internal* authority, and left us in no doubt as to what that authority is; it is, without question, spiritual insight. But now he comes to the *external* authority, and we must expect him to be highly critical. In fact, in view of the argument so far, it is not clear that there is any place for an external authority at all. But Oman does not proceed to this radical conclusion. He points out that the revelation which is essential to our freedom, and so to our whole well-being, is indeed to the individual, but to the individual in his place. And his place is society; and a man can learn true freedom nowhere else. So the revelation is to the race, and the wise men of the race, the prophets, the holy and the loving, build up a treasure of understanding and truth into which we all enter, and to which we all may add a little. Thus revelation takes place in history, and a historical reve-

[1] ibid., pp. 62–84

lation is a necessity of man's position in the world. Thus revelation, also of necessity, is transmitted to each generation in turn by a religious society, and we 'must all build on the foundation of the apostles and prophets'–who are those who have obeyed the divine call and recognized the divine teaching. We depend on the good and faithful in the past; they form our ancestry and kinship and our true Church. Our debt to this Church is incalculable, and its authority must in some way be acknowledged. But it must be acknowledged in freedom, not servitude, and how we are to reconcile authority and freedom is the question that occupies the rest of *Vision and Authority*.[1]

Oman first investigates the possibility of accepting 'the authority direct', and in the process makes what is surely the classic statement of the case against an external, infallible authority. We are often told, says Oman, that there is no peace and security for the human soul or for the human race if the Church does not speak and man obey; if the Church is to speak, and so produce this human obedience, it has to be a Church which is the mouthpiece of a divine revelation, an absolutely reliable guardian of divine oracles, and a sure interpreter of what God has revealed. And this argument is not completed until we go on to conclude that a Church which is an infallible mouthpiece, guardian and interpreter requires a single head. Those who tell us this are ready to add that Rome provides exactly and in all respects what the argument requires.

Others deal in another way with the alleged need of the human soul for an authority to which it can unquestioningly yield obedience. They argue to the necessity of a Church which gives infallible teaching, as in the other case, but they claim that infallible teaching must be provided by a Scripture which can be misunderstood, but can never be doubted or questioned.

To the claim of Rome to supply infallibility we must give the preliminary answer that it contradicts the facts of history. To those who argue for an infallible Bible we must reply at this stage that, though the Bible's persuasive power over the

---

[1] ibid., pp. 87–91

minds of men has never been greater than it is today, the demand made on its behalf for submission without persuasion has never been more dubious. The infallibility of verbal inspiration is really no longer a tenable view.

We cannot evade the difficulty in which everyone who believes in infallibility is placed by invoking the authority of the traditional Church while accepting the scientific criticism of the Bible; that is, by positing an infallible Church with a fallible Bible. The people who feared that the dissolution of the Bible's authority endangered every claim to infallible authority were perfectly justified in their fears. An infallible Church with a fallible Scripture is a ludicrous conception. If God did not give us an external guarantee in the past, when the Bible was written, what possible reason is there for supposing that he gave one a few years later, or gives one now? The undermining of the infallible Scripture has undermined the infallible Church.

Above all, to believe in the necessity of unquestioning submission to external authority is to exalt necessity over freedom, and to disbelieve in the advantages of freedom. If God really requires men to submit without discussion or question, why did he not create us in the same way as he created the planets and the other objects in the universe which obey the necessary laws of nature? On the showing that God demands unthinking obedience of man, he is just plainly incompetent in making man with a desire for freedom. But if freedom is the highest thing in human life, as surely it is, the toil and turmoil of human life are explained and justified, and we see that the environment of man is the divine workshop of human freedom.[1]

In fact, we know that truth and knowledge are imparted to man progressively, according to man's capabilities and responsiveness. Progress comes at all times by building on the foundations laid by others. In the succession of good men and true who have received and passed on God's revelation, the prophets of the Old Testament are the most important guides for us. They were children of freedom; they were buffeted by incredible disasters. Yet they continued stedfastly in the path

[1] ibid., pp. 92–7

of freedom, insight and loyalty to truth; and as they advanced in knowledge their conceptions of God and the world became less and less materialistic. Always they appealed for free response, never for blind submission. And Jesus, who understood them more profoundly than anyone else has ever done, and in his person and message brought them to fulfilment, never quoted them as a final warrant for the truth of what he said; his appeal was always to the living hearts of men.

Jesus himself is the greatest in the succession of prophets. He spoke as man to men with great humility, unfolding the meaning of Scripture, creation and time. Men were ready to accept anything on the authority of others then as now. But Jesus refused to ask them or encourage them to do so. Rather, he based everything on the authority of mind and conscience. He did not appeal to external witnesses; he was his own witness to himself. He never opposed the authority within the human soul. His words, 'I say unto you', *began* the inquiry into truth; they were not intended to end it, and did not end it. This is why it is true that to accept Christ as teacher is intellectual emancipation, not subjection. As he was in his mode of teaching, so he was also in his mode of saving the world. He could have done it by the exercise of divine omnipotence, and there were, and are, some who believe this to be the method he should have adopted. But Jesus did his work of salvation by dying on the Cross.[1]

The case of Simon Peter is clearly crucial for the whole argument, for he stands in the Church and before the world as the symbol and head of an ecclesiastical institution which negates almost everything which Oman has been saying, and in Scripture the passage in which he salutes Jesus as the Messiah and is called (at least, on the traditional interpretation) 'the Rock' is the chief support for the claims of that institution to be the true and only Church. Oman, therefore, comes next to 'The Blessing of Simon', and affirms that Simon was addressed by Jesus in the words, 'Blessed art thou, Simon Bar-Jona', not because of what he had said, but because of the manner in which he had come to see the truth which he expressed. He had seen this truth *for himself*–this is

[1] ibid., pp. 98–118

155

what Jesus meant by saying that flesh and blood had not revealed it to him, but his Father in heaven; he had not taken
it on the authority of others. Thereafter, and throughout his
life, Simon made many mistakes; indeed, 'with how much
human limitation and even error the Divine certainties may
be consistent, Peter's life seems designed to show'. Immediately after being called 'the Rock', he says something which
Jesus ascribes to diabolic inspiration; a few weeks later he
denies his Lord at a moment of crisis; later on he is seriously
confused on the subject of the Gentiles' admission to the
Church, where he seems to have grasped the Lord's intention
very inadequately, and is at the mercy of a 'few troublers of
the Church whose bigotry was the measure of their persistence'. But it remained true of him that what he opened no
one shut, and it remained true, not because he made no mistakes, or because what he decided God was committed to
sustaining, but because he had the gift of approving and con-
demning what God approves and condemns.[1]

This gives us the clue to what is meant by the saying, 'On
this rock I will build my Church.' The Church was built on
Peter because he was a man of insight, and also on other men
of insight. All these men had hesitations, all these men made
mistakes, but their trust was in God. They *were* the Church
in its beginnings, and to this Church Jesus gave the task of
transmitting his message to posterity. He was careful not to
write the message down, for a written, autographic record of
the message would have put it beyond the reach of all
dubiety, and caused it to become rigid and legalistic, to be
received by the faithful with implicit obedience. Instead, he
passed on his message to the Church, that is, to living men,
in a more vital and memorable way than writing it down
would ever have achieved. To the Church, thus, was given
the task of spreading and interpreting his teaching in a rich
and dynamic way. The time came, of course, when the message had to be written down, but this was simply a case of
practical necessity, not divine instruction.[2]

In the course of this chapter on 'The Founding of the
Church' Oman has to meet the argument that the 'guarantee

[1] ibid, pp. 119–24   [2] ibid., pp. 125–30

of a literal and absolute transmission of the truth . . . was assured by the promise given to the disciples of a special endowment of the Holy Spirit'. For 'did not Jesus Himself say that the Holy Ghost would bring all things to their remembrance, whatsoever He had told them'? To this Oman replies that the promise of the Spirit's aid was 'an assurance, not of an infallible, but of a living transmission'.[1]

We are now ready to receive the true meaning of 'apostolic succession'. Who is the true successor of Peter, the fisherman, who in his lifetime sat 'in a chair of the plainest wood that could keep him from the ground'? The Pope, sitting on the throne of the Caesars, 'elected with much intrigue by the princes of the Church'? The Archibishop of Canterbury, 'the proud spiritual head of a prosperous nation that esteems itself second to none upon earth'? Or the Moderator of the General Assembly of the Church of Scotland, maintaining inviolate the whole edifice of the faith in his palace of infallibility beyond the Grampians? Or, to put it otherwise, is the Pope a truer successor of Peter when he presides at Church Councils, or when he kneels before God in penitence and uncertainty? Or the Archbishop when he sits on an ancient and stately throne, or when he mixes with ordinary men in their state of inadequate cleanliness and is willing to unite with any Christians if the thing can be made possible? Or the Moderator, when he speaks as a Son of Thunder to the applause of the Celts, or when he visits a lonely shepherd on the moorland on a winter's night? The answers which Oman gives are already obvious. The true succession to Peter and the other apostles is found when men can truly say of themselves: 'We toil, working with our own hands; being reviled, we bless; being persecuted, we endure; being defamed, we entreat.'[2]

Oman has by this time stated and elaborated his main thesis, and the rest of the book contains a good many repetitions, from many points of view, of what he has already made clear. But we may pick out from it various implications and applications of his theory of authority which both illuminate it and test it in practice. He has much to say, for instance, on the question of Christian unity. He insists that the original

[1] ibid., p. 127f.   [2] ibid., pp. 131-8,

unit of Christian fellowship was the meeting of two or three gathered in the name of Christ, constituting in essence a new social order. When men and women meet thus in his name, they may not agree on all matters, but they remain harmonious, because they are bound together in allegiance to personal insight. Christ is their Regenerator and Saviour, not their Reformer and Ruler. It is therefore wrong to insist on a unity of organization. But it is not wrong to believe in the true sort of unity, that is, in being perfected into one. Such unity is always in the future, but always to be worked for. And the right method of working for it is through a unity of those who seek for the truth together by the use of the spiritual insight that God gives to them, and are for ever discontented with any form of unity which is not the best. They eschew the unity 'of the quarry', and all hasty endeavours at uniformity, all short cuts through difficult and dangerous territory. Nor do they think it worth while to distil all doctrines into one mixture or to make a compound of all organizations, or to gain a unity of creed founded on compromise. At all times they preserve the method of freedom, just as Paul, even at the height of the controversy about circumcision, prayed, not that his opponents should submit to him, but that they should receive knowledge and discernment. This way forward and upward is slow and costly, and there are many setbacks. But it is the only right way. And the end is unity in life and charity, faith, hope and love–a unity which binds together Franciscans and Salvationists.[1]

But how, on this view, can we discern the true Church and its members, and the true message of the Church? We alone, ourselves, can judge whether we are members of Christ's Church. The Church itself has no right to judge us, and can therefore exclude none. Similarly with Christian truth. We must select and appropriate the treasure handed down from the past–but discern the truth for ourselves. This is freedom, and when we have gained it we shall find that the authority without and the authority within are in perfect agreement.[2] There is no help to be gained from trusting an infallible Church or an infallible Bible, for such trust stems from a

[1] ibid., pp. 139–58   [2] ibid., pp. 167–76

desire to have truth established on other than religious conditions.[1]

And what of Church tradition? In the beginning the Apostles were identified with their message, but later ages have separated them. Then the Church proceeded to interpret the message by the methods of the Jewish scribes whom Christ repudiated, claiming that divine inspiration suspended all the human qualities of the writer and turned them into machines. Or it put them in 'the Cave of Polyphemus' (the legendary giant who herded men into a cave as if they were beasts), for instance by clamping a particular theory upon the history of doctrine, forgetting the human personalities of the men who preached and wrote the Gospel, and neglecting the plain meaning of their words. Or it reduced the whole apostolic witness to a cold scientific system to be proved by reasoning.[2]

The alternative is not, Oman claims, to consign Scripture to purely private interpretation or private opinion. Scripture, of course, springs from personal experience, but this does not give every man liberty to make of it exactly what he wills or finds congenial. The true interpreters of Scripture are those who have made the experience of its writers their own, and contended for the truth which they have seen against all hardships and obstacles.[3]

But what shall we say of the 'ideal of Hildebrand', which constantly rears itself up against any theory of personal liberty in matters of religion? The Church, it is argued, can be maintained only if its ruler is absolute and its doctrines are regarded as infallible. Hildebrand, Pope Gregory VII, attempted to put this into practice. He did not entirely succeed, and his measures led to strife in Europe, but this was because he was not himself perfect. If we could find one who is perfect, should we not put him in a position of absolute control, and demand man's total subjection to him? No. Hildebrand's error was not to ask for too much, but to ask for too little. He asked for submission to himself, and used human methods to gain it. He should have asked for total submission of heart and will to *Christ*, and used Christ's methods to gain it. Thus he would have founded a real kingdom of free men. The Church, when it seeks worldly power in order to secure the truth, always falls into professionalism and the inordinate love of precedent. Supreme power is in any case too much for any man to have; if we are to have a Papacy, let us put it into commission![1] Not that the Church must not be visible. The visible Church is not final or eternal, but it is a means to the glory of God, and for that end needs rules and discipline; but never at the cost of freedom.[2]

Thus the Church has order. It is not Christian to avoid the 'office of a bishop' on the ground of man's sin and folly. The office should be accepted, not for the power it gives, but in humility and helpfulness, and especially in times of danger. The Church throughout its history has owed much to men who have been willing to do this.[3]

But, finally, does not the promise of Christ that the Gates of Hades will not prevail against the Church imply a promise of earthly power and a sanction of earthly methods? This cannot be so, for Christ himself in the wilderness rejected the temptations to provide material good for mankind, to compromise with earthly society and its methods, and to impress the world with pomp. He deliberately chose the way of self-sacrifice and service. To get round this, the Church has distinguished the Christ of humiliation from the Christ of exaltation, and in the name of the second Christ has used the methods of coercion and false authority. But there is only one Christ; Christ remains the same in his exaltation as he was in his humiliation, and he still proceeds by the methods of love and freedom. It is clear that the Church that will prevail against the Gates of Hades is not the visible, institutional Church; in fact, *this* Church will be defeated by the Gates of Hades, for all earthly things ultimately perish. The Church that will prevail is the Church that is made up of those who are faithful in love. It cannot at present be separated out from among men, and gathered into a pure society. But it exists. Its progress is constantly being retarded, and its success slow to come. But its progress will come to consummation, and its success is assured. And its leaders are those who

[1] ibid., pp. 263–80   [2] ibid., pp. 280–8   [3] ibid., pp. 289–92

are bravely meek, working amid the common life of men, and seeking only a free response.[1]

This whole argument contends for a view of authority which has been, and should be, and will be in these pages, much criticized. But as an account of the Christian's approach to the central truths of his religion, it stands high. This is perhaps to say that its religious value is greater than its theological value; but it is also to say that its religious value is very great indeed, as those who, like the present author, were considerably influenced by it in their formative years will gladly testify. For it puts out of the way the notion, fostered from time to time by all the great denominations of Christendom, that religious faith consists in adherence to and acceptance of a pre-formulated system of thought. It makes even more irrelevant and impossible the notion that faith is the blind acceptance on authority of the customs, institutions and manner of life of a particular body of Christians. It is a plea, insistent and in the end undeniable, for 'authentic' Christianity, for the free response of free men to a gracious, personal God, who will go to any lengths to win, but will do nothing to coerce, the allegiance of his children. Moreover, it vindicates, as part of men's knowledge of God, the quality which he calls spiritual insight—a quality hard, if not impossible, to define, but recognizable as distinguishing the man who 'sees things for himself' and passes on to others, however obscurely, what he has seen, from the man who has to be content, and is sometimes complacently content, to pass on what he has been taught by others.

Oman's argument also establishes the existence through the Church's history of a succession of men who had this gift of insight and by their use of it have placed the Church at large permanently in their debt. He calls it the true apostolic succession, and recognizes no other. This nomenclature is not very useful, because we have no evidence at all that the apostles, apart from Peter and Paul, and perhaps one or two others, were men of spiritual insight to any high degree, and even in the case of Peter there are more recorded examples of his spiritual obtuseness than of his spiritual insight. If we are

[1] ibid., pp. 318–52

to believe in an Apostolic Succession, which we are not required by history or Scripture to do, we do best to hold that the succession consists of men whose task it has been rather to administer the Church and conserve the deposit of Christian doctrine, and also, it is to be hoped, to be true *pastores pastorum*, than to exhibit special gifts of insight and spiritual discernment, though those qualities have by no means been entirely lacking in many of the bishops of the Church. Oman would have done better to speak always of the succession which he had in mind as *prophetic*, as indeed he frequently does. But he has certainly shown that this succession exists, and it is not without significance that when we think of the men and women who undoubtedly belong to that succession—Irenaeus, for instance, Origen, Athanasius, Augustine, Benedict, Francis, Abelard, à Kempis, Luther, Calvin, Loyola, George Herbert, Richard Baxter, Wesley, Newman, F. D. Maurice, William Temple, John XXIII (we may make what list we want, within limits), the last question that we ask, if we ask it at all (except, perhaps, in the case of John XXIII), is whether they were bishops, though we are interested to find that some were and some were not, and that some were not even ordained.

Nor is anyone likely to question the validity of Oman's well-documented attack on the use of earthly power to achieve a spiritual end. No doubt in the temper of modern times the physical enforcement of obedience to outward authority would in any case have passed away—at least so far as religion is concerned; in the realm of politics this happy state has not yet been reached. Nor is it conceivable that the attempt, in Spain and Latin America, to force Protestants to become Roman Catholics by material sanctions, or the attempt to force Roman Catholics to become Protestants, wherever this has been made, will ever be resumed once it has been dropped. But the effect of Oman's book is to drive out of the mind of his readers any lurking thought that perhaps one ought to make sterner efforts to prevent the young from going astray into agnosticism or atheism, or the wrong denomination.

And, surely, Oman has made it more difficult than ever

before to put up a case for a doctrine of ecclesiastical or
Biblical infallibility, or for any external infallibility whatsoever. By Biblical criticism 'Scripture is shown to be mighty as
an appeal to the heart and the conscience, but to have nothing of the infallibility of a proclamation which directly
claims submission.'[1] Can this verdict on the assured results of
Biblical scholarship be seriously doubted, except in the
interests of a theory about the Bible which has been formed
quite apart from the impartial investigation of the Bible itself? And can such a theory, however ingenious, be har-
monized with the facts of the Bible as scholarship has disclosed them?

The condemnation of the view that, although we have no
infallible Bible, we have an infallible Church which tells us
exactly what the Bible is saying through the medium of its
insight, errors, contradictions and variegated authorship, is
equally devastating. 'Conclusions which show that the Spirit
of God did not give an external guarantee of truth in the
past, make it probable that He does not give it in the present.'[2] Is it not very implausible, to say the least, to suggest
that God, having decided not to provide an absolutely correct
record of his thoughts and purposes for the people of Israel
and the Early Church (who might perhaps be thought to need
such a record even more than we do), determined later on to
nullify his earlier decision by giving the Church the authority
to declare infallibly what the Bible really means?

But the decisive consideration, which makes a doctrine of
external infallibility finally incredible, is stated by Oman
thus: 'Uninquiring submission to external authority is neither
God's method with man nor a desirable method of human
obedience, but mere exaltation of necessity over freedom.'
But grant, for the sake of argument, that God wishes for this
uninquiring submission:

> Would not the end required have been better served, had
> God absolutely subjected man to Himself from the begin-
> ning? . . . If the obedience of mere submission will satisfy
> the heart of God, then we can only say that the method
> God has employed with man is chiefly distinguished from

[1] ibid., p. 93   [2] ibid., p. 94

the method he has employed with the planets by the chaos it has permitted.[1]

We may put the same point rather differently:

The infallibilists must have it one way or the other. They can say that God requires absolute submission; in which case they must explain why God has shown himself so woefully inefficient in obtaining it. Or they can say that God respects human freedom; in which case, how do they reconcile the doctrine of infallibility with their statement?

These are negative but important virtues of Oman's argument. Does he replace the theories which he rejects by a theory which will meet the facts which he uncompromisingly points out? Does the concept of spiritual insight give us what we have been seeking throughout this book? It is already clear that 'spiritual insight' is, in the strict sense, all that Oman has to offer in place of an infallible authority, though he speaks of the educative process by which man rises according to his capacities to the apprehension of higher and higher truth, and of the accumulation of spiritual treasure which comes from the insight of prophetic men who build on the wisdom of those who come before them. Does spiritual insight give us something which we can trust, not of course unquestioningly, but as a guide which will lead us on to greater and greater understanding? Unfortunately, Oman's whole argument on its behalf rests on the presupposition that spiritual insight always provides knowledge of the truth as *Christians* see it, always a fuller understanding of the *Christian* Gospel—as though God had somehow guaranteed that no honest seeker could fail to find Christianity. But, quite apart from the fact that it is not really consistent with Oman's approach to suggest that God guarantees anything in the field of truth at all, it is demonstrably untrue to say that spiritual insight always leads to a Christian view of the world or of God, unless we are going to deny blankly that there is any spiritual insight to be found in the founders or followers of any non-Christian religion; and it is unlikely that we shall feel justified in doing this. But if spiritual insight as Oman has taught us to think of it leads a man to Buddhism, or agnosticism,

[1] ibid., p. 94f.

or atheism, or Mormonism, or even (horrible for Oman to contemplate) to Roman Catholicism, what can we, or anyone, say in rebuke or correction? In the end, it will only be our spiritual insight against his. Who shall 'judge the spirits, whether they be of God'? Are we not back at the very beginning of our quest for religious authority?

In the cases where spiritual insight does lead to recognizably Christian truth, Oman asserts that it leads also to the only proper kind of unity–a unity of faith and love (instead of a false unity of the kind which is imposed from above) and a unity which includes Christians of all varieties of thought and expression. But history does not bear out this optimistic affirmation. When the whole emphasis is placed on spiritual insight, the result is greater disunity, not a growing together in love and faith. The further the divided denominations of Christendom go towards insistence on the sanctity of individual judgement, the greater the proliferation of division. Many devout souls have been shocked and surprised by this lesson of history, but it is the lesson of history nevertheless. If we love and prize the unity of all Christians, we cannot honestly put all our reliance in the matter of authority on the individual conscience or on personal insight into truth, though we shall of course have to find an important place for both of these.

And finally, Oman offers no real comfort or hope to the many men and women, probably the vast majority, who have no gift of spiritual insight. They have to rely on the spiritual insight of others. But whose? That of the man or group of men who seems to them to have the deepest spiritual insight? But it needs much spiritual insight to discern this very thing, and this is what they have not got. For all that Oman can say to the contrary, they will be wisest to rely on the stored-up wisdom of the oldest Church they can find, so long as they do not ascribe infallibility to it. But this is not a very happy solution either.

So we must sadly conclude that Oman has not succeeded in reconciling authority and freedom in religion, though he has not failed to show that other proffered solutions are no longer open to us.

Chapter Seven

THE HIGHEST POSSIBLE AUTHORITY

Peter Taylor Forsyth (1848–1921), most notable of modern Congregationalist divines and for many years Principal of Hackney College, Hampstead, was in his lifetime the object of veneration, though not always of understanding, not only among Free Churchmen, but also among those thoughtful Anglicans who were coming to see that creative theological ideas in this country were not limited to members of the Church of England. In his later years liberal theology was in the ascendant, and his writings did not receive at the time the cool and sober appraisal which is normally granted to those of a senior theologian, the scheme and pattern of whose ideas have become apparent. But when Barth had re-asserted the claim of the Bible to speak as the Word of God, and of theology to exist in its own right, those who happened to take up Forsyth again noticed, with some surprise, that much of what Barth was saying had been said, at least in embryo, by Forsyth in such works as *The Work of Christ* and *The Cruciality of the Cross*. Thus he has entered, somewhat belatedly, on the esteem which he deserved from the beginning.

But it must be admitted that another reason for the failure, even of theologians, to grant him proper recognition in the past, and, indeed, still today, is the orotundity and complexity of his style. He writes in a spacious and rhetorical manner which men of the twentieth century, both now and fifty years ago, have found trying and difficult; and to abbreviate his periods and summarize his ideas, if it can be done fairly and intelligently, does him no disservice. Forsyth himself thought that it was his emphasis on the necessity of theology that prevented him from being much more than a voice crying in the wilderness, and this explanation cannot be discounted. But, if he had used words more lucidly and economically, those who journeyed out into the wilderness to hear him and join his company would have been far more numerous. Theologians, of course, live permanently on the horns of a dilemma: if they are clear and straightforward, they are dismissed as shallow and superficial; if they are obscure and mysterious, they may gain a reputation for profundity, but are not read or understood. Forsyth in effect, though not in intention, adopted the second alternative.

His *Principle of Authority*, described by him as an 'Essay in the Philosophy of Experimental Religion', was published in 1913, and is integrally related to the rest of his theology. It can best be understood and appreciated if a number of things about the author and his theological approach are laid down and remembered.

In the first place, like Schleiermacher and Oman, but with more complex results, which will be pointed out, he is free from the necessity to uphold an existing institution and to support a pre-determined scheme of theology, but at the same time he is committed to the general body of Christian doctrine. This situation results from his place in the orthodox Congregationalist tradition (there are other Congregationalist traditions, with which we are not concerned). He has no Thirty-Nine Articles to render consistent with what he says, or even to demonstrate to be utterly out-of-date; he has no Church of England by law established whose foundations he must not undermine, however much he may question the value of some elements in its superstructure. On the other hand, the person and work of Jesus Christ furnish the sole reason for his existence as a theologian and a Christian. But whereas Oman and Schleiermacher carry their rejection of the visible Church as a divine institution and the Creeds as definitive to the point of questioning the claim of the visible Church, as such, to have preserved any divine revelation at all, and so have the *comparatively* simple task of erecting a theology on the basis of human understanding alone, Forsyth takes seriously *both* his emancipation from the institutional Church and its dogmas *and* the basic fact of revelation through the Church, and has the extremely delicate task of reconciling freedom and revelation without downgrading either. In a sense, Forsyth attempted to do for English Free Churchmen what *Lux Mundi* attempted for Anglicans; for Oman had raised the same standard of 'subjectivistic' revolt in the non-Anglican Churches as *Essays and Reviews* had raised in the Church of England.

In the second place, Forsyth remains in all arguments and discussions fundamentally convinced of the absolute priority of 'the Holy'. 'The Holy' is, in fact, the theme of all his theology. In this matter he professes himself to have broken away entirely from the old rationalistic conception of Christianity, and asserts that we should and can no longer ask whether our religion is in conformity with *a priori* principles and the axiomatic standards of philosophic and scientic truth. We ask rather in what relationship it puts us with 'the Holy'; and since the time of Kant we have seen that 'what Christianity means by the holy is best expressed in ethical terms as the absolute moral Reality. We too are holy according to our relation to that power, or rather according to his relation to us.' For Kant has shown us that 'the ethical' is 'the real'.[1]

In the third place, Forsyth's thought is dominated by the idea that God's act for us in Christ is objective and autonomous. 'It is not religion that is really valuable, but God.'[2] 'The only final authority for Christian faith is its Creator–God Himself acting on us in the Christian way of a new creation, *i.e.* God asserting His holy Self in Christ's historic and regenerative work.'[3] 'The main thing, the unique thing, in religion is not a God Whom we know but a God Who knows us.'[4] 'Over the God with a supreme value which we enjoy is there not the God with an inextinguishable right which we must serve?'[5] God does not serve us, he is not God because of his value to us; he is God in himself alone, with absolute authority over all things and all men. Otherwise he could be exploited for human purposes. And God's act of redemption and reconciliation in Christ is the supreme, objective fact of all history and all existence.

---

[1] *The Principle of Authority* p. 5   [2] ibid., p. 55   [3] ibid., p. 59
[4] ibid., p. 167   [5] ibid., p. 409

This means, in the fourth place, that religious experience is experience of *God*, and thus the means by which truth is appropriated. But Forsyth counts it a grievous error to conclude that religious experience is the source of truth. The only source of truth is God himself:

> The more we fix our attention on the object of our certitude, the more we humbly realize that it is a something *given*. Its source is not in us. It is of grace. The men of discovery, of inspiration, tell the same tale. Truth finds them, not they it.[1]

And, fifthly, the fact that God makes himself known to us in and through experience, and that it is *God* who makes himself known, is for Forsyth the justification and necessitation of theology. The purpose of theology is not to provide us with the presuppositions of our thought about God–that is rationalism, now wholly discredited. Nor does theology provide us with a set of truths to be faithfully and unquestioningly believed on the authority of the Bible or the Church. Its function is to explicate the experiences of God which comes to us through Christ, and such explication is clearly necessary if man is to give his total allegiance to God in Christ:

> No form of religion can live in modern society, with its growing education and its consequent rationality, unless it have a theology. A religion of the free spirit without the fixed word is nebulous, and trails off in vapours which only ascend and do nothing. A temperamental and romantic religion is doomed to a wide area, a weak effect, and a brief life. It revolves in a subjectivity which is the final ruin of real religion, because it is the destruction of authority. . . . Experience is the field where our theology arises, but it is not the spring. The matter of such theology, its Word, is a Revelation which speaks the language of experience but with the voice of the eternal God. Christianity at least cannot live without a theology which sets forth such a Revelation. . . . [Theology] is the intelligible content, the inevitable statement (spreading out to the elaborate exposition), of the act and person given in a historic revelation.[2]

[1] ibid., p. 91   [2] ibid., p. 237f.

In the light of these key considerations, we can now look at Forsyth's arguments for his conception of authority. The Prologue to his book puts the central issues squarely before us, and hints at the solution which he will in proper course expound. The principle of authority, he claims, is the whole religious question, for all authority comes ultimately from the relation of the soul to God. For all questions are, in the end, moral questions, and all moral questions run up into religious ones, so that all turns, in the last resort, on man's relation to the supreme ethic, which is the action of the Holy One. There is no future for society without a truly constituted and acknowledged authority, and the one practical authority for society is the God who comes in Jesus Christ to judge and redeem. We know that Kant has put it beyond doubt, that the ethical possesses absolute primacy in human life, and that the Holy is identical with the supremely ethical. In life we experience this reality in a dualistic manner, through the conflict, waged within the self, between instinct and obligation, the natural law and the moral norm; and experience leaves us in no doubt that it is the moral norm that should prevail. But only in God does the ethical ideal find its consummation; God wills good because he is good, he is good because he wills good. Thus the moral norm and the ultimate reality of the world are the same.

The difficulty for men is that the moral norm is inaccessible to us—we cannot apprehend it, and we cannot fulfil it—unless God makes it accessible by a miracle. But this is what he has done: by divine revelation and divine grace

the unapproachable approaches, enters, tarries, lives, dies, conquers among us and in us, knows us into our only knowledge of itself, subdues all things to its sanctity, and establishes its good and blessed self in us and on us all.

But to know the ethical ideal is at once to be judged by it, because our life does not and cannot match it. The revelation comes to us, therefore, not by the enunciation of propositions, but by God's act in redeeming us from sin through the Cross: 'the Cross is the creative revelation of the holy, and the holy is what is above all else revealed in the Cross, going out as love and going down as grace.'

The task of the Church in enabling us to know and do the divine will lies in securing our freedom, and this it does by providing an authority which creates freedom, and that is the authority of the Gospel and of the Saviour. The Church has not always performed this task with success or in the right way. Sometimes it has detached liberty from authority, laid too much emphasis on one or the other, and brought about its own decay. It is all-important that the authority that is exercised is the right kind of authority. For the performance of the ethical ideal the only true authority is an authority for action over the whole field of life and on the scale of all life. Only the action of God on the Cross satisfies the requirements. The sinlessness of Jesus, taken by itself, is not adequate. It must be the full work of Christ as Saviour and Lord; Christ has ultimate authority through his death and resurrection, and the proclamation of these events is laid upon the Church. But authority is not purely objective and impersonal; on the contrary, it is religious and personal, centred in obedience to a person.[1]

The Prologue, thus, sets out the theme, and leads straight into the main argument. We can never say, argues Forsyth, that the authority of a Book or of the Church is final, and that what the Book or the Church teaches must be accepted without question. Such a statement carries conviction no longer. In fact, nothing carries conviction except an experience of personal salvation. But when a man is conscious of that, the fact of such salvation carries its own conviction–it is as true for a man as his own soul and his own sin. Thereafter his life is impregnable to doubt; he lives on the inner power of his religion, he speaks from within the special order, the inner fortress, of holy love and grace which belongs to Christ's redemption.

This is, plainly, not an external authority, but an authority for the person, and for his soul. In youth we believe things on the authority of others–this cannot be avoided. But when we come to maturity, we accept no other authority than the 'creative object of our religion', which is the activity of God's creative self-revelation in the Cross and Resurrection. Holy

---

[1] ibid., pp. 1–15

men are the best argument for the Christian religion; we trust an apostle, not for his veracity, or for his competence as a reporter, but as giving a consistent expression in life of his personal experience. The words of Jesus himself are supremely valuable to us, not as an external authority speaking from above, but as transcripts of his own experience.

So far, it might almost be John Oman speaking. But Forsyth goes on at once to ask: Is this not self-delusion? And this is plainly a crucial question. Forsyth's answer at this point is twofold. He urges that the personal experience which is here described becomes for us and all who have it 'not only recurrent but continuous, and masterful'. It becomes, in fact, the source and principle of what can only be called a new life; we become new men in a manner of which we ourselves by ourselves are completely incapable. And this process is repeated over and over again in people of every kind and in every place. All the people who undergo it refer it 'to the same fontal historic source'–the fact of Christ. It has been subjected to all necessary tests, and by these tests the merely visionary and individual elements have been eliminated, while the experience itself survives all questioning and scrutiny. It is true that similar experiences are found from time to time among Muslims and Buddhists. But they are so rare, and so lacking in ethical content, and so much confined to people of mystical temperament, that we can safely discount them. The unity of witness to the experience of new life coming to men through Christ is so deep that it is not destroyed by all the ecclesiastical divisions of Christendom.

He urges, in the second place, that 'the chief guarantee of the value of an experience is not given by its actual universality, by its popularity, but by its content'. The content is the only thing that takes us beyond the purely psychological to the truly religious significance of an experience. 'The content transcends in reality the experience whose language it speaks, and whose psychology it follows. Faith is a religious experience, but religious experience is not faith.' The content of Christian experience is, on the one side, God–'an active God, an approaching, revealing, recreating God'–, and on the other side our act of surrender. This twofold event, this 'reciprocal act', enables us to 'acquire our souls for life', 'it completes our personality', 'it really gives us to ourselves'. When this happens we can be utterly sure that our experience is objective, for 'can anything be surer to a personality than that which realises it?'[1]

There is here, unfortunately, no real answer to the charge of possible self-deception. We cannot argue from the fact of new life in Christians to the truth of Christianity. Forsyth greatly underestimates the number of instances of new life to be found in non-Christian religions. Every religion, or at least every higher religion, has its saints. It also, of course, has its hypocrites and scoundrels, but so also has Christianity. We cannot dispose of this fact by saying that all those who have 'new life' in other religions are of mystical temperament, for the same could be said of the Christians with 'new life'. If there are more Christians with new life, proportionately, than Buddhists, as there may be, for all anyone knows, this establishes nothing beyond itself; for the truth of a religion cannot be judged by any form of 'counting heads'. Indeed, it is not only religions that produce 'new life'. No one who was in Germany before and after 1933 can doubt that National-Socialism produced 'newness of life' in millions of Germans, and Communism in many countries has done the same. It could be replied that the 'new life' thus produced is highly inferior to the 'new life' produced by Christianity, but that is a judgement that presupposes the truth of Christianity, and it is the truth of Christianity that the argument is seeking to show.

And even if, for the sake of argument, we were to concede that new life is found only among Christians, the proof still fails. For we should be in a situation in which Christianity produces the kind of life which it seeks and professes to produce and that nothing else does—and this would be reassuring to those who are inclined to wonder if Christianity does, in fact, do what it claims to do—,but we should be no nearer to making the connexion between the 'success' (in this sense) of Christianity and its truth. And we cannot get any nearer to this until it has been demonstrated that only a true religion

[1] ibid., pp. 25–31

can produce the 'new life' of which Christianity speaks, and no proof of this is offered to us.

But what of the objectivity that is said to be established by the 'content' of Christian experience? This content is double—God acting in us and our response by surrender to him. If we knew for certain that our experience is of *God*, and is not purely psychological, or induced by outward forces, perhaps in the form of economic or social conditions, then it would clearly follow that religious experience for Christians established the existence and goodness of God, and many other of the things which Christians say about him. But whether the experience is of God, or only an inner psychological state, is precisely the question under discussion. So the 'content' argument to objectivity simply begs the question.

That is not to say that religious experience has nothing to do with the truth of the Christian religion. If it never, or only rarely, produced, or seemed to produce, the 'new life' of which Forsyth speaks, Christianity could indeed still be true in a limited sense; it could still give a correct account of the being and character of God, of the nature of the life after death, and of other matters. But included in Christianity as it is usually interpreted is the affirmation that Jesus Christ renews and regenerates men and women, and if it were shown that this renewal and regeneration never in fact happen, a great deal of Christianity would have to be discounted, and the rest of it would not be likely to retain much of a hold on the minds of men. But the converse is not true: it does not follow that if renewal follows Christian experience, then Christianity is true. This means that 'new life' can be used, and indeed should be used, as a *test* of the truth of Christianity, but not as a demonstration of it.

The point can be illustrated from two lines in a hymn of Charles Wesley which are part of a prayer to Christ, in which he asks that he may:

> *The truth of my religion prove*
> *By perfect purity and love.*[1]

The meaning of these lines is uncertain, since 'truth' and

[1] Methodist Hymn Book, No. 605, verse 5

'prove' can each be interpreted in two ways. 'Truth' may mean 'correspondence to reality' (if this will serve as a definition of truth in the ordinary sense of the word), or it may mean 'genuineness'. 'Prove' may mean 'demonstrate', or it may mean 'test' (as in the expression, 'The exception proves the rule'). Thus four meanings of the lines are possible:

(a) I pray that my purity and love may demonstrate my religion to be true.

(b) I pray that my purity and love may demonstrate my religion to be genuine.

(c) I pray that my purity and love may test the truth of my religion.

(d) I pray that my purity and love may test the genuineness of my religion.

(d) gives a very weak sense, and should be ruled out, but it is hard to decide between the other three. If the argument of these pages is sound, (a), if the right interpretation of Wesley, would nevertheless be a prayer for the logically impossible. (b) and (c) would both express legitimate aspirations for the Christian to cherish. Let us hope, if we are admirers of Wesley, that one of these two things is what Wesley meant to say.

But we are only at the beginning of Forsyth's book, and we must go on to see if he is able to present, later, a more convincing view, or the view already given in a more convincing fashion. After rebutting in the way that we have indicated the suggestion that his view involves the possibility of self-deception, he points out a very considerable advantage in falling back on experience for authority and certainty: we are thus preserved from regarding faith as 'a piece of [the soul's] property', or as 'a deposit of truth', or as 'a refuge from conflict. For, with this conception of faith, we are bound to realize that it is something which has to be continually re-acquired and never taken for granted; that we have to fight to retain it; that it develops as we grow older; that we and everyone else have to verify truth for ourselves and are not at liberty to take it on trust from others.[1] Once again, this could be John Oman speaking.

[1] *The Principle of Authority* pp. 34–7

But from this point onwards Forsyth's thought begins to develop on somewhat different lines, though it never entirely loses contact with what he has already said. The certainty of a Christian, he affirms, resides in its object, God. It is, in fact, communion with God, who plants in us the certainty of himself. I stand, as a sinful man, confronted with the absolute demands of God's holy love, and must ask myself whether this holy love is for me or against me. I see myself to be guilty before God. But God answers me, not by condemnation, but by his salvation, whereby his justice becomes mine and a new creation takes place in me. Then I commit myself, absolutely and wholly, to Christ my justifier, and certainty is born in me.[1]

At this point Forsyth makes partial use of a distinction which we have already found in Newman, between 'certitude' and 'certainty'. His argument would have been more clearly expressed if he had carried the use of this distinction right through: 'certitude' in this case being what resides in a man who is certain, 'certainty' being what belongs to that of which he is certain. It will be convenient to make strict use of this distinction ourselves. The seat of authority, then, according to Forsyth, is subjective to us; it is inner certitude. But its source and sanction are not subjective. For Christian certitude is certitude about something–something which is experienced, but which emerges in experience without being evolved from it. It is, in fact, certitude about *God*: God in action, bestowing upon us the divine life. And God, of course, has the quality of certainty. Thus authority lies not in the Christian consciousness, but in God. We start from the Cross, God's act, the ultimate act of universal moral reality, consummating all things. The Cross acts, miraculously, on man's guilty conscience, and man, by responding to it, receives the evangelical experience of regeneration. So the individual soul is the sphere and medium of revelation, redemption, authority, and possesses certitude; but it is not its source, for its source is the divine act, an act of absolute authority and certainty. And this act is not a mere event of history; it is a historic *word*, in the Biblical sense of a word that both utters

[1] ibid., pp. 38–53

and effects the divine will. We may say, indeed, that the final authority is a person communing with us.[1]

This viewpoint enables Forsyth to handle the problem of the relation between psychology and theology. He points out that if we put faith's foundation in personal experience we are in danger of subordinating the former to the latter. To do that would be to hand over the content of faith to the single individual and ignore the Church. The source of authority must not be placed in the feelings, though we must give liberty to the psychologists to insist on analysing men's feelings as the sphere in which authority operates. Psychology is a descriptive science. We must not deal with the problem by warning our critics off the ground; but, equally, we must not give up our belief in God as the source of experience, and concentrate on the experience.[2]

Much of Forsyth's position so far has relied on the facts of the historic Christ. But this reliance, he sees, opens him to the criticism that he has neglected the saying of Lessing (which, says Forsyth, 'still holds its ground in many uncritical quarters') that 'the accidental truths of history can never become proof for the necessary truths of reason'. Put otherwise, the problem is: How can the historic Jesus be part of my present life? Forsyth deals with this criticism and solves this problem by making a distinction, which has become common coin since his time, between *Historie* and *Geschichte*. These German words means, he says, respectively, 'history as it may be settled by the methods of historical science', and history as 'the evolving organism of mankind'. What Lessing may be taken to mean, on this showing, is that the eternal truths of *Geschichte* cannot be proved by the detailed facts of *Historie*. No, says Forsyth, but they may be *conveyed* to us in this way. So the historical facts of the life of Jesus *convey* the grace of God and the new life which he gives to us in the present. It is thus possible to claim that the historical Jesus founded an absolute faith. This claim cannot be logically established. The making of it always arouses opposition. But, once it is made, it confronts us, condemns us, drives us to despair, and then justifies and redeems us. 'The certificate of

[1] ibid., pp. 54–68   [2] ibid., pp. 82–90

the Gospel to us is really its own unique and unimpaired work with us.' And we can justifiably move on from this to say that 'our ultimate authority . . . which justifies every other authority in its degree and measure, is the Creator of the New Humanity as such'.[1]

These facts about Christian faith help us to distinguish Christian certainty (or, as he might have done better to say, certitude) from other type of certainty. Faith does not differ from other certainties in being a faculty distinct from other faculties, for faith is not a faculty, but an act of a whole personality. And it is distinguished from other acts of the whole personality by its object, which is God. The unique thing about religion is not that we know God, but that God knows us. If it be asked why it is that not all men have this faith, since it comes from God, the answer is that God does not impose it on any man. He offers it to all, but not all receive it, and God respects man's freedom to reject it.[2]

Many would argue at this point that Forsyth has drawn the wrong conclusion from the acknowledged facts. Granted that faith is a response to the action of God, it surely follows that there must be something in man to which revelation can appeal? And is not that 'something' the real authority in religion? Forsyth seeks to forestall this criticism by admitting that there is indeed something in us which responds to revelation, but claiming that this 'something' is not reason, but will; for the holy is revealed to us, not as something congenial and readily acceptable to our reason, but rather as something contrary to us, something which holds us up to the light and judges us, something which deals a severe blow at human nature. The divine comes to us, in fact, not as that which continues and completes what we are already aware of, but as a contrast to our ways of thinking.[3] As Forsyth says in a later passage, when discussing the relation between reality and dreams, religion shows its reality by integrating us into the wholeness and depth of life; but this is not an integration into a preconceived system of ideas, but into an experienced system of guilt and grace.[4]

[1] ibid., pp. 125–36   [2] ibid., pp. 165–86   [3] ibid., pp. 187–98
[4] ibid., pp. 220–2

And where is the place of theology and the Church in all this? So far we have spoken as if the only thing in religion were the action of God on the individual and his response in faith. But this, of course, is not the true state of affairs, and the balance must be restored. Theology is necessary as the explication of revelation, and the Church is necessary to give an authoritative theology. In the Church, divided as she is, theology is weak and incompetent to do its proper work (there is an important passage at this point of the book on the necessity for the 'proportion of faith' and on the evil of sectarianism).[1] There is need for variation in theology, so long as it does not include the toleration of heresy: grace the answer to guilt, Christ crucified and risen, are essential to the faith and life of the Church.[2] But how do we decide what is true doctrine? Majorities are fitted to decide only unimportant things–the faith is not at the mercy of a plebiscite,[3] nor is the Church a democracy. Nor can the apostolic word of Christ crucified and redeeming be dispensed with by the Church under any circumstances whatever if it is to remain the Church.[4]

At this point someone will adduce the 'Reformation principle' of private judgement. To this we must reply by a question: 'Is the private judgement of a Protestant youth of any doctrinal value beside the public judgement of a Catholic theologian? Or a village evangelist's against Bishop Gore on Church, Sacrament and Ministry?' The truth is that the principle of private judgement comes from the Renaissance and the Revolution, not from the Reformation. The Reformation did not destroy 'the hierarchy of competence'. The Reformation said, indeed, that the layman with the Bible has the Holy Spirit as his expositor; and that everyone alike has the same Holy Spirit to help him. But it never denied that the ordained minister had a teaching authority not given to the layman. The layman has the authority of personal experience under the Gospel, and is entitled to preach–this is the 'liberty of prophesying'. But to *teach*, and to preach beyond personal experience, requires qualifications and equipment,

[1] ibid., pp. 237–44   [2] ibid., pp. 244–52   [3] ibid., p. 253f.
[4] ibid., p. 285f.

which, of course, every man is entitled to obtain. He obtains these in the 'true school of thought' which is 'the living tradition of the Church'. Thus we grant to the Church 'authority in the second degree'–and authority in the first degree to God alone.[1]

The authority which the Church could exercise, so long as it is moral and inspiring, not coercive, is immense. Perhaps it would have to be exercised by a federation of Churches with equal rights. We ought not to give such authority to an institution, for all institutions are liable to corruption and lies. So the seat of authority must be more religious than an institution; it should be a truly evangelical Christianity, preached in a Church which has been redeemed by the absolutely Holy and has the authentic power and note of the Gospel. Thus the authority exercised would be the authority of saving grace.[2]

This authority is in the last resort miraculous, not evolving from our own nature, but invading it from outside; for authority with its source in us is no true authority. It is rational, not in the sense that it appeals to our reason, but in the sense that it springs from a spiritual nature which is akin to our own. Yet it speaks to us only among our own psychological conditions–through our faculties of mind and feeling, and in the midst of our own intimate experiences. It is in fact a 'gracious God in salvation'; and all other authorities are hierarchically arranged under it. The first authority is religion; the second is theology; the next is the Church of the worshippers and the saints, the community which confesses the faith.[3]

And Forsyth sums up his whole argument at the end thus: For the Protestant, authority is of grace, not truth; whereas for the Catholic it is of a body of guaranteed doctrine. We give our supreme allegiance to Christ the Redeemer, given, objective and historical:

The last authority of the soul for ever is the grace of a holy God, the holiness of His gracious love in Jesus Christ. And

---

[1] ibid., pp. 319–29   [2] ibid., p. 337f.

[3] ibid., pp. 339 ff. There is a slight inconsistency here with what is said just above – that the Church has authority in the *second* degree.

this is the last reality of things, the last rest of all hearts, and the last royalty of all wills.[1]

We have followed the second direction of Forsyth's thought to its goal. And surely we find ourselves presented, perhaps for the first time, with a doctrine of authority which is fully theological–or it may be that we should say, theocentric. There is no preoccupation here with the need of the Church to be coherent and effective and conclusive, or to have a compact body of teaching with which to evangelize and convince the world; still less is there any call to provide the individual believer with an authority which he need not question, and which therefore blesses him with peace of mind, freedom from doubt and spiritual comfort. The emphasis is entirely on God. That it is more important that God should know us, than that we should know God, we are clearly told. Therefore the supreme authority must belong to him. But God is for ever active, for ever taking the initiative, for the salvation of mankind. He has made himself known in Jesus Christ. But he has done more than that. He has also redeemed us in Jesus Christ. And he has done even more than that. He has miraculously transformed the historic Christ into a present, contemporary reality, a Redeemer who in this present time of our existence bestows on us new life and makes us new people. And all this without any prompting or petition from us, and certainly without any merit on our part. Therefore the supreme authority which belongs to God is not the authority of a credal statement, or of a *summa* of doctrines, or of an institution or book or pontiff, but of a holy, living, active, saving God who out of pure grace regenerates and renews all those who respond to his love and put their trust in him. He is the source of all truth and knowledge; there is nothing that we can know or think or experience which corresponds to the truth of the universe that does not come from him.

Here is a view of authority which springs naturally and logically from the New Testament doctrine of grace. According to this, God does all that he does on his own initiative, and all that he does is prompted by his love. It follows that when he reveals himself to us, or indeed makes known to us anything, even the smallest thing, that it is good for us to know, he acts *ex gratia*. Charles Wesley's verse:

> *Thy ceaseless, unexhausted love,*
> *Unmerited and free,*
> *Delights our evil to remove,*
> *And help our misery,*[1]

applies just as much to God's disclosure of the truth as it does to the work of our salvation. Revelation falls as completely within the realm of grace as does redemption.

And just as the offer of God's love in redemption is not compulsory but voluntary; just as we appropriate it, not mechanically or automatically, but in the freedom of loving trust: so the offer of his love in revelation is made to us as free beings, and is appropriated by us in an act of free response. We speak of God's grace as sovereign, but we are not driven to speak of predestination; we speak of God's truth as authoritative, but we are not impelled, or allowed, to suppose that it drives itself into us by the exercise of power or the force of unanswerable logic. We believe what God reveals to us because it makes the impact of truth upon us.

So far, this vindicates itself as an essential part of any Christian doctrine of authority, since Christianity stands or falls by the Biblical doctrine of grace (whatever else may flow from it in the form of Christology, Soteriology or Pneumatology), and Forsyth's conception of divine authority follows from it. But when the divine authority is acknowledged, when the divine truth is believed, what is the situation of the believer? Does he now *know* the truth, is he completely assured of it, is the problem of religious authority solved for him? What is the manward side of the doctrine?

For Forsyth's answer we have to turn back to the direction of his thought which we found in the early chapters of his book. A man, redeemed by Christ and given new life by him, has no further doubts about God's love or the basic truths of his religion. He has been granted certainty (or, as we have seen it could be better called, certitude). He has new life, full-

---

[1] Methodist Hymn Book, No. 49, verse 1

ness of life, life of a kind which leaves no doubt that its source, and the truths on which it rests, are from God. And if this should still seem to allow of doubt, that doubt can be banished when we remember the *content* of his experience, for the content is God himself. The objectivity of God guarantees the objectivity of man's certainty. We could certainly discredit religious experience, however intense and deep, if its source were man. But its source is the holy God, and we cannot, therefore, discredit it. God reveals himself through our psychological processes and in the human situation in which we find ourselves; but it is God who reveals himself. The processes and the situation may be said to convey the truth to us; but in no sense do they originate it.

We have seen that this line of thought does not really deal with the charge of self-delusion that can be brought against Forsyth's teaching on religious experience.[1] The new life which is granted to Christians may be said to *test* the truth of Christianity, but it furnishes no ground for certitude. But now that we have looked at Forsyth's full account of what he means by saying that God is the *content* of our experience, can we not find more to say for his view that this content of experience vindicates its objectivity, even if we must agree that the claim to certainty has fallen down?

Unfortunately we cannot. For the precise issue of religious authority is whether God *is* the content of our religious experience. If he is, then all our problems admit of a speedy answer, and it would even be possible to claim certainty for our beliefs. But we cannot show that he *is* the content simply by asserting that he is. Yet this is what Forsyth, if we strip his words down to their precise meaning, and neglect the strong and genuine religious feeling that suffuses them, in fact does. Thus the crucial question is begged from the outset. The bridge between God, active, holy, revealing and redeeming, and our religious experience, is not yet built theologically, however sure we may be in our heart of hearts that it exists.

[1] see p. 174 above

183

Chapter Eight

THE REVISION OF INFALLIBILITY

It goes without saying that the Roman Catholic Church, like all the other communions of Christendom, has been heavily battered during the present century by the storms of doubt and the cold winds of criticism. Until recent years the effects of this experience have been concealed from the eyes of non-Romans, but now they are clear for all to see. It has often been said that in Roman Catholic countries and communities the only alternatives are complete adhesion to the tenets of the Roman Church and complete scepticism, but this, if it has ever been true, is certainly true no longer. It is perfectly possible to be and remain a faithful member–even a faithful priest–while doubting, not the existence and nature of God, but some of the dogmas of the Church which has declared that all its dogmas are unquestionably true; and while accepting, almost in full measure, the critical methods of modern Biblical scholarship. In certain quarters this was probably the case before the pontificate of John XXIII; it is the case now in all those areas of Roman Catholicism which have not resisted, in all but name, the decrees of the Second Vatican Council. It is instructive therefore to seek to find out what changes, if any, have been made in the Roman Catholic doctrine of authority, and to do so, by comparing, first, the pronouncements on Scripture and Tradition made by the Council of Trent with those made by the Second Vatican Council, and, secondly, the pronouncements on infallibility of the First Vatican Council with those of the Second.

The sacred and holy, oecumenical and general Synod of Trent, . . . keeping this always in view, that, errors being removed, the purity itself of the Gospel be preserved in the Church; which (Gospel), before promised through the prophets in the holy Scriptures, our Lord Jesus Christ, the Son of God, first promulgated with His own mouth, and then commanded by His Apostles to every creature, as the fountain of all, both saving truth, and moral discipline; and seeing clearly that this truth and discipline are contained in the written books, and the unwritten traditions which, received by the Apostles from the mouth of Christ himself, or from the Apostles themselves, the Holy Ghost dictating, have come down even unto us, transmitted as it were from hand to hand: [the Synod] following the examples of the orthodox Fathers, receives and venerates with an equal affection of piety and reverence, all the books both of the Old and of the New Testament–seeing that one God is the author of both–as also the said traditions, as well as those appertaining to faith as to morals, as having been dictated, either by Christ's own word of mouth, or by the Holy Ghost, and preserved in the Catholic Church by continuous succession.[1]

Then follows a list of the books officially acknowledged as Scripture. The list contains not only those accepted as belonging to the Old and New Testaments by all Churches, but also the books of what is usually called by non-Romans the Old Testament Apocrypha.[2]

So spoke the Council of Trent in 1546. Now for 1965:

In His gracious goodness, God has seen to it that what He had revealed for the salvation of all nations would abide perpetually in its full integrity and be handed on to all generations. Therefore Christ the Lord, in whom the full revelation of the supreme God is brought to completion (cf. 2 Cor. 1: 20; 3: 16; 4: 6), commissioned the apostles to preach to all men that gospel which is the source of all saving truth and moral teaching, and thus to impart to them divine gifts. This gospel had been promised in former times through the prophets, and Christ Himself fulfilled it and promulgated it with His own lips. This com-

---

[1] P. Schaff *Creeds of the Greek and Latin Churches* p. 79f.
[2] ibid., p. 8of.

mission was faithfully fulfilled by the apostles who, by their oral teaching, by example, and by ordinances, handed on what they had received from the lips of Christ, from living with Him, and from what He did, or what they had learned through the prompting of the Holy Spirit. The commission was fulfilled, too, by those apostles and apostolic men who under the inspiration of the same Holy Spirit committed the message of salvation to writing.

But in order to keep the gospel for ever whole and alive within the Church, the apostles left bishops as their successors, 'handing over their own teaching role' to them. This sacred tradition, therefore, and sacred Scripture of both the Old and the New Testament are like a mirror in which the pilgrim Church on earth looks at God, from whom she has received everything, until she is brought finally to see Him as He is, face to face (cf. 1 Jn. 3:2)

And so the apostolic preaching, which is expressed in a special way in the inspired books, was to be preserved by a continuous succession of preachers until the end of time. Therefore the apostles, handing on what they themselves had received, warn the faithful to hold fast to the traditions which they have learned . . . This tradition which comes from the apostles develops in the Church with the help of the Holy Spirit. For there is a growth in the understanding of realities and the words which have been handed down. This happens through the contemplation and study made by believers, who treasure these things in their hearts (cf. Lk. 2:19, 51), through the intimate understanding of spiritual things they experience, and through the preaching of those who have received through episcopal succession the sure gifts of truth. For, as the centuries succeed one another, the Church constantly moves forward toward the fullness of divine truth until the words of God reach their complete fulfilment in her. . . .

Hence there exist a close connection and communication between sacred tradition and sacred Scripture. For both of them, flowing from the same divine wellspring, in a certain way merge into a unity and tend toward the same end. For sacred Scripture is the word of God inasmuch as it is consigned to writing under the inspiration of the divine Spirit. To the successors of the apostles, sacred tradition hands on in its full purity God's word, which was entrusted to the apostles by Christ the Lord and the Holy Spirit. Thus, led by the light of the Spirit of truth, these successors can in their preaching preserve this word of God faithfully, explain it, and make it more widely known. Consequently, it is not from sacred Scripture alone that the Church draws her certainty about everything which has been revealed. Therefore both sacred tradition and sacred Scripture are to be accepted and venerated with the same sense of devotion and reverence.

Sacred tradition and sacred Scripture form one sacred deposit of the word of God, which is committed to the Church. Holding fast to this deposit, the entire holy people united with their shepherds remain always steadfast in the teaching of the apostles. . . . The task of authentically interpreting the word of God, whether written or handed on, has been entrusted exclusively to the living teaching office of the Church, whose authority is exercised in the name of Jesus Christ. This teaching office is not above the word of God, but serves it, teaching only what has been handed on, listening to it devoutly, guarding it scrupulously, and explaining it faithfully by divine commission and with the help of the Holy Spirit; it draws on this one deposit of faith everything which it presents for belief as divinely revealed.

It is clear, therefore, that sacred tradition, sacred Scripture, and the teaching authority of the Church, in accord with God's most wise design, are so linked and joined together that one cannot stand without the others, and that all together and each in its own way under the action of the one Holy Spirit contribute effectively to the salvation of souls.[1]

This is from the Constitution on Divine Revelation of the Second Vatican Council. The first point that emerges from the comparison that we have made is that there is very close resemblance on many important matters between the decrees

---

[1] *The Documents of Vatican II* pp. 114–18

of Trent and the Constitution of the Second Vatican Council. In fact, for a great deal of its length, the Constitution is a commentary on and elaboration of the Tridentine Decree; at other points it expounds the Decrees on Revelation and Faith and Reason of the First Vatican Council.[1] There is the same parity of veneration accorded to tradition and Scripture, the same importance ascribed to the episcopal succession in the transmission of truth through the ages, by Trent and Vatican II. And, if we compare Vatican I and Vatican II, we shall find that the teaching office, the *magisterium*, of the Church is put on the same lofty pedestal.

But at two points a difference can be observed between Trent and Vatican II (at each of these Vatican I is on the side of Trent). The Tridentine Decree, without much doubt, is so framed as to allow the Church to promulgate doctrines as part of divine revelation which are not to be found in Scripture, on the theory that they were received from the apostles by the bishops in the historic succession, concealed for the time being on divine instructions, and in due course divulged to the Church on instructions from the same source. The Constitution of Vatican II, though it does not explicitly exclude such promulgation, is so framed that it deals only with the doctrines which *are* contained in Scripture. This seems to show that the doctrine that Scripture contains all doctrines necessary for salvation is encouraged, though not required.

But, of course, the Church has promulgated doctrines since the time of Scripture which are not explicitly set down in Scripture. And this is the second point at which difference is to be observed. It is stated by Vatican II that there has been a development of doctrine in a sense not mentioned, or, probably, contemplated, at Trent. The Spirit, we are told, has guided the Church in the progressive understanding of what the Scripture says; and under his guidance, we may infer, the Church has brought into explicit utterance what was only implicit in Scripture. Thus there are no non-Biblical doctrines in the teaching of the Church; but there are Biblical doctrines, to the full understanding of which the

[1] for the text of, see Schaff, op. cit., pp. 234–56

Church has only gradually been led. This doctrine of development is, of course, very nearly the same as that which was propounded by Newman a century before,[1] and by no means welcomed for many years within the Roman Catholic Church. Now it has come into its own.

Some further comments on the Constitution seem to be called for. Earlier in this volume it has been maintained that it is now no longer possible to make a sharp distinction between Scripture and tradition, since the process of tradition has already begun within the pages of the New Testament, and, in fact, within the Gospels themselves.[2] The Fathers of the Second Vatican Council, however, proceed as if this were not so; they retain the distinction in the old, Tridentine form, and no defence against the attacks which have been made on the distinction is offered. The distinction made is, of course, between Scripture and *unwritten* tradition, and it may at first sight seem absurd to object to this on the ground that the Bible contains unwritten tradition, since anything in the Bible is obviously written. But the point of those who object to the distinction when it is made in a hard and fast form is that some of what the Council of Trent and Vatican II describe as unwritten tradition has already reached the stage of being written down before the end of the New Testament. Here, it seems, not enough account has been taken of modern knowledge.

Then, when all has been truly said in the Constitution about the place of Scripture as the repository of all necessary doctrine, it remains as the assertion of Vatican II that the interpretation of Scripture belongs inalienably to the *magisterium* of the Church. Now it is notorious that interpretations of Scripture reached by exegetes in various communions, and, no doubt, sometimes within the Roman communion, often differ and conflict. In such cases the tradition of the Church has frequently decided the issue, and Roman Catholics are taught that the interpretation thus reached is the one to be believed, and that the question is no longer an open one. In other cases, where tradition has not given a ruling, or the meaning of its ruling is disputed, the matter is

[1] see pp. 76ff. above   [2] see pp. 24ff. above

referred to the *magisterium*, and its decision is final. This surely places tradition above Scripture, and the *magisterium* above both. This superiority is illustrated by the analogous case of the Supreme Court of the United States of America. This works out as follows. Certain laws are on the statute book of that country about the equality of all its citizens. The legislature of a particular State authorizes a course of action which discriminates against the Negroes in that State. The Supreme Court, when an appeal is made to it, rules that the State in question has acted against the Constitution of the United States, and its ruling is final. This did actually happen in 1954, and showed, if it needed to be shown, that the Supreme Court was superior to all State legislature, and to the legal code of the United States–to the former absolutely, to the latter in so far as it, and it alone, could say what the laws of America really meant. So in the Roman Church the *magisterium* decides which traditions are valid, and what the Bible really means.

But on what grounds are we asked in the first place to believe that the *magisterium* has this authority? Not on the testimony of Scripture, though this is often claimed for it. The meaning of the passages in Scripture which are held by Rome to assert the authority of the teaching Church is itself very much disputed. The *magisterium* has ruled that the 'Roman' interpretation is the correct one. In other words, it has ruled in its own favour. But why should anyone accept this ruling unless he has already acknowledged that the *magisterium* possesses the *charisma veritatis*, the divine gift of truth? But the question whether the *magisterium* has the *charisma* is exactly the question which we are expecting Scripture to answer. The argument for the authority of the *magisterium* seems to be incurably circular.

But there are many parts of the Constitution which can be unreservedly welcomed as showing an appreciation of the Bible and of modern Biblical scholarship which all Christians can share–not least the earnest and emphatic exhortation to all teachers to study the Scriptures attentively and to all the faithful to read them with prayer and patience;[1] and the

---

[1] *Documents of Vatican II* p. 127f.

account of divine revelation as given by deeds as well as by words.[1] Noteworthy also is the insistence that due attention must be paid to the various literary forms employed by the writers, and to their circumstances, culture and habitual modes of expression–so that the Christian is no longer asked to accept as history what belongs to the poetic or prophetic form of discourse; with the further consequence, presumably, that when he reads what is intended as history he should pay due regard to the limitations of ancient historians and their methods of investigation.[2] It is true that the historicity of the Gospels and their apostolic origin are unequivocally asserted.[3] It is to be hoped that this will not debar Roman Catholic scholars from playing their proper and valuable part in those inquiries into the relationship between myth and history in the Gospels which are being vigorously prosecuted in other parts of the Church.

But we must turn back to the *charisma veritatis*, for it is a subject which brings us directly to the second comparison between Roman conciliar statements which we need to make. The First Vatican Council leaves those who read its decrees in no doubt whatever as to the primacy of Peter and his successors in the See of Rome; the perpetuity, power and nature of that primacy are set out in detail, and any denial of what is said on the subject is condemned in unmistakable terms. For instance, it is stated that 'it has at all times been necessary that every particular Church . . . should agree with the Roman Church'. The opinions of those who hold that the primacy was not bestowed immediately upon Peter himself, but upon the Church, and through the Church on Peter as her minister, are condemned as perverse. And the Council further teaches that

in all causes, the decision of which belongs to the Church, recourse may be had to his [*sc.* the Pope's] tribunal, and that none may re-open the judgment of the Apostolic See, than whose authority there is no greater, nor can any lawfully review its judgment. Wherefore they err from the right course who assert that it is lawful to appeal from the judgments of the Roman Pontiffs to an oecumenical

ibid., p. 113 [2] ibid., p. 120 [3] ibid., p. 123f.

Council, as to an authority higher than that of the Roman Pontiff.

All this prepares for and leads up to the famous decree 'on the Infallible Teaching of the Roman Pontiff'. This begins by claiming that the Pope's 'supreme power of teaching' has been affirmed by Scripture, and has been acknowledged through Christian history by the Councils of the Church. It goes on to say that the purpose of this gift of teaching was not that new doctrine should be propounded by the Pope, but that the 'revelation or deposit of faith delivered through the Apostles' should be inviolably kept and preserved by him. And it culminates and concludes with these words:

> Therefore faithfully adhering to the tradition received from the beginning of the Christian faith, for the glory of God our Saviour, the exaltation of the Catholic religion, and the salvation of Christian people, the sacred Council approving, we teach and define that it is a dogma divinely revealed: that the Roman Pontiff, when he speaks *ex cathedra*, that is, when in discharge of the office of pastor and doctor of all Christians, by virtue of his supreme Apostolic authority, he defines a doctrine regarding faith or morals to be held by the universal Church, by the divine assistance promised to him in blessed Peter, is possessed of that infallibility with which the divine Redeemer willed that his Church should be endowed for defining doctrine regarding faith or morals; and that therefore such definitions of the Roman Pontiffs are irreformable of themselves, and not from the consent of the Church. But if any one–which may God avert–presume to contradict this our definition: let him be anathema.[1]

The Second Vatican Council's Constitution on the Church contains much that is moving, impressive and challenging. The full and profound description of the Church as the People of God, the reinstatement of the laity as the brothers and co-workers of those in the ordained ministry, possessing its own apostolate, the acknowledgement that members of other communions are 'in some real way joined with us in the Holy Spirit', the assertion of episcopal collegiality–all

[1] Schaff, op. cit., pp. 256–71

these are welcome signs that the Roman Church has gone through the process of entirely re-thinking the doctrine of the Church in a way in which many Protestants have not even begun to do. We look therefore with a sense of expectancy at what the Constitution has to say about the authority of the Church and about infallibility.

The Church, propagated and governed by Peter and the other apostles, is 'the pillar and mainstay of the truth' (1 Tim. 3:15). 'This Church, constituted and organized in the world as a society, subsists in the Catholic Church, . . . although many elements of sanctification and of truth can be found outside of her visible structure'.[1] In the matter of its hierarchical ordering, we are told:

> In order that the episcopate itself might be one and undivided, [Christ] placed blessèd Peter over the other apostles, and instituted in him a permanent and visible source and foundation of unity of faith and fellowship. And all this teaching about the institution, the perpetuity, the force and reason for the sacred primacy of the Roman Pontiff and of his infallible teaching authority, this sacred Synod again proposes to be firmly believed by all the faithful.[2]

After reiterating the traditional Roman doctrine of apostolic succession, the Constitution goes on to say that, as Peter and the other apostles formed one apostolic college,

> so in a similar way the Roman Pontiff as the successor of Peter, and the bishops as the successors of the apostles are joined together.

> But the college or body of bishops has no authority unless it is simultaneously conceived of in terms of its head, the Roman Pontiff.

> The order of bishops is the successor to the college of the apostles in teaching authority and pastoral rule; or, rather, in the episcopal order the apostolic body continues without a break. Together with its head, the Roman Pontiff, and never without this head, the episcopal order is the subject of supreme and full power over the universal

[1] *Documents of Vatican II* pp. 23; there is a clear reference to Vatican I.
[2] ibid., p. 38

Church. But this power can be exercised only with the consent of the Roman Pontiff.

The supreme authority with which this college is empowered over the whole Church is exercised in a solemn way through an ecumenical council. A council is never ecumenical unless it is confirmed or at least accepted as such by the successor of Peter.[1]

And finally:

In matters of faith and morals, the bishops speak in the name of Christ and the faithful are to accept their teaching and adhere to it with a religious assent of soul. This religious submission of will and of mind must be shown in a special way to the authentic teaching authority of the Roman Pontiff, even when he is not speaking *ex cathedra*. That is, it must be shown in such a way that his supreme *magisterium* is acknowledged with reverence, the judgments made by him are sincerely adhered to, according to his manifest mind and will. His mind and will in the matter may be known chiefly either from the character of the documents, from his frequent repetition of the same doctrine, or from his manner of speaking.[2]

Although the individual bishops do not enjoy the prerogative of infallibility, they can nevertheless proclaim Christ's doctrine infallibly. This is so, even when they are dispersed around the world, provided that while maintaining the bond of unity among themselves and with Peter's successor, and while teaching authentically on a matter of faith or morals, they concur in a single viewpoint as the one which must be held conclusively. This authority is even more clearly verified when, gathered together in an ecumenical council, they are teachers and judges of faith and morals for the universal Church. Their definitions must then be adhered to with the submission of faith.

This infallibility with which the divine Redeemer willed His Church to be endowed in defining a doctrine of faith and morals extends as far as extends the deposit of divine

[1] ibid., pp. 42–4
[2] The Papal Encyclical on Contraception (July 1968) seems to be a clear example of what is meant here. See *Additional Note*, p. 223 below

revelation, which must be religiously guarded and faith-fully expounded. This is the infallibility which the Roman Pontiff, the head of the college of bishops, enjoys in virtue of his office, when, as the supreme shepherd and teacher of all the faithful, who confirms his brethren in their faith, he proclaims by a definitive act some doctrine of faith or morals. Therefore his definitions, of themselves, and not from the consent of the Church, are justly styled irreform-able, for they are pronounced with the assistance of the Holy Spirit, an assistance promised to him in blessed Peter. Therefore they need no approval of others, nor do they allow an appeal to any other judgment. For then the Roman Pontiff is not pronouncing judgment as a private person. Rather, as the supreme teacher of the universal Church, as one in whom the charism of the infallibility of the Church herself is individually present, he is expound-ing or defending a doctrine of Catholic faith.

The infallibility promised to the Church resides also in the body of bishops when the body exercises supreme teaching authority with the successor of Peter. To the resultant definitions the assent of the Church can never be wanting, on account of the activity of that same Holy Spirit, whereby the whole flock of Christ is preserved and progresses in unity of faith.[1]

As they read this passage, those who have some experience of ecumenical conferences can easily imagine the drafts and re-drafts, the assertions, withdrawals and concessions, the word-for-word scrutinies of every sentence, the sub-commit-tees and the private conferences, which must have preceded the acceptance of the final wording by the Theological Com-mission. In particular, it is tempting to think of both the supporters of the increase of episcopal authority, and those determined to maintain the Papal authority unimpaired, as striving by might and main to ensure that their point of view is not submerged by the opposite one. On the whole, both sides succeeded in their efforts. First, we are told that the bishops can teach infallibly, especially when assembled in ecumenical council; and we know that a council is not

[1] ibid., p. 48f.

ecumenical unless called or approved by the Pope. Then we are told that the Pope, as the supreme teacher of the universal Church, can speak infallibly in his own right, in virtue of his office, and the divine assistance promised to Peter. From this we must conclude that the doctrine of the Pope's infallibility, as enunciated by the First Vatican Council, remains inviolate; but also that the body of bishops, when united with the Pope, or even when dispersed, so long as they agree with each other and the Pope in what they say, is also infallible. In other words, the Pope does not require the consent or presence of the bishops in order to make an infallible pronouncement; the bishops require the Pope's consent if they are to make one.

There is, then, no great advance on Vatican I in the exposition of the doctrine of infallibility, except in the place, important, but not necessary, given to the college of bishops. This Constitution of Vatican II at this point is still open to all the familiar arguments against infallibility. But at least it does not pronounce an anathema on those who think differently!

It must be confessed that the lack of any revision or modification of the doctrine of infallibility casts a blight on any hopes that we may cherish of fruitful conversation and eventual reconciliation with Rome. For it seems to follow from the doctrine as it is still formulated that any communion of Christendom which denies the doctrine, or any other doctrine promulgated by Rome, is already adjudged by Rome to be in error. Thus vital matters, and this one of authority above all, are settled before any conversation starts, and no conversation seems to have any chance of success. Logically, the old claim to submission remains unchanged, though we know that in practice, and, indeed, in certain parts of this very Constitution, the attitude of Rome to those outside her fold is very different from what it was–that she has, in fact, eaten many of the words that she spoke at Trent and at the First Vatican Council. Charity may yet prevail over logic; but it would have been better if Vatican II had found a way of reconciling its doctrine with its undoubted charity. This task still remains to be done.

Yet perhaps a start has been made. Hans Küng, in *Struc-*

tures of the Church, has a very thorough discussion of infallibility, written before the Constitution on the Church of Vatican II, and no doubt not without some influence upon it. His point of departure is the criticism of the Roman doctrine of infallibility made by Karl Barth in 1939,[1] but, according to Küng, not sufficiently attended to by Roman theologians. Barth charges the Roman Church with failing to distinguish between the Church and revelation, or rather, with identifying the two. This identification is to be seen as far back as the writings of Irenaeus; it became more pronounced at Trent and continues into the present time. And since Trent it has been more seriously erroneous than ever before, since the post-Tridentine Church has thought of itself as being the Church and the whole Church, so that revelation has been identified with the actual Roman Church. In 1870 things went from bad to worse, for in that year the Roman Church proceeded to identify the Church with the Roman Pontiff, so that on the Roman view the Pope and revelation are the same. Küng quotes Barth: 'Since the Vatican Council we can know what, after all this, had not been previously known, viz. where and who *in the concrete* is the Church which teaches revelation.' And later he gives the sentence of Barth, which, he says, constitutes the crucial objection to the Roman doctrine: 'I cannot hear the voice of the Good Shepherd from this "Chair of Peter".'[2]

Küng defends his Church against the Barthian attack in various ways. He contends, for instance, that Vatican I did not identify the Pope with revelation, since it denied that the Pope could promulgate new doctrines, and claims that the Decree on the Pope's infallibility means that the charism of infallibility bestowed on the successors of Peter gives him the function of explaining and supporting the revelation already given, and not of anything more than that. But he acknowledges that the Church would do well to deepen and strengthen the distinction between the revelation of God and the word of the Church. For the Pope teaches only in obedience to the Holy Spirit; this is the right way to think of his infalli-

[1] in *Church Dogmatics* Vol. I, 2 (T. & T. Clark, Edinburgh 1956), pp. 548–51
[2] *Structures of the Church* pp. 314–26

bility, and this is the way on which the faithful should be taught to think of it.[1]

Passing on from his treatment of Barth's criticism, he further affirms that Vatican I's Decree on infallibility did not extend the Pope's infallibility, but limited it against the extravagant claims made for it in certain quarters. For, in spite of its assertion 'that the definitions of the Roman Pontiffs are irreformable of themselves, and not from the consent of the Church', Vatican I did not separate the Pope from the Church; on the contrary, it declared him to be infallible only in so far as he represented the Church, and did not allow him to issue a definition without consulting the mind of the Church. 'No doubt, there exists no absolute necessity for the pope to consult with the Church or the episcopate in a definite way, but there is certainly a relative necessity' (we are bound to point out that this interpretation of the Decree is not very plausible).[2]

Küng adds that Vatican I does not teach that infallibility belongs exclusively to the Pope. It is true, he admits, that it does not expressly state that infallibility belongs to others too; but this is its implication. For it says emphatically that the Pope may not define truths against the mind of the Church. And it certainly does not confuse infallibility with impeccability; what infallibility means is a *de jure* freedom from error. Not only is it true that he *non errat*; it is also true that he *errare non potest*.[3]

It is, however, in the last few pages of his book that Küng encourages the birth of a hope that Rome will one day consider at least the re-formulation of its doctrine. In these pages Küng brings into prominence some 'problematic aspects of the question of infallibility'. He expounds with great sympathy the Protestant objection to the ascription of infallibility to a man or group of men, and shows that Protestants no less than Catholics believe the Church to be in essence 'indestructible, permanent, infallible', because it is united with Christ, while at the same time holding that the concrete history of the Church in *all* its members is ever anew a history of sin and error:

[1] ibid., pp. 320–6   [2] ibid., p. 330f.   [3] ibid., pp. 334–6

For Protestant Christians the continuity and indestructibility of the Church does not depend upon the infallibility of certain utterances but upon the Spirit, which operatively permeates the frailty and fallibility of human beings as well as their utterances.

From this he is led to point out that the Decrees of Vatican I were formulated in reply to the errors of Gallicanism, and do not directly meet the Protestant objections. The task of elaborating Catholic doctrine in its relation to Protestant theology has still to be carried out, and until this is done it is very likely that Protestants will be unable to appreciate the real strength of the Catholic position on the question of infallibility.

But while this task remains unperformed Küng ventures to offer some considerations which may help the ecumenical dialogue. In relation to the Protestant idea that the authority of Church and Pope overrides the sacred rights of human conscience, he says, quite definitely, that the Roman Church teaches the absolute supremacy, he says, quite definitely, that the Roman Church teaches the absolute supremacy of conscience in all matters of ethics, and that a man is required to obey his conscience even at the risk of excommunication. Then he argues that we ought to distinguish between faith and its formulations: the divergencies between Churches are sometimes not really matters of faith, but of formulation only; and formulations are to be understood and evaluated in the light of the historical circumstances in which they are made. In particular, statements of doctrine with a polemical intent are apt to be inadequate. They are apt to concentrate on the error which they wish to confute, and so to miss the kernel of truth contained in the error. 'The ecumenical task of theology on both sides is seriously to consider the truth in the error of the others and the possible error in their own truth.'[1]

If it is seriously meant that individual conscience is to be obeyed, if necessary, against the declared mind of the Church, then the doctrine of papal infallibility is found to admit of exceptions: I am no longer required to believe it if my con-

[1] ibid., pp. 336–51

science forbids me, and those whose conscience so forbids them cannot be placed outside the frontiers of the true Church. And if there is error in truth, and truth in error, then not even an infallible Pope or Church can declare infallibly that what he or it promulgates is true without dilution of error, or that what it denies is false without admixture of truth.

As Küng rightly suggests, these considerations could be the beginning of that real dialogue between Catholics and Protants which a little while ago seemed to be quite out of the question. Of course, this is not yet any reason for thinking that the proposals of Küng will be taken up by his Church.

Chapter Nine

THE ECUMENICAL DIMENSION

It will not be hard to show that the Ecumenical Movement has had a profound effect on the way in which the problem of religious authority must be handled today. But since the words 'ecumenical' and 'ecumenism' have been so seriously debased in common usage, it may be as well to indicate the sense in which they are mostly used by those who are nearest to the heart of the Ecumenical Movement.

It is not ecumenism when ministers of different denominations meet together for discussion, or even join together to lead parties from their denominations to the Holy Land, listen together to lectures on unity and other subjects, and say their prayers together. This is fraternization of a kind happily common among those who would not venture to describe themselves as ecumenical.

It is not ecumenism when members of different denominations engage together in a worthwhile activity of service to the community or share in the work of Christian Aid. This is Christian co-operation of a kind which is perfectly possible for those to join in who are opposed to all the ideals of the Ecumenical Movement.

It is not ecumenism when Christians of different denominations but the same theological standpoint forgather at Keswick or elsewhere to strengthen one another in their common faith. Such a gathering is, of course, interdenominational, and interdenominational gatherings of this kind served in some areas as precursors of the Ecumenical Movement. But community of view across the denominations does not constitute ecumenism.

Still less is it ecumenism when representatives of many

branches of the same confessional family meet in conference or launch common enterprises. This is, indeed, ecclesiastical internationalism, but the Ecumenical Methodist Council (which seems to have been the first, in 1881, to use the word 'ecumenical' in a modern context outside the Orthodox and Roman Churches) was quite right to change its name in 1951 to the World Methodist Council.

Nor is it ecumenism when one Church in an exchange of theological views or any kind of meeting to promote unity sets out to convince the other participants that it is right and they are wrong in small or great matters, or to persuade other Churches to surrender their particular witness and be absorbed, however honourable the terms of absorption may be. Such an attempt will be styled 'denominational imperialism', or 'zeal for the revealed truth of God', according to the point of view; it is not ecumenism.

The activities which we have been describing, except for the last, are not, of course, *anti*-ecumenical. In fact, in most cases they may well promote the cause of ecumenism, though the other possibility is usually present. But it leads only to confusion of thought when 'ecumenical' and 'ecumenism' are used as blanket words to cover anything which is done together by members of different denominations. If such a usage were legitimate, it would be possible to say that ecumenism began when the first marriage took place between a Catholic and a Protestant, or between members of the Eastern and Western Churches after the Schism!

We come nearer to ecumenism when Christians of various communions pray together, following the example and teaching of the noble Abbé Couturier, for 'the unity which God wills in the way he wills'. But if the matter ceases there–as it did for many years, and still often does, for many Christians–and still more if prayer for 'the unity which God wills' is used as an excuse for not promoting any actual scheme of unity in case it should be the wrong sort, ecumenism has not come into full existence.

For ecumenism comprises thought, and study, and dialogue, and planning, and action, as well as prayer and worship. The Ecumenical Movement happens when separated

Churches, through their appointed representatives, come together, in an atmosphere of shared prayer and worship, to make known to and discuss with one another their traditions of faith and worship and thought and order, in the conviction that they have something to impart and to receive from one another, with a view to eventual, however long delayed, organic union within the restored wholeness of the Body of Christ. It is a movement in which *Churches*, as such, not individuals or groups, participate. They do not try to defeat each other in any matter of difference between them, for they acknowledge from the start that they have no monopoly of Christian truth or understanding. The dialogue between them is not for the purpose of persuasion, though this may, of course, occasionally happen, but for the reconciliation of diverse truths within the wholeness of the Faith, or at least for the inquiry whether such truths are at present reconcilable.

The unity which is the end in view is not uniformity of faith and practice, but is constituted out of diversity; it does not spring from the domination of one form of the Church over all others, but from the coming together in harmony of many forms; it is neither purely inward nor purely outward, but both inward and outward (for inward unity is the prerequisite of any worthwhile outward unity, and outward unity the necessary expression of inward unity); it is therefore *organic* union. It embraces faith and order, life and work; it is for the sake of the world much more than for the sake of the Church; it finds its full sacramental expression in the gathering of all God's people round the Table of the Lord.

If this is the true nature of ecumenism, it is clear that those who are ecumenically minded are debarred from certain views about the *locus* and nature of authority in religion which have been widely held in the past. Sometimes, of course, it is the abandonment of these views which has convinced their previous holders of the value of ecumenism; sometimes the adoption of an ecumenical attitude or theological approach has led to the abandonment of these views. In either case, ecumenism has been found to be inconsistent with the views we have here in mind.

One of these views takes the form of a claim that the interpretation of Scripture which is maintained in such and such a Church or group–usually the Church or group to which the claimant belongs–is authoritative, or even infallible. This claim has been made on behalf of and by the Roman Church; it has been made for and by the Conservative Evangelical wing of the Church of England; it is made for and by the Mormons, the Jehovah's Witnesses, and the other sects; it is made most stridently and persistently of all by the Exclusive Brethren. The fact that the interpretations offered by the various groups and Churches differed violently from one another, and sometimes were diametrically opposed to one another, and yet were asserted to be authoritative for all Christians, always puzzled Christians of a less dogmatic frame of mind. Now, within the Ecumenical Movement, these interpretations can be offered, not as authoritative, but only as those which are accepted within certain communions; they cannot be imposed on those communions which have decided to reject them. Those who intend to adhere to their own interpretations as authoritative cannot join the Ecumenical Movement–and this is one of the reasons why the Witnesses, the Mormons, the Missouri Lutherans, the Southern Baptists, the Exclusive Brethren, and, indeed, the Open Brethren, cannot join. They are still convinced that their interpretation of Scripture is the right one, and that those who hold a different one are simply wrong.

This point can be illustrated in a number of ways. Conservative Evangelicals, who are notable for having accepted the Calvinistic 'plan of salvation' as being necessarily and exclusively implied by the words of Scripture about the dealings of God with man, now in many cases want to take part in ecumenical conversation, and have begun to do so. They are at once involved in talking with Christians who interpret the Bible in quite a different way, and find themselves tacitly accepting the possibility that other interpretations of the Bible than their own are legitimate, at least on some matters. Again, Roman Catholics, also wishing to take part in ecumenical dialogue, frequently find themselves hampered by the pronouncements of their Church to the effect that the

Roman interpretation of various important passages in the Bible, for instance about the Apostle Peter, are not subject to amendment; and these pronouncements have not been withdrawn by Vatican II. The real awkwardness of this situation has so far been concealed by the extreme courtesy–very welcome after the centuries of recrimination–with which Catholic–Protestant discussions are at present carried on and by the present tendency on each side to give the other side the benefit of the doubt. But as discussions become franker, as they must, the true condition of affairs will be revealed. It is, in fact, hard to see, from a human point of view, how the Roman Church can be a full participant in ecumenical activity until and unless her not-yet-withdrawn claims to inerrant interpretation of Scripture are in fact withdrawn. Then, the Ordinal in the Book of Common Prayer states in its Preface:

> It is evident unto all men diligently reading holy Scripture and ancient Authors, that from the Apostles' time there have been these Orders of Ministers in Christ's Church; Bishops, Priests and Deacons.

But it is no longer evident, for scholars both of the Anglican and other communions cast serious doubt on the version of history which the Preface repeats. Clearly, Anglican participants in ecumenical discussion must be prepared to regard this version as only one possible one among several.

Next, commitment to the Ecumenical Movement involves, by the same token, the repudiation of all claims on the part of any denomination, whether it is a member of the World Council of Churches or not, to proclaim the Christian Faith authoritatively and completely. For ecumenism implies the willingness to be taught by other denominations with different theological standpoints, and this in turn implies the possibility of error in one's own standpoint; and we have seen that no denomination is entitled to enter the Ecumenical Movement with the intention of winning others over to its own point of view. The first few decades of the Faith and Order Movement, the theological sector of the Ecumenical Movement, were spent in comparing the statements of the different communions on Christian doctrine, and a great deal of pleasure and surprise was recorded at the substantial measure of agreement on major issues which embraced all the denominations. But there were and are still, disagreements on such matters as the Church, the Ministry and the Sacraments, and the Faith and Order discussion goes on in the hope of reconciling them. But it could not go on if the participating Churches, or any of them, asserted that their point of view was irrefragably right and indubitably complete. Faith and Order Conferences frequently approve reports which state that 'some of us hold that . . ., while others hold that . . .'; and no anathema is put on either opinion. Rather, it is assumed that both opinions hold their place within the totality of Christian truth, though it may be hard at present to see how they can be reconciled with each other.

Thirdly, the Ecumenical Movement, for those who believe in it, puts finally out of court any doctrine of infallibility. And this must be said, in spite of the fact that the Roman Church is eager to take part in the Movement and has nevertheless shown no signs of relinquishing its doctrine of Papal infallibility. For, as every Church participating hopes to share its insights with others, and to learn from others, so it must risk the possibility that on certain points it may find itself confessing itself to have been in error, or at least to have stressed what should not have been stressed, and it must envisage the further possibility that it may convince another Church of the partial error of its ways. But if any one Church, or group within a Church, claims infallibility on any doctrinal point, the road to understanding, and to mutual correction and amplification, is barred from the start. To take what may, indeed, be the most difficult case, how can the Church as a whole do what badly needs to be done, consider again the place of the Virgin Mary in the faith of Christendom, without the prejudice and sentimentality which have so often been found in both Protestant and Catholic camps, but Scripturally and objectively, if it be held by some of those taking part that the dogma of the Assumption has been infallibly declared and is not open for discussion? It may be possible for Protestant theologians to demythologize this particular dogma in such a way as to refer it to the Church, rather than to the human mother of Jesus, and so to urge its acceptance on Protestants. But it is impossible to see how Roman Catholics can take it in this sense, and still maintain the infallibility of the Papal promulgation of the doctrine. Ecumenism and infallibilism do not go together.

So far, the effects of the Ecumenical Movement on our inquiry seem to be largely negative, and opinions may differ as to whether they represent a gain or a loss. But there are three further effects which will be generally acknowledged to represent a substantial gain. The Churches which take part in ecumenical discussion—this does not, alas, apply to those who still remain aloof—can now re-consider their own tenets, and allow others to help them in this re-consideration, without the defensiveness that has characterized such re-considerations in the past (when indeed they have been undertaken at all). Those who have been charged with the task of revising denominational statements have previously felt themselves obliged, often against their natural or Christian inclinations, to defend at all costs those things for which their denomination 'has always stood', lest they be suspected of 'selling the pass', or, much worse, actually diluting the Gospel as it was delivered to their fathers. This is why the militant and aggressive note is often to be found in such statements; each denomination tends to picture itself in the role of *Athanasius contra mundum*. Those who represent their Churches at ecumenical conferences still, of course, feel themselves obliged to state and defend the point of view of their Church fairly and persuasively—or else the purpose of such conferences would be lost. But if they are invited to scrutinize afresh, with Christians of other denominations, an issue on which their Church holds a certain view, they will no longer feel bound to defend every jot and tittle of what their Church believes and insist that every part of it should find a place in the report of the conference, for the views of no Church are under attack, and when no one is aggressive, there is no need for anyone to be defensive. Thus each Church reaches a better, because non-defensive, understanding of its own position, and of the position of others at the same time.

Secondly, it is now becoming possible to think of certain

apparently contradictory doctrines, once thought to be mutually exclusive, as mutually complementary. This has already happened over wide areas of eucharistic doctrine, especially when traditional disputants have gone back together to the Scriptural sources of all eucharistic doctrine. Even the doctrines of the ministry, as held by 'Catholics' and 'Protestants', and now submitted to the piercing gaze of those who see sociological as well as theological factors operating in the development of the priesthood and the episcopate, do not now seem to be as widely discrepant as they once undoubtedly were. If we acknowledge on all sides, as is now often done, that baptism is incorporation into the salvation of mankind effected by the life, death and resurrection of Jesus, it could cease to be a matter of ultimate controversy whether a child should be baptized, in prospect of the personal faith into which the Church, of which he becomes a member by his baptism, hopes to lead him, or only adults, in token of the faith into which they have already come.

Thirdly, and most relevantly to the question of authority, it is not too much to say that we can see the slow emergence of the common mind of the Church on issues which have divided it for centuries. In the early days of the Church the rise of heresies compelled the Church to discover and publish its common mind on the questions of the Person of Christ and the Trinity, and it is of course true that the rise and strength of anti-Christian forces is compelling the Church to do the same on many fundamental questions of belief, and the Ecumenical Movement provides a convenient means to that end. But this is by no means the only thing that is happening. The constant, almost continuous, certainly regular, meeting of men and women of all traditions determined to discover together what the Church really is, what its function is in the modern world, what meaning and validity can be ascribed to its teachings in the face of all the criticisms levelled against them, is leading steadily, though painfully, to conclusions which all Christendom may one day accept; and here, of course, the accession of Rome to the ecumenical dialogue is immensely valuable, in spite of its retention of infallibilism (which from time to time in such discussions it seems conveniently to forget). Can it be that we are approaching that re-statement of Christian doctrine which has long been necessary, but entirely prevented by the divisions of the Church? It would be unduly optimistic to say this. Yet the consensus of Christian thought on an increasing number of subjects clearly points to the possibility of finding a new *locus* of authority in the considered pronouncements of a fully ecumenical body such as the World Council of Churches essays to be. Infallibility is, as we have seen, out of the question; but authority, in a sense which we shall try to define in the next and final chapter, may yet be capable of discovery.

Chapter Ten

ONLY ONE WAY FORWARD

It must surely now be clear that the gift of infallibility in matters of religious truth is granted to no one and nothing –no book, no person or group of persons, no institution. There is in religion no such thing as infallibility; it is a concept which has no equivalent in reality. In answer to the challenge of Schleiermacher, consciously or unconsciously recognized as highly dangerous to all forms of authoritative religion, many theologians have made attempts, some of which are described in this book, to defend a doctrine of infallibility; and Churches, in their understandable, if not always laudable, desire to counteract the erosions of modern scepticism and secularism, have made great efforts to build guarantees of inerrancy–as, for instance, the argument that God *must* have made provision for an infallible guide, or else mankind would have been left in total darkness–into their theological systems. But the attempts and efforts have all failed; and their very frequency and variety, the continuing disputes among infallibilities as to *where* infallibility is to be found, and the shifts to which they have sometimes been reduced in order to render plausible the notion that human beings can in some circumstances be lifted above error, are eloquent testimonies to their failure. Infallibility is disproved theologically, since it implies a doctrine of God and man which is anti-Biblical and inconsistent with the rest of Christian faith; it is disproved empirically, since no claimant to infallibility has appeared who can stand up to the attacks of Biblical, historical and philosophical critics or to the counter-claims of his rivals.

And, even if, for the sake of argument, we were to agree

that it is theoretically possible that there is somewhere an infallible authority, we should still never be able to identify it, unless we were ourselves gifted with infallibility. We might, of course, have a strong personal opinion that infallible authority is to be found in the Bible, or in the Papacy, or elsewhere; but since strong personal opinions are often, as all agree, mistaken, we should never know whether the pronouncements of the body or book or person whom we had elected to regard as infallible were in fact infallible. Roman Catholic writers, from Newman to Bishop B. C. Butler, have tried to circumvent this difficulty by distinguishing certitude (or certainty) from infallibility–certainty being limited to the occasion when we accept the Roman Church as infallible, infallibility being a permanent gift granted to the Roman Church and its head. But this does not really help their case very much, for, on this view, certainty is a kind of temporary infallibility, and temporary infallibility is, if anything, more difficult to locate than the permanent sort. Moreover, it is even more open to objection than the permanent infallibility of the Church; an individual, deciding whether to become a member of the Roman Catholic Church, is surely even less likely to be exempt from error than the majestic Roman Church, with all its history, wisdom and experience.[1]

So infallibility is out. The claim to possess it, and the belief in its existence, are seen to be attempts to short-circuit the endless questionings which arise within the human mind and soul about the nature and purpose of existence, by the assertion, itself claimed to be infallible, that *here* is the place where all doubts are laid to rest. All doctrines of infallibility are psychological, not theological or logical; as such they may be highly successful in achieving the end for which they were in fact created–widespread peace of mind. But we cannot in our time be content with any doctrine which achieves this but is otherwise untenable: nor, perhaps, will it much longer achieve even this.

But are we not in a much better position if we withdraw the claim to infallibility, wherever it has been made, and say

[1] I have argued this point at somewhat greater length in *Why I am a Protestant* pp. 56–61.

that a measure of authority which is sufficient for the spiritual and intellectual needs of the Church and its members is to be found in the Catholic Creeds, or the Roman Catholic Church, or the Pope, or the Bible, or in human conscience, or in human reason? By 'a measure of authority which is sufficient for the spiritual and intellectual needs of the Church and its members' we should perhaps mean something like this: Granted that we cannot know the truth of the Christian religion *for certain*, or the truth of any particular doctrine *for certain*, we can be enough convinced of their truth to live by them without awareness of any contradiction between them and the rest of what we believe to be true: and an 'authority' which can convince us in this way and to this extent is 'sufficient'.

This conception of 'sufficient authority' is, as we shall perhaps see in a few minutes, a useful one. But can we ascribe this authority to the Pope, or to the Creeds, or to the consensus of the Church Catholic, or to reason, or to the spiritual insight or Inner Light of the individual Christian, or to Christian experience, or to conscience, or even to Scripture? The conclusion to be drawn from the preceding chapters is that we cannot. By 'the Pope' we of course mean 'the Pope speaking *ex cathedra*', or, since Vatican II, 'the Pope speaking with the bishops of the Roman Church'. 'The Pope', in this sense, lacks 'sufficient authority', not because he is not to be trusted at all as an exponent of Christian truth–no Christian would wish to deny that *ex cathedra* pronouncements can faithfully expound Christian truth–but because among *ex cathedra* pronouncements there are some, for instance the one on the Immaculate Conception of the Virgin Mary, which have no chance of obtaining the consent of the whole of Christendom and are thought by many Christians to be contrary to the Christian Gospel as they have accepted it. The Creeds are nearer than 'the Pope' to possessing 'sufficient authority', and there are few sections of Christendom which would entirely deny a measure of authority at least to the Apostles' and Nicene Creeds. But the measure is not 'sufficient', because at certain points–not many, it is true–they state dogmatically what must be regarded as still open to inquiry–the Virgin Birth, for instance, and the Descent into Hades. And the Nicene Creed suffers from the additional disqualification in that it is said in two versions in different parts of the Church, one containing the *filioque*, and other not. Nor can we ascribe 'sufficient authority' to the consensus of the Church Catholic, for although the consensus of the ancient Church is to some extent, as we have seen, available in the Creeds, the divisions of the Church have made it impossible for the consensus of the Church through all the ages and in all places to be ascertained.[1]

The claims of reason, conscience, spiritual insight and the Inner Light are on a different level, but equally unacceptable. The chief objection to them is, of course, their individualistic character. One man's reason is another man's irrationality; one man's Inner Light is another man's darkness. One man's spiritual insight is another man's misguided prejudice. And within the Church–indeed within individual communions–consciences differ and conflict most profoundly. But even when reason, conscience and the rest can free themselves of their individualistic taint, we must still ask: What is the reason or conscience or insight, even of a large number of people agreeing together, to set itself up against the accumulated wisdom and experience of the Church at large (for this is what they are venturing to do if they claim 'sufficient authority')?

The case of the Bible is different. Here, surely, is a source of authority by which all communions of Christendom, and almost all individual Christians, profess themselves willing to test their doctrines and their practices. Surely here, at least, we have 'sufficient authority'? But even here the claim cannot be conceded. The historical and scientific errors of the Biblical writers do not matter at this point (they are important only if the alleged *infallibility* of Scripture is being discussed). But the Old Testament conflicts at many points with the New Testament, and the New Testament at some (not many) points conflicts with itself. These discrepancies cannot be resolved from within the Bible itself, despite the efforts of theologians since the very beginning of Christian

[1] see pp. 208f. above.

history, and especially since the Reformation, to resolve them. To attempt such a resolution involves preference of one passage above another, and who shall determine the preference? And, much more seriously, as the Roman Church has clearly and consistently taught, the Bible needs an interpreter; it does not bear its plain meaning on its face. There are in existence many hundreds of interpretations of the Bible, several of them claiming to be infallible. A book which is at some points in conflict with itself, and is patient of many conflicting interpretations, cannot be said to possess 'sufficient authority'. And if the Bible does not possess it, the last and most promising candidate has fallen out of the race.

To some readers the contention made in the last few pages will seem, if true, to be a sentence of death on the Christian Faith. If we have no infallible guide, if we have not even any person or body of persons, or any collection of writings, or any gift within ourselves, by whose prescriptions and pronouncements we can live without contradiction or serious doubt, they will perhaps say, how can we be expected, or expect others, to accept the Christian Faith? If we cannot know that we are right when we recite the Creeds or believe the Bible or submit to the Church, we are, far more than those who 'for this life only . . . have hoped in Christ', of all men most miserable. Christianity is not able to deliver the goods which it advertises, and we must turn elsewhere. And there seems nowhere else to turn.

But in fact, what seems to be a sentence of death is a charter of life and renewal and unity. Up till recently Christians have believed that there is a source of authority to which it is the duty of all to submit. Those who have been sure that the authority recognized in their own communion is the correct one have anathematized, persecuted and despised the subjects of other authorities. And those who have taken seriously the Lord's refusal to call down fire from heaven, at the suggestion of his disciples, on the Samaritan village which rejected him, have been puzzled and distressed by the Babel of authorities and by Christians' mutual destructiveness, and they have sought to mitigate in practice the rigours of the doctrine to which they have been committed.

But now we know that there is not, and never has been, an infallible guide, and that there is not, and never has been, one authoritative source of truth. At last, the real truth about our human situation is revealed, and we are free from the compulsions and constraints of the past. Immediately, of course, we are called to repent of our intolerance, our aggressiveness and defensiveness; and, although we may hope that God will wink at the times of our ignorance, to be conscious of the enormity of our offences against charity and humility. But at the same time we are enabled to approach the whole question from an entirely new position, without presuppositions and presumptions, and, although so ancient a problem will not be quickly solved, we can hope that a new beginning will lead to more rapid progress than has ever been possible before.

We can indicate the way forward in the simplest possible terms. A man becomes a conscious Christian when he commits himself to Jesus Christ. The nature of this commitment is that, with all his faculties in full possession and use, and in full awareness of the other theories of the world and the other patterns of life which have been propounded to him, he accepts for himself Jesus Christ as the meaning of the world and of human existence. That is, he recognizes God as Father, and he recognizes the principle, which can briefly be called the principle of love, asserted by Jesus in life and teaching, in death and resurrection, to be the principle on which the universe is created and sustained, as being in fact the principle which underlies all things; and, at one and the same time, he declares his intention of living by the same principle, so far as it lies within his power and at any cost. If we wish, as many of us probably will, to put this in more religious terms, we shall say that to become a Christian means to accept Jesus Christ as Lord, Master, Saviour, the Son and Word of God, and the supreme authority for thought and life.

This self-commitment is an act of faith, not an assertion of knowledge. Indeed, by making this act of self-commitment, a man forgoes and forswears the claim to *knowledge* about God and the universe and human life. He says, in effect, that in a world in which certainty on ultimate questions is impossible, and knowledge is confined to the vast but limited area of science, he is prepared, because he is aware of powerful reasons which appeal to his total personality (though they stop short of demonstration), and of no objections strong enough to counterbalance them, to put his personal trust in Jesus Christ and to live the life which is involved by that trust right through to the end. He can be said, from one point of view, to have accepted the most probable hypothesis, and to have adopted (as Bishop Joseph Butler recommended) probability as the guide to life; from another point of view, he deliberately lives by faith, and not by knowledge.

At this point a linguistic philosopher who happens on these pages may object that a Christian, in this case, is one who confuses his categories. For he has taken note of the life and teaching of a historical personage, and attached to them ontological significance and an ethical evaluation. These, according to many linguistic philosophers, are highly illegitimate things to to do. Historical events and personages belong to one universe of discourse; attributions of ontological significance, if indeed they are allowable at all, belong to another, and ethical valuations to yet another. It is not possible to argue from a statement in one universe of discourse to a conclusion in another.

It must at once be conceded that the a-scription of meaning to Jesus Christ—which is what we maintain that a Christian makes—combines in one assertion what the objector claims to be two, or even three, universes of discourse. If this is illegitimate, then all religious statements are illegitimate, as in fact the logical positivists have alleged. To answer the objection satisfactorily would require a total defence of religion, for which this is not the place. Here it can only be pointed out that the illegitimacy of the 'combination of universes' is not by any means undisputed among philosophers. But it can be added that what we have here in mind, when we speak of the faith of a Christian, is not a proposition about God, man and the universe, but the declaration of a 'policy of life'; and as such it is not vulnerable to the objection of the

linguistic philosopher above set out. The theological statements to which we shall shortly come may be open to it, but
the basic faith of a Christian is not.

Historians may come up with a further objection. A Christian, they point out, has now been defined as a man who has
commited himself to a personage who, whatever else is
asserted of him, is admitted on all sides to be historical. No
one nowadays doubts his historical existence, but there is very
considerable uncertainty about the course and details of his
life as they are narrated in the Gospels, and very little certain
knowledge of his actual words. Is what is known about him
enough to justify self-commitment to him? The answer to
this must be that, although we should very much have liked
to know more about Jesus' historical career, we do know
enough for the purpose. Historical research into the Gospels, which has been carried out in a more radical spirit than
in virtually any other area of history, has left us at least with
the outlines of the life and the central elements in the teaching of Jesus, it has verified in general the Gospel account of
his death, and although it has certainly not removed the
doubt which hangs over the personal resurrection of Jesus
from the dead, it can be said quite definitely to have vindi-
cated the historicity of the disciples' 'resurrection experience'.
Moreover, it has left it open to less radical schools of historians to accept the historicity of a good deal more than we
have just given, and to do so without loss of their academic
respectability. We have enough for faith, though not enough
to satisfy our legitimate curiosity.

But at this point, and on the same general theme, a theological objection may be raised. Is not the Christian, as we
have described him above, putting himself far too much at the
mercy of historical contingency? After all, it might one day be
demonstrated that the whole Gospel is legendary; although
this mode of attack has for the time being been dropped,
perhaps some new historical discoveries or doubts may bring
it to life again; and then where would our Christian faith be?
If Christianity is to be asserted as true, there must be some
guarantee of its truth outside history–the Holy, Catholic
Church, for instance, whose existence not even the most

hardened sceptic can deny. We have seen already that no guarantees can, in fact, be available. And to the main burden of the objection we can reply that when the Christian commits himself to a historical person, he knows, or should know, exactly what he is doing. He is committing himself precisely to one who, on his own showing, although he was uniquely related to God, has deliberately chosen to enter the realm of historical contingency, and has thus put himself at the mercy of any historian who claims to have proved his non-existence. God, as Jesus speaks of him, is exactly of such a character as to put himself and his revelation, in his desire to respect the freedom of human beings, at such a risk as this. To deny the submission of Christ to historical contingency is to deny the Incarnation, and turns Christianity into a kind of Gnosticism, according to which historical events are interesting but can be dispensed with by the intelligentsia.

The act of faith which is self-commitment to Christ has two immediate and lifelong consequences. The first is that by such commitment a Christian is incorporated into the Church, which is the historical fellowship of those who are thus committed. The second is that he is involved in working out the implications for life and thought of his commitment. The implications for thought make up what is called Christian theology, and take the form of doctrines and doctrinal teachings. The Christian works these out, assisted and guided (though not infallibly) by the Holy Spirit (as he firmly believes), by the use of his reason, by his spiritual insight (which is the best name for the Inner Light, since it does not imply, though it does not deny, that there is something of God in every man) and by his conscience. He does this in the context of worshipping and teaching life of the Church, and thus enters into its agelong heritage of theological thought and controversy.

At an early stage in this process, perhaps when he first stumbles on the fact that Christians dispute about many articles of the faith, there arises in his mind the problem of authority. Granted that reason and conscience and insight, and the teaching of the Church to which he belongs, point in a certain direction of thought, but granted also that teachers of another Church, or other teachers in his own Church, point in a different direction, how is he to know what to believe? And once the problem of authority has arisen for him, it is likely to remain his constant companion until he comes to terms with it. We have discarded several ineffective ways of dealing with it. What is there left? And here we must urge the replacement of the word 'authority' by the word 'witness'. In the first part of this chapter we found a certain usefulness in the conception of 'a measure of authority sufficient for faith'. But now we can plainly say that the word 'witness' corresponds much more accurately to the functions which we are now about to describe, and to the basic assertion, already made, but now made more explicitly and definitively, that for the Christian the supreme authority is Christ himself, to whom he has committed himself in faith.

The assertion of the supreme authority of Christ is essential to the position which this book represents. It means that there is no going behind Christ for further information about God, that in Christ is everything, implicitly or explicitly, that we need to be told about God and his purposes for the world and for us; it means also that we depend on faith just as much in the realm of authority as in any other part of the Christian religion. For we cannot know (the word is here used in the Pauline sense) Christ except by faith.[1]

This is the authority of Christ, in whom we trust. But our trust in him requires us to find out as much as we can about him and to work out as much as we can of the implications of trust in him for faith and life, as we have already said. And for this we require, not unimpeachable *authorities*, but trustworthy *witnesses*. And trustworthy witnesses are what we in fact have. Before all others, the Bible–which first of all is the record of the preparation for the coming of Christ in the history of Israel, its leaders and its prophets, and in its second part is the testimony of the only eye-witnesses to Jesus that we can ever have, set down by themselves or by

[1] The fact that the commitment is in faith and claims no certainty helps us to avoid the awkward logical problem raised by all assertions of absolute authority; see p. 16 above.

those on whom they relied to do the task for them. After the Bible comes the undivided Church, which formulated in the Creeds what it clearly understood, after much argument, to be the main content of Scriptural teaching. The Bible and the Creeds make up the major and the minor part of the Tradition which is the whole Church's most valuable possession. Then come the great liturgies of the great Churches of Christendom, the writings of the Fathers of the Early Church, and of the Fathers of the Middle Ages and of the Reformation and of later times. And then the 'traditions' of the various communions into which the Catholic Church has been divided. And finally, but only just over the horizon of the future, is the prospect, held out by the Ecumenical Movement, of the reunion of Christendom and the re-assertion and re-formulation of Christian truth by the once-again undivided Church.

The testimony of these witnesses needs to be adjudged and evaluated by the individual believer as he lives in and with the Church, and applies his reason, his conscience, his insight and his experience to it. These faculties and capacities of the believer are not witnesses in their own right, to be compared with the witnesses already mentioned and sometimes set over against them, and even preferred to them. Rather they are the means by which the witnesses are tested before they are accepted. They are the preparation for faith. Faith does not require indisputable evidence, nor is such evidence available; but it does require conviction that no contradiction of what is already believed or approved on good evidence is involved in the act of faith; and this conviction is provided by our human capacities as they are quickened by the Holy Spirit. For of course the acceptance of the witnesses is still an act of of faith, however well-grounded in reason, conscience, insight and experience that act of faith may be and should be.

The order in which the witnesses have been mentioned is, as will have been seen, an order of priority. Yet no single witness, as we have also already seen, has a 'sufficient measure of authority' in and by itself—not even the Bible or the consensus of the reunited Church. But in convergence and combination this measure of authority *can* be claimed for them. Not in *any* convergence and combination, for it is impossible that any witness who gives the lie to the Bible, even in harmony with another witness, should be believed, for the Bible is and must always remain the primary witness to the truths of the faith, for the simple reason that nothing else provides a first-hand account. But God is a God of order and coherence, and we may suppose therefore that when all the witnesses concur the authority which they possess will be as high as any authority we shall find anywhere in this world. This authority belongs to the future, not the present, since the Churches are not yet reunited. Meanwhile the concurrence of the others has very high authority indeed, the concurrence of the two parts of the Tradition an authority almost as high. But when the witnesses are in conflict, the authority of each of them (unless one of them is Scripture, and its testimony is absolutely clear) is in suspense until further light is granted to the Church. When only one witness offers testimony–unless that witness be Scripture–then the testimony can only be tentative until confirmation comes from another quarter; in the case of Scripture, its testimony can, if necessary, stand alone, with a strong claim upon our faith.

This gradation of our witnesses is certainly not free from difficulties; but the very difficulties serve to emphasize the essential features of our Christian existence. We are committed to Christ, and we live by faith in him. As we grow in the knowledge of him, we explore more and more deeply the truth as truth is in him. In our exploration we are assisted by many witnesses, not one of which either alone or in concert with the rest relieves us of the responsibility of thinking and deciding for ourselves, or puts us out of the reach of doubt or perplexity, but all of which help us to see the truth for ourselves. Sometimes the witnesses are in harmony, and we advance rapidly in understanding; sometimes they are in conflict, or seem to us to be, and we are impeded and puzzled. But we go forward in the same faith as that in which we started the journey, surely trusting, because we believe that Christ holds the meaning of all life, that, if not to us on earth, at least to the Church after us, will be granted unity in the truth. For the promise that the Holy Spirit will guide us into all the truth is the promise, not of a Spirit-proved inerrancy, but of a Spirit-guided exploration of the unsearchable riches of Christ.

Additional Note

THE PAPAL ENCYCLICAL ON
CONTRACEPTION

The Encyclical 'Humanae Vitae' was published subsequently to the preparation of this book for the Press. It plainly poses the problem of authority in an acute form. No doubt after much consultation with his personal and ecclesiastical advisers, and in conformity with previous Roman teaching, but in contradiction of the judgement communicated to him by the majority of the special commission appointed by his predecessor to advise him on the subject of contraception, and without associating with himself the judgement of the bishops, the Pope has 'laid down the law'.

It must be considered surprising that so soon after Vatican II's pronouncement that the Pope and the bishops acting together constitute the 'magisterium' of the church,[1] the present Pontiff has chosen to issue this important Encyclical on his own sole authority. Diplomatically and psychologically this appears to be a grave error. But theologically it can be justified by the sentences in the *Constitution on the Church* of Vatican II which, taken over from the decrees of Vatican I, still grant *magisterium* to the Pope without the bishops: '. . . his definitions, of themselves, and not from the consent of the Church, are justly irreformable. . . . Therefore they need no approval of others, nor do they allow an appeal to any other judgement'.[2]

Morever, as has been frequently pointed out, no claim to infallibility is made for the Encyclical. The authority of the Encyclical is rather that of a pronouncement of the Vicar of Christ which must be taught by the priesthood, and ac-

---

[1] *Dogmatic Constitution on the Church*, para. 22 (*Documents of Vatican II*, p. 43)
[2] ibid., para. 25 (*Documents*, p. 49)

cepted and acted upon by the faithful, until and unless it is contradicted, corrected or consigned to oblivion by a subsequent Encyclical or infallible pronouncement. What is demanded by it is canonical obedience, not assent to it as to an article of faith.

This notion of 'provisional infallibility' has the merit that it stops short of committing the Papacy, in selected instances, to the view that its pronouncements cannot conceivably be corrected, while requiring obedience meanwhile to what the Pope, on good evidence, believes to be undeniably true. It also allows for the exercise of conscience by those who are not persuaded that these pronouncements are true, and hope for their future amendment, but can be expected to conform outwardly as loyal children of the Church.

Thus, taken by itself, it is a more plausible doctrine than that of absolute infallibility. But it breaks down because of its attempt to 'have it both ways'. It requires the faithful to act upon certain pronouncements *as if* they were infallible, while admitting that they are not yet known to be so. So we have statements that are not infallible in theory, but must be regarded as infallible in practice. This may be perfectly in order for the multitudes who have not been able to give theological attention to the question pronounced upon and will regard the pronouncement as infallible anyway (and it is no doubt for these multitudes that the Pope was making provision when he issued the Encyclical). But it places an intolerable strain, not only upon the consciences, but also upon the mental powers of those in the Roman Catholic Church who have studied the question in a serious theological way and have come to a conclusion which is different from that of the Pope, but is in accordance with a great body of informed Roman Catholic opinion.

It is to be expected that a Church which has a 'doctrine of Encyclicals' will at some time or other put it into operation. But it would surely have been better in this case not to have done so, but rather to have re-stated the Christian doctrine of marriage, and left the matter of contraception to the individual's pastorally-guided conscience. But it would be better still not to have the 'doctrine of Encyclicals' at all.

INDEX

225

232